PHILOSOPHY OF
NONSENSE

D1610386

Why are we, and, in particular, why are philosophers and linguists so fascinated by nonsense? Why do Lewis Carroll and Edward Lear appear in so many otherwise dull and dry academic books? In this amusing, yet rigorous new book, Jean-Jacques Lecercle shows how the genre of nonsense was constructed and why it has proved so enduring and enlightening for linguistics and philosophy.

Lecercle claims that nonsense makes sense, philosophically speaking. Nonsense texts reverse the usual positioning of text to theory by reading their theory in advance: they are the reflexive, active interface between literature, linguistics and philosophy of language. Nonsense texts, like all texts, must be read in the light of philosophical and linguistic concepts, but they turn the theory back upon itself to open up new ways of thinking and theorising about language. *Philosophy of Nonsense* examines the philosophical pillars which structure the nonsense text, but also explores the innovative philosophy which nonsense gives rise to. Lecercle asserts that this new philosophy is no less than a confrontational reappraisal of the analytic and continental traditions of the philosophy of language.

Jean-Jacques Lecercle is Professor of English at the University of Paris. He is the author of *Philosophy Through the Looking Glass*, *Frankenstein: Mythe et Philosophie* and *The Violence of Language*.

PHILOSOPHY OF NONSENSE

The intuitions of Victorian nonsense literature

Jean-Jacques Lecercle

London and New York

First published 1994
by Routledge
11 New Fetter Lane, London EC4P 4EE

Simultaneously published in the USA and Canada
by Routledge
29 West 35th Street, New York, NY 10001

© 1994 Jean-Jacques Lecercle

Set in 10/12 pt Garamond by Megaron, Cardiff, Wales
Printed and bound in Great Britain by T. J. Press Ltd, Padstow,
Cornwall.

Printed on acid free paper

British Library Cataloguing in Publication Data
A catalogue record for this book is available from the British
Library

Library of Congress Cataloging in Publication Data
Lecercle, Jean-Jacques.
Philosophy of nonsense: the intuitions of Victorian nonsense
literature/Jean-Jacques Lecercle.
p. cm.
Includes bibliographical references and index.
1. Nonsense literature. English–History and criticism–
Theory, etc. 2. English literature–19th century–History and
criticism–Theory, etc. I. Title.
PR468.N6L43
827.009–dc20
93-5384

ISBN 0–415–07652–8 (hbk)   0–415–07653–6 (pbk)

For Edward

CONTENTS

CONTENTS

ACKNOWLEDGEMENTS

The diagram on p. 102 is reproduced by permission of Longman. Section 2 of the introduction first appeared in *Substance* (1993). The five lines from Mervyn Peake's *Book of Nonsense* are quoted by permission of Peter Owen Ltd.

INTRODUCTION: READING
NONSENSE READING

READING NONSENSE

There is a sense in which Alice is like Dracula. Not in outward appearance or feeding habits, but in the fact that she belongs to a text that has come to acquire the status of a myth. There are as many signs of this in the case of the *Alice* books as there are with Bram Stoker's novel. First, versions of Alice have proliferated across the various media, from stage Alices to Kafkaesque film versions to, *horresco referens*, pornographic novels based on *Alice's Adventures in Wonderland*. Second, the tales, in spite of the fact that they have been admitted into the canon of English Literature (in a minor capacity, it is true), have managed to keep remarkably alive, far beyond the range of the professional interest of academics. To the point that one could indulge in the usual game – ask the woman in the street what the name 'Alice in Wonderland' suggests to her, and elicit the same sort of response as in the case of 'Frankenstein' – the account would be reasonably accurate, except that the name of Walt Disney would have pride of place, over and above Lewis Carroll, even as Boris Karloff tends to overshadow Mary Shelley.

My aim in this book is to give an account of this mythical power, or force, which the *Alice* books, and beyond them the works of Victorian nonsense, possess to such a striking extent. I shall produce another symptom of this, which will be the centre of my enquiry. The books have proved to be an inexhaustible fund for quotation and allusion for linguists and philosophers alike. The average linguistics textbook, usually in the middle of the first chapter, offers an analysis of the coined words in 'Jabberwocky' (this book will be no exception). And philosophers, both Anglo-Saxon and continental, have always been fond of trying to solve the puzzles in which Carroll ensnares his readers, or of referring to

1

the *Alice* books for the purpose of serious, and sometimes jocular, illustration of their pet problems.

I shall set about answering the question raised by the existence of nonsense as a literary genre (which is another way of formulating my initial question: why have the texts retained such mythical power?) in two ways. I shall give a synchronic or rather anachronic, account of the genre, showing that the persistence of its mythical power is due to the quality of the intuitions, linguistic, pragmatic and philosophical, embedded in the text – there is a sense in which the works of Lewis Carroll anticipate the main aspects of the current philosophical debate, or the discoveries of generative grammar. And I shall give a diachronic account, showing that the emergence of the genre in the Victorian period is due to the fact, which accounts for their mythical force in the sense of Lévi-Strauss or Vernant,[1] that they attempt to solve by imaginary means a real contradiction in the historical conjuncture.

The anachronic account will deal with the intuitions of nonsense. My thesis, developed in Chapters 1 to 3, is that the negative prefix in 'nonsense' (in a sense the whole of this book is an analysis of the various senses of this negative prefix) is the mark of a process not merely of denial but also of reflexivity, that non-sense is also meta-sense. Nonsense texts are reflexive texts. This reflexion is embodied in the intuitions of the genre. Nonsense texts are not explicitly parodic, they turn parody into a theory of serious literature; Lewis Carroll's metalinguistic comments on points of grammar (the Duchess's unintelligible sentence, the Duck's comment on a cataphoric use of 'it', etc.) can be fully understood only in the light of Chomskyan linguistics – although Carroll was in no way a grammarian or a philologist himself, he was a century in advance of contemporary specialists; Edward Lear's omnipresent reference to an aggressive 'they' in his limericks is crying out for an existentialist or Heideggerian account.

In the course of the anachronic account, two subsidiary theses will be defended. The first concerns the characteristic style of nonsense, the linguistic and literary structures whereby such intuitions are made manifest. I am struck by the fact that nonsense is on the whole a conservative-revolutionary genre. It is conservative because deeply respectful of authority in all its forms: rules of grammar, maxims of conversation and of politeness, the authority of the canonical author of the parodied text. This aspect, which I confess is not the most obvious or the most celebrated of the genre, nevertheless becomes apparent when the texts are read carefully and in detail. It is inextricably mixed with the opposite aspect, for which the genre is justly famous, the liberated, light-fantastic, nonsensical aspect of nonsense, where rules and maxims appear to be joyously subverted. My thesis is that the genre is structured by the contradiction, which I shall eventually formulate in terms of a dialectic, between over-structuring and de-structuring, subversion and support. In other words, I shall seek to account for nonsense in the terms, familiar to contemporary French thought in the fields both of psychoanalysis and philosophy, of the dialectic of excess and lack. I have already formulated the linguistic version of this dialectic – of which nonsense is the best possible illustration – in the following terms: the speaker is always torn apart between the two poles of the contradiction of language, 'language speaks' (it is language, not I, that speaks, the words come out of my mouth 'all wrong') and 'I speak language' (I am in full control of my utterance, I say what I mean and mean what I say).[2]

The second subsidiary thesis seeks to account for this state of affairs. The strong perlocutionary effect of nonsense texts will be ascribed to a powerful affect, the need to understand what not only passes understanding but also forbids understanding by withdrawing sense. The deep-seated need for meaning, which nonsense texts deliberately frustrate in order to whet it, will be accounted for in terms of the non-transparency of language, of the incapacity of natural languages reasonably to fulfil their allotted task of expression and communication. Nonsense both supports the myth of an informative and communicative language and deeply subverts it – exposes it as a myth in the pejorative sense (thereby acquiring mythical force in the positive sense). The crux of this development will be the question of metaphor – of its centrality or marginality in language, and why nonsense texts carefully avoid it. We understand why nonsense is a reflexive genre better: if the thesis is correct, there is a close link between the practice of literary nonsense and the tradition of hermeneutics. Nonsense is the reflective image of our practice of interpretation, as philosophers or literary critics – it is interpretation gone wild, but also lucid, as clearly appears in the works of those extreme practitioners of (non)literary nonsense whom we call *fous littéraires* after Raymond

Queneau or, after Michel Pierssens, 'logophilists'.[3] The anachronic analysis of the genre will concentrate on these 'meta' characteristics, which account for the title of the book: there is an implicit philosophy in nonsense, a philosophy in act or *in nuce*; and nonsense texts reflect and comment on the practice of philosophers.

The diachronic account will seek to explain the emergence of nonsense in the Victorian context, its function in a determinate historical conjuncture. The main thesis will be that nonsense as a genre is a by-product of the development of the institution of the school, that the texts provide an imaginary solution to the real contradiction between the urge to capture an ever wider proportion of the population for the purpose of elementary schooling, and the resistance, religious, political and psychological, that such a cultural upheaval inevitably arouses. There is an obvious link between this historical thesis and the second subsidiary thesis above. The school is the institution that develops the need for meaning and a reflexive attitude towards language, and channels them in socially acceptable ways. The school is the institution where not only rules of grammar, but also maxims of good behaviour, linguistic and otherwise, are learnt. Thus, nonsense will be seen to have a part to play in the acquisition of cultural capital, to speak like Bourdieu.[4] Of course, such a thesis has a strongly paradoxical flavour, as it is immediately apparent that nonsense texts aim at (and choose their characters from) the type of child who has not yet been captured by the institution – children of nursery age in the case of Lear, little girls in the case of Carroll, who loved children 'except boys', that is except the part of the population who benefited from what Virginia Woolf enviously calls 'Arthur's education fund'. Alice does not go to school; but she has a governess at home, and the school as theme is present in nonsense texts, albeit usually in indirect fashion. We are back with the negative prefix of 'nonsense', which here appears as a mark of Freudian negation – nonsense reflects the changing state of schooling; it also phrases the resistance to this change.

A historical account of nonsense will also have to face another paradox. Any attempt to write a history of the genre is bound to founder upon the paradox of the sudden emergence, which can be dated with considerable precision, of a genre that is offered complete with a long tradition of predecessors. Victorian nonsense has both no history – it is a Victorian creation, an event in the field of literature – and a long history, which dates back, according to the inventiveness and enthusiasm of the critic, to Chaucer, Shakespeare or Sterne. It has no direct ancestors (Carroll is nobody's 'ephebe', to speak like Harold Bloom,[5] unless he is the ephebe of his contemporary, Tennyson) and yet the genre is a repetition, in a vastly different conjuncture, of medieval French *fatrasies*, those absurd short poems which might, four centuries in advance, have been written by Edward Lear. The solution to this paradox is not hard to find. We shall duly denounce the retrospective, *après coup*, nature of the invention of such a tradition (literature is not the only field in which such invention is at work – see Hobsbawm on the royal family).[6] But if we linger a few moments within the bounds of the paradox, perhaps a theory of what a literary genre is, and how a literary text, as a singularity of a specific kind, works, will emerge.

One word about my corpus, and its apparent lack of coherence. I have adopted the practice of anthologies of nonsense, i.e. I have chosen a variable corpus, with a centre and a periphery, as practised in what is known as prototype semantics. Anthologies of nonsense are all built around a hard core of texts by Carroll and Lear. Consequently, most, but not all, of my analyses will deal with the two masters. But the anthologies also include other members of the tradition they inevitably construct, both before and after Victorian nonsense. I shall, within strict limits, indulge in the same practice. All the more so as the first part of my account is a- or ana-chronic. This is a book about Lewis Carroll. It is also a book about the philosophy of language. Perhaps my main thesis is that the link between the two is unavoidable.

NONSENSE READING: LEWIS CARROLL AND THE TALMUD

My second subsidiary thesis states that nonsense is an *a contrario* reflexion on the tradition of hermeneutics. Nonsense texts, as is apparent in the emblematic figure of Humpty Dumpty, mimic the activities of literary critics and philosophers, only in an excessive and subversive way. In so doing they express intuitions that often escape more serious practitioners of the art. They also, of course, fail to produce the same result – a coherent interpretation of the text being read: excess always compensates for lack. The lack of results, of seriousness, can be seen as the necessary loss in order to gain new intuitions. In their nonsensicality or 'madness', nonsense texts are often more perceptive, or imaginative, or intuitive, than straightforward readings. This power of intuition may be extended to many *fous littéraires*. Beneath the delirium of Brisset or Wolfson,[7] implicit or explicit views about the workings of language emerge, which are of the utmost interest to us. The detour through madness in which they engage for other reasons pays a dividend in terms not only of epiphanic revelation, but of truth as disclosure. There is intuition in their madness, to the same extent as there is madness in their method. Wolfson's total translation is an impossible attempt, but it tells us important things about the speaker's relationship to her mother tongue, and, on the rebound so to speak, about the nature of all translation. Brisset's demented etymologies belong to the unrespectable tradition of speculative etymology, yet they offer intuitions about the part desire and the body play in ordinary linguistic exchange.[8] That such discoveries are accompanied by a mixture of pain and elation, even jubilation, only goes to show that the *fous littéraires* are in possession of a form of gay science.

Through an account of the work of another *fou littéraire*, Abraham Ettelson, I shall try to show that a manifestly demented interpretative practice, founded on an equally demented revelation, because it is based on traditional techniques, produces textual effects that have something to do with truth and knowledge. Even as Brisset's demented intuition, because it is based on the traditional techniques of grammarians (the analysis that yields paradigms, the synthesis that yields syntagmata), ends up producing linguistic knowledge of a sort. Nonsense or madness not only subvert, they also disclose and construct.

In 1966, an American Hasidic Jew, a medical doctor by profession, Abraham Ettelson, published – I suspect the publisher is what is known as a vanity press – an 80-page pamphlet entitled '*Through the Looking-Glass' Decoded*. The paratext is rather complex, as the text begins with a foreword by Rabbi Adam Neuberger, from Phoenix, Arizona, who celebrates the 'tremendous research' accomplished

INTRODUCTION

by the author and his 'scholarly' deductions, and informs us that he is a direct descendant of the Baal Shem Tov, the founder of Hasidism. The text itself fulfils the expectations one may derive from the title, since it demonstrates that *Through the Looking-Glass* is a cryptogram for the Talmud, that the subtext of Carroll's tale is made up of references, not even allegorical but cryptic, that are both literal and coded, to the Jewish ritual and what Ettelson calls 'the Jewish way'. The text has a material appearance that will be familiar to anyone who has ever opened a Jewish biblical commentary, or read Derrida's *Glas*.[9] There are two columns of text on each page, the left-hand one being made up of quotations of or textual references to Carroll's text, and the right-hand one being devoted to the deciphering and commentary. Chapter titles refer to the chapters of Carroll's tale, whereas subtitles all refer to episodes of the Jewish ritual. The only exception to this arrangement is the deciphering of the poem 'Jabberwocky', where the commentary, which is longer and more detailed than usual, almost takes the form of a short critical essay. There is nothing unusual in this, since the same situation obtains in Martin Gardner's *Annotated Alice*:[10] the notes to Jabberwocky fill several pages and interrupt Carroll's text. The following quotation will give a fair idea of the arrangement and contents of Ettelson's text:

>   *Rosh Hashonah*
>   (Jewish New Year)
> Paragraph 9
> And I do so . . . . means that Dodgson wishes it *would*
> *wish* it was true!   be a Happy New Year for himself! On
>   Rosh Hashonah Jews *wish* each other a
>   Happy New Year. But Dodgson was
>   *not* a happy man.
>   After Yom Kippur (in the fall) comes
>   winter: snow covers up the fields with
>   a white quilt, and they sleep till
>   summer; and wake up in the summer,
>   then the Jewish High Holy Days roll
>   around again in the autumn, when the
>   leaves are turning brown.[11]

As the quotation shows, Ettelson is not particularly respectful of Carroll's text. So few constraints are imposed on this interpretation that I feel capable, by using the same interpretative

7

technique, of proving that Carroll was a Corsican nationalist. This is, of course, where Ettelson's interpretation is 'demented': since he allows himself every possible interpretative move, the only rule he follows is 'anything goes' – because too much is allowed, the interpretation is null, or empty, like a definition that, being so wide as to encompass all the phenomena, would utterly fail to define the intended subpart. I mean, however, to go beyond this obvious reproach, which is so true as to be trivial. And the best way to progress is to try and understand what Ettelson is doing, for instance by reading the introduction to the pamphlet, where he gives an account of the origin of his intuition, which, we may imagine, must be linked to a moment of revelation, to an epiphany. Alas, we shall be disappointed, as the introduction is rather bizarre. Ettelson devotes one paragraph to an outline of Carroll's life, and goes on to quote two pages from Derek Hudson's biography. He regrets that paragraphs in *Through the Looking-Glass* are not numbered, like verses in the Bible, and in the last two paragraphs he suddenly reveals the contents of his intuition:

> Strange as it may seem, the 'Alice' books are written in code, and this book is a decoding of one of them. In the decoding process, it was found by trial and error that a search had to be made for certain key words in each paragraph, in order to arrive at the hidden meaning, while some words had to be examined through a mirror and read backwards.
>
> It will no doubt come as a surprise to the reader to learn that 'Jabberwocky' is the code name for the Baal Shem Tov of Medzhbish, in the Province of Kamenetz Podolsk in the Ukraine, on the Bug River! He was also known as the Rov of Podolia. It may also come as a surprise to discover that the first stanza of the poem beginning with 'Twas brillig, etc., etc.,' is not 'nonsense writing' at all, but contains within it one-half of the Hebrew script alphabet.[12]

This text has a familiar Carrollian ring. It reminds us of the principle of inversion that provides a structure for *Through the Looking-Glass*. But it also provides an interpretation for this inversion: it is not only textual, involving the process of reading backwards, in a mirror; it is also Jewish. Inversion is the symbol of the Jewish way, as made manifest by the inversion in the direction of reading in English on the one hand, and in Yiddish or Hebrew on the other. And what indeed is Yiddish, if not German read through the looking-glass?

8

There is something missing in Ettelson's introduction. It does tell us about the intuition at the centre of his interpretation, and about the end-product of his reading of Carroll. But it fails to say anything about the moment of revelation. One of the reasons is that the epiphanic moment is alluded to on the very first page of the pamphlet, the dedication page. The text is 'fondly dedicated' to the author's 'own child-friend' who, 'one day in May' let him read her copy of *Alice in Wonderland*. Without this epiphanic reading, his own book 'would never have come to fruition'. On the whole Ettelson is a rather shy and ascetic *fou littéraire*: he alludes to the epiphany in the most discreet and indirect manner (why, for instance, does he decode *Through the Looking-Glass*, if the revelation came to him through a reading of both *Alice* books?). I suspect that the reason for this is truly Carrollian. This dedication is bound to remind the reader of the anecdote of the little girl holding an orange in her left hand which, Carroll claims, is the origin of *Through the Looking-Glass*. (The puzzle is: why does the little girl hold an orange in her left hand, whereas her mirror image holds it in her right hand?) This intertextual reference, whether it is deliberate or not on Ettelson's part, is food for thought. It is clear that his intuition is not merely demented, but also faithful to Carroll.

However, revelation and intuition are not enough. They have to be materialised in the form of a device – a logophiliac is worth what his device is worth. Had Brisset merely been a lover of frogs, he would soon have disappeared in oblivion – as an etymologist, of the most imaginative type, he still captures our attention. Without his translation device, which uses *traducson*, or translation according to sound, Wolfson would be just one more paranoiac. Ettelson, too, is interesting because of his device. I should say his devices, as he uses two, which I propose to call the *symbolic* and the *rhetorical* devices. His *symbolic* device is typical of interpretative excess – its main characteristic is the uncontrolled use of the copula, 'x *is* y', in order to mark relations of identification or equivalence. Such unrestrained use of brutal assertion is the very emblem of interpretative violence, what the French language calls a *coup de force*. Thus, the phrase 'eyes of flame' in 'Jabberwocky' is glossed: 'When Israel held the page before his eyes, his face became aflame, his eyes glowed as if they had pierced into the heart of the earth – Thus the "sword" (*Book of Wisdom*) had been passed to the Baal Shem Tov.'[13] The device works in three stages. An equivalence between signifiers ('flame'/ 'aflame') is transferred to the level of the signified (Carroll's tale/the Book of Wisdom), which is taken to be an allusion to the Baal Shem Tov's life. This *is* is indeed a copula in the etymological sense of the word: it links a word in *Through the Looking-Glass* to a word in the hypotext, the Talmud, the Jewish ritual or the life of the prophet. Sometimes this copulative relation even dispenses with the material link between signifiers. The 'ball of worsted' with which Alice's kitten is playing becomes the wool from which the Tsitses is made (this is in no way irrational, as 'worsted' is the name of a twisted woollen thread – the Tsitses is a tassel of twisted cord worn by orthodox Jews at the corners of certain garments), and the association, which, even if not unmotivated, is far-fetched, to say the least, is followed upon, as the kitten 'curled up in a corner' evokes 'the four corners of the Tsitses'.[14] It is clear that the symbolic device imposes minimal constraints on interpretation. Such analysis, even if it is coherent, is closer to simile than to metaphor, at least if we follow Davidson's theory of metaphor.[15] According to him, simile is trivial, because too easy, because always possible (everything is 'like' everything else in at least one respect), whereas metaphors, being blatantly false at the literal level, are at least non-trivial.

Ettelson's *rhetorical* device is more immediately interesting, if only because it is more varied. In the course of his commentary on 'Jabberwocky' he interprets the title of the poem by dividing the word into equal parts, 'Jabber' and 'wocky' and reading each in the mirror, which gives 'Rebbaj Ykcow', Rabbi Jacob, who, of course, is the Baal Shem Tov (we are on dangerous ground here, as the analysis seems to yield results which we can no longer dismiss as arbitrary with the same ease as before). The 'Jubjub' tree, when looked at in the mirror, yields 'Judjud', that is 'Yude Yude', Jew Jew. (Of course, Ettelson is cheating – all logophiliacs do – the word 'jubjub', when read in a mirror, does not yield any coherent word, or at most, if we decide to read the letter 'j' as symmetrical in certain scripts, 'dujduj', but certainly not 'judjud' – Ettelson has in fact read only the letter 'b' in the mirror.) Lastly, Ettelson remarks, which is entirely correct, that the word 'Bandersnatch' contains an anagram of 'Satan'. The interest of this rhetorical device is clear. By playing on signifiers, on the material side of language, it imposes real constraints on the result of the interpretation, the constraints of language (that these effectively constrain is revealed by the temptation to cheat). This has two important consequences:

(a)This device is substantially the same as the one Carroll himself, through Humpty Dumpty his creature, has adopted – it is a quasi-etymological device, reminiscent of Brisset: thus Ettelson reinterprets 'frumious', the adjective coined by Carroll, as a combination of Hebrew 'frum', meaning 'orthodox Jew', and English 'pious' – this is what, since Humpty Dumpty first used the word, we have called a portmanteau-word; (b) Apart from clear cases of cheating, the analysis yields real results – what Ettelson finds is actually there, in the words where he finds it. We are no longer dealing with the facility of arbitrary pronouncements, as was the case with the symbolic device – the 'Satan' anagram is not hallucinated by Ettelson.

Naturally, being sceptical rationalists, we shall dismiss this under the name of coincidence or, more relevant still, by reducing it to a childish game one can always play with language. I am sure children's magazines and pre-prandial television programmes are full of games where one has to find as many words as one can in a given word. I am sure that a scrabble enthusiast could do better with 'Bandersnatch' than Ettelson does: five letters is not a lot. The fact is that the result of the rhetorical analysis is pre-programmed, that Ettelson inevitably finds what he was looking for, and that his interpretation is deeply unfaithful to Carroll, who was a deacon of the Church of England and had strictly nothing to do with the Talmud and the 'Jewish way'. The problem is that the device is also deeply faithful to Carroll's own devices. Portmanteau-words, words read in a mirror, anagrams: Carroll is fond of all these games, and *Through the Looking-Glass* is the text where he most obviously practises them (which may account for Ettelson's choice of this tale over its more illustrious predecessor). The cleverness and skill of the logophiliac are of the same order, and of the same degree, as that of his model, the canonical author. Parodying the famous slogan from the May '68 events in France, we can only exclaim: '*Lewis Carroll, Humpty Dumpty, Ettelson, même combat!*'

To speak like Lyotard, in *Le Différend*,[16] we have to acknowledge that there is such a thing as an 'Ettelson-phrase', a mode of expression, a style of interpretation, which are both entirely coherent and in a specific relationship with their model, the 'Carroll-phrase'. The Ettelson phrase has two variants, one symbolic, the other rhetorical, but its 'regimen' is not in doubt: it is

11

a descriptive phrase, which phrases apodictic judgements. The next question, however, is that of linking, of the constraints on the phrases that follow the apodictic judgement – the question of the genre to which Ettelson's text belongs. The question is open, as we could seek to understand (and absorb) Ettelson by inserting his text in different genres.

The simplest solution is to decide that Ettelson is indeed mad. His text, therefore belongs to the genre of the case history, a primary source for a psychiatric and/or Freudian-style analysis, where Ettelson is this author's judge Schreber (the judge is, as we know, the author of *Memories of my Mental Illness*, and the object of one of Freud's 'five case studies'). The text is a classic instance of interpretative delirium, what Michel Thevoz calls *'un texte brut'*.[17] This solution to the genre puzzle is interesting only in one of its complex versions: what we are dealing with is a demented intuition coupled with an interpretation machine that is paranoid, therefore methodical, therefore coherent, therefore lucid up to a point. Ettelson in this version is indeed worthy of judge Schreber. The problem with this interpretation is that it is merely a means to get rid of Ettelson, to ascribe a place to his text, to triangulate it as Deleuze and Guattari might say – unless we remember the last words of Freud's analysis of the Schreber case: the delirious patient is also more keenly aware than the most imaginative of analysts.

Because my main interest lies in literature, I offer a second solution, which puts the first into perspective. Ettelson's text seems to be a case history because it is a postmodern novel. We may remember that Wolfson, too, dreamt of writing the Great American Novel, that he wanted to emulate E.E. Doctorow, whom he had met at school, and that his second book, *Ma Mère* ...[18] is, in its own way, his version of the said novel. Ettelson has written the fiction of Carroll's Talmud, as someone else has written the fiction of Flaubert's parrot. He is using the banal post-modernist strategy which turns canonical texts into sources of new fiction, as in the case of Hunter Steele's *Lord Hamlet's Castle*.[19] Nor are devices unknown to metafiction, witness the novels of Roussel, or Walter Abish's *Alphabetical Africa*,[20] where the first chapter contains only words beginning with 'a', the second words beginning with 'a' and 'b', and so on till Chapter 52, the progression being inverted after the twenty-sixth chapter. Ettelson's device is hardly more bizarre than this.

12

Neither of my two solutions seems quite right. They are both unjust to Ettelson, because they fail to capture the specificity of the logophiliac text. Ettelson's text claims to state the truth about Lewis Carroll. It is situated in a universe where truth is opposed to fiction as the serious to the non-serious. There is no attempt at pastiche or humour in Ettelson. Unless, of course, the whole exercise is a practical joke, of which the reader (this reader) is a victim. Apart from the fact that, in imagining this, I am sailing dangerously close to paranoia myself, I have a conviction (should I say an intuition?) that such is not the case. Ettelson possesses the most striking characteristic of the genuine logophiliac: his exorbitant claim to truth is the price he has to pay for the indirect expression of truth-bearing insights. There must be a third solution to the problem of the genre of the text: there is a distinct logophilist tradition (here I abandon the pejorative, quasi-psychiatric suffix '-iac' for good), in which the logophilist-phrase is defined through a dual relation to knowledge, the established knowledge it draws upon, and the new knowledge it anticipates. Ettelson belongs to the tradition of the 'other' Saussure, the 'demented' discoverer of anagrams: the very madness of his intuition is a way of access to truth.

The science explicitly mentioned by Ettelson belongs to his culture: it is the tradition of midrash. I shall briefly venture into a domain which remains largely alien to me. For it is only too obvious that Ettelson's commentary of Carroll has the shape of a Talmudic commentary. Following the collection of essays on midrash and literature edited by Geoffrey Hartman,[21] we can see that four characterisics of the tradition also concern Ettelson's text: (1) The commented text is, both with the midrashists and with Ettelson, cut off from the intention of meaning of its author, of any will-to-say. This is particularly important in the case of Carroll, who would have blushed when reading Ettelson; (2) There is no remainder, nothing is left over, either in the text or in the commentary. The object of the commentary is the whole text, not only its meaning as derived from its words: the sounds, the shape of the letters, the frequency of occurrence of the signs, the number of lines or pages are objects of equal interest to the hermeneutist. Even semicolons give rise to interpretation. Carroll would have liked such minute attention to detail: he had firm opinions on inverted commas and the position of apostrophes in the negative forms of the English auxiliary verbs; (3) Midrash is another embodiment of the old paradox: how can we produce the new out of the old? In a sense, everything has already been said in the commented text and on it. Since the tradition is centuries old, the accumulated strata of commentary are extremely impressive. Yet each new commentary starts afresh, as if everything had to be reinvented. This is indeed what Ettelson is doing to Carroll: the critical violence of his intuition sweeps away the interpretative sediments that clutter the text, and starts anew. Yet, of course, his interpretative technique is no different from that of his predecessors; (4) As a consequence of this, interpretations proliferate – they succeed, but do not cancel, each other, like the innumerable re-analyses of the same phrase according to Brisset's device. Ettelson's interpretation of Carroll claims to be the only true one, since Ettelson is the only one to have discovered that *Through the Looking-Glass* is a cryptogram of the Talmud. But, in order to do this, Ettelson uses other interpretations, by quoting, for instance, Hudson's biography of Carroll (which was published in 1954), and by using Carroll's own devices, which means that his own discovery is only one more stage in a cumulative progress towards knowledge.

It is nevertheless also obvious that as a midrashic commentator Ettelson is somewhat of an eccentric. If only because he inverts the direction of midrash. He no longer goes from an ancient text, the revealed text, which is the pre-text of a novel, and perhaps imaginative, commentary. On the contrary, he starts from a substitute text, modern rather than ancient, imaginative but not revealed, and uses it as a pre-text for the rediscovery of the ancient text. Such a reversal has important consequences: (a) Carroll's text is placed in the position of a revealed text, which is perhaps no more than stating that Carroll's tales now belong to the canon. Each culture has the revealed texts that it can have or wishes to have; (b) The existence of Ettelson's commentary of Carroll induces an infinite sequence of commentaries. If Ettelson is right, the Talmud is the source of Carroll's tale, which is the source of Ettelson's commentary. But since the second moment is a repetition of the first, there is no reason why the process of repetition should stop here. As a result, Ettelson's text is the source of new commentary, mine for instance; (c) However, we are still within midrash here, within the sedimentation of inter-pretations. But there is another aspect to this perverse relationship that should now attract our attention. The Talmud is both Ettelson's source and inspiration and the result of his discovery, the contents of his commentary (which, compared to Brisset's, is not imaginative in the least – there is at least something strikingly new in Brisset's theory about the origins of human language in the croaking of frogs). The proof of Ettelson's talent does not lie in the contents of his discovery, which are poor, but in the path he follows in order to reach them. As a result, we have not only an infinite chain of commentaries, in which the first link is an arbitrary and violent origin, the word of God, and the last the beginning of an *en abyme* lineage (Ettelson is part of an infinite sequence of commentators), but also a closed circular structure, whereby the Talmud and *Through the Looking-Glass* are mirror-images of each other. Indeed, the best commentary of Ettelson is not my own, but the commentary only Pierre Ménard might give, which, starting from Ettelson's Talmud, would reproduce *Through the Looking-Glass* word for word – Pierre Ménard's Carroll, as Borges wrote 'Pierre Ménard's *Quixote*'.[22] This type of circularity is already present in Ettelson's commentary. Thus, the 'worsted' in Carroll's tale is assimilated to the 'Tsitses' in the Talmud; this Tsitses refers back to the word 'corner' in Carroll, which in turn evokes the corners of the Tsitses. The circularity, the *va et vient* of inter-pretation establishes a metonymic relationship between 'worsted' and 'corner' in *Through the Looking-Glass*, whereas they have only the most distant and tenuous syntagmatic relationship, as two unrelated words on the same page.

Ettelson's 'gay science', even if hopelessly caught up in the circularity and closure of the Lacanian imaginary (I am attempting to give a slightly more precise meaning to Ettelson's 'madness'), produces effects, if only an effect of construction. An arrangement of interpretative utterances emerges, an interpretative machine that projects and structures a complex intertext. Such a construc-tion also produces a truth effect – a form of implicit knowledge about the workings of language.

There is such a thing as an Ettelson interpretative machine, which relates various texts in order to produce a new text. The text in question may be called ana-, cata- and meta-phoric. It is anaphoric in that it draws on the results of an already constituted knowledge – on a tradition, a lineage, like the lineage of the Baal Shem Tov, whose descendant Ettelson is. It is cataphoric, in that it anticipates the infinite chain of commentary in which it is merely a link, but also in that it gives instructions for use that will allow future explications to unfold – in Lyotard's terms, it claims to be an element in a *montage en parallèle*, a faithful reflection of holy origin, but it is really part of a *montage en série*, an unending chain of ever emergent commentaries.[23] Lastly, it is metaphorical, in that it reflects and displaces the interpretative techniques of literary criticism, which we practise daily. The result of this interpretative arrangement is not, of course, a hierarchic tree of knowledge, but a rhizome (see Figure I1).

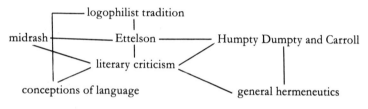

Figure I1

In Figure I1 the importance of Ettelson becomes manifest at last. It now appears that the interest of his text lies not in the mad contents of his interpretation, but in the fields of knowledge that it intertextually links, in the rhizome that grows in and around it. I shall explore a few of the rhizome's shoots.

I have already shown that Ettelson was both faithful and unfaithful to Carroll. His interpretation device is very close to Humpty Dumpty's, therefore to Carroll's. In Chapter 6 of *Through the Looking-Glass*, Humpty Dumpty comments on the poem 'Jabberwocky' for Alice's benefit. He uses the same symbolic and rhetorical devices as Ettelson. Thus, a 'borogove' is 'a thin shabby-looking bird with its feathers sticking out all round – something like a live mop'; whereas 'toves' are 'something like badgers – ... something like lizards – and ... something like corkscrews'.[24] – in their arbitrariness, such accounts belong to the symbolic mode. Whereas the accounts he gives of 'slithy' ('lithe and slimy'), of 'brillig' ('four o'clock in the afternoon – the time when you begin *broiling* things for dinner'),[25] playing as they do on signifiers, belong to the rhetorical mode – they are noticeably less arbitrary than the other ones, to the point that Alice, who has understood the rule that governs them, is able to anticipate Humpty Dumpty's explanations. Such similarities in technique, of course, are in no way surprising: Ettelson, like Alice, like any reader of Carroll, is Humpty Dumpty's disciple. But the interplay is more complex, as Ettelson takes Humpty Dumpty's advice to the letter, and does systematically, with a vengeance, what Alice dares to do only hesitantly and occasionally: he reflects Humpty Dumpty like his mirror-image. If Ettelson is mad, so is Humpty Dumpty, which is not at all strange since the world of nonsense, as the Cheshire Cat reminds Alice, everybody is mad. But mirror-images multiply, as in the last scene in Orson Welles's film *The Lady from Shanghai* – Humpty Dumpty is the mirror-image of the hermeneutically inclined reader. Something crucial is happening in this interplay of mirror-images, which I shall analyse in three stages. The first stage takes place at Madame Tussaud's.

Ettelson is you or me seen in a magnifying mirror, the caricature of a critic, who utters truths about our daily practice that are painful for us to hear. We too have produced interpretations using the symbolic, and the rhetorical mode. Some of these interpretations are simplistic (if we use the arbitrary 'x is y' without due precaution), others are more complex, and more pleasurable (if we slalom down the slopes of the signifier) – all are worthy of Ettelson, even if generally more prudent, less obviously mad. To come back to Carroll, we have inevitably said or read that the White Rabbit is a small penis; and we have also read or produced infinitely more convincing accounts couched in the language of Lacan[26] – all these interpretations, nevertheless, are, to a point, worthy of Ettelson. Of course, the difference is not hard to tell – as responsible critics, we show the commented text all the respect that is due. And under the name 'respect', we must understand Kant's concept, based on the autonomy of the critic (who imposes constraints on herself) and on a hermeneutic categorical imperative ('interpret the text so that you treat it as an end, not as a means'). Ettelson's imperative is problematic, not categorical: if you wish to discover the Talmud in Carroll's text, use Carroll's own interpretative devices to explain the text. At this Madame Tussaud stage we know why and in what Ettelson is mad.

At the second stage, Ettelson is no longer mad, but intuitive. In his irrepressible compulsion to force meaning out of the text, he tells us something about the workings of language. He refuses to respect the text, in the person of its author, for instance, whose deeply felt religious convictions he ignores, but also in its preferred meaning (and it appears that even a nonsense text can be interpreted wrongly, against the grain of its sense – this is one of the main lessons of Ettelson's attempt). All Ettelson shows respect for is the letter of the text, which is no proper object for respect (according to Kant, we respect the moral law, and human beings in so far as they accept it – in textual terms, we respect the laws of grammar, and the will-to-say of the speaker who appropriates them to express her meaning), because it is easy, too easily manipulated. To force meaning out of the text is to be deliberately reductive, to 'fix' meaning as varnish fixes paint, to anachronise in order to go beyond the surface of the text. Like all interpreters, Ettelson knows how to make the text blab. But such a reduction (his interpretation reduces the meaning of the text to one single meaning, the Talmud for short, at the expense of all others) is not necessarily a loss. It is the result of the operation of the symbolic-rhetorical machine, but also the point where interpretation goes wild, and lines of flight appear. Lewis Carroll had nothing to do with the Talmud, but, in the terms of Deleuze and Guattari, there is a becoming-Talmud of *Through the Looking-Glass*, which is made manifest in Ettelson. The interpretation, caught in this process of 'becoming', becomes interminable, like Freudian analysis. And this does not mean that, because too few constraints are imposed upon it, in the way of interpretation anything goes. This does not apply, even to Ettelson. His reduction, his forcing meaning out of the text, is linked to an awareness of the workings of language. They provide the main constraint: Ettelson's interpretation, like all interpretations, merely ex-plicates the virtualities of meaning which language contains in its folds. What Ettelson discovers is invented in the archaeological sense of the term, it is always already there in a fold of language. Ettelson's interpretation is a paradoxical object, in that it seems to give the text a *sens* (meaning) which is determinate, that is which is also a *sens* (direction – Deleuze's 'logic of *sens*' plays upon this pun),[27] but that the manifest folly of its contents draws the text back not towards designation, manifestation and signification, the three parameters of fixed meaning in Deleuze's theory, but towards the fourth element, 'sense', a bundle of potentialities of meaning, without a fixed direction, where meaning and nonsense coexist. This 'sense' is another name for language – this is where Ettelson makes a statement about the workings of language which is of the order of truth.

We have reached the third and last stage, where the logophilist is not only intuitive, but also the possessor of knowledge. This is not the constituted knowledge of the tradition he draws upon; nor is it the knowledge which he implicitly transmits, without being fully aware of it. It is a form of knowledge and truth that is the object of a conscious quest. The time has come to take Ettelson seriously. In the language of Deleuze and Guattari, I am struck by the fact that his interpretation turns Carroll's tale, which has been absorbed by the canon, into a *minor* text again. For *Through the Looking-Glass* does not belong to 'major' literature.[28] Ettelson gives it back its most precious possession – its madness. By madly trying to turn it into a Jewish text, he produces a wonderful symbol of the minority of Carroll, of the constitutive de-territorialisation of his text. That Ettelson immediately re-territorialises Carroll into the Talmud is not important. What counts is that he is faithful to the minority of the text, in which little girls and language are objects of desire. Ettelson's interpretation, therefore, is (a) deeply worthy of Carroll's genius; (b) worthy of the workings of the English language, and of the way Carroll dwells in it, to use Heidegger's metaphor: and (c) easily inserted in a philosophical tradition, which I will mention briefly under the name of Walter Benjamin.[29] Like all logophilists, Ettelson is essentially a translator – his device is a translation device. But in his case translating does not simply mean a passage from one language to another, but rather an intimate relationship, a convergence, between two idioms, here Victorian nonsense and the Talmud. We understand why Ettelson's goal is to recover the Talmud in Carroll's text. Not so much in order to capture a canonical text for his religious persuasion (this is certainly his conscious aim, but intention, here as elsewhere, is of little importance – it would be too easy to dismiss his text as an attempt, from a marginal point in Anglo-Saxon culture, to join the mainstream), as because the revealed word is the very embodiment of that 'elusive' element in the original text, which is 'the primary concern of the genuine translator'.[30] Only the Talmud can provide an echo worthy of Carroll's text, the echo of his minorisation of Victorian culture, within another historical conjuncture. The following quotation from Benjamin's essay on the task of the translator is fully relevant to Ettelson's attempt:

as regards the meaning, the language of a translation can – in fact, must – let itself go, so that it gives voice to the *intentio* of the original not as reproduction but as harmony, as a supplement to the language in which it expresses itself, as its own kind of *intentio*. Therefore it is not the highest praise of a translation, particularly in the age of its origin, to say that it reads as if it had originally been written in that language. Rather, the significance of fidelity as ensured by literalness is that the work reflects the great longing for linguistic complementation.[31]

Not only is Ettelson far from simply mad, but his symbolic–rhetorical translation of Carroll is the only faithful one. There is food for thought in this.

REREADING NONSENSE: 'JABBERWOCKY'

Ettelson is too nonsensical: he seems to break through the bounds of common sense and historical verisimilitude, and gives free rein to his hermeneutic imagination. And yet he is not nonsensical enough by half. He postulates a single and unitary meaning behind the text he analyses, the intentional meaning that Carroll must have encoded in his tale, and beneath this the Meaning that God, in his mysterious way, intended to reveal, both to Carroll and Ettelson. A nonsense text, on the other hand, plays with the bounds of common sense in order to remain within view of them, even if it has crossed to the other side of the frontier; but it does not seek to limit the text's meaning to one single interpretation – on the contrary, its dissolution of sense multiplies meaning. This is because a nonsense text requires to be read on two levels at once – two incompatible levels: not 'x means A', but 'x is both A and, incoherently, B'. In other words, nonsense deals not in symbolism but in paradox. Because this is a little abstract, we shall read the first stanza of 'Jabberwocky' again:

> 'Twas brillig, and the slithy toves
> Did gyre and gimble in the wabe:
> All mimsy were the borogoves,
> And the mome raths outgrabe.[32]

I do not intend to provide a new and original reading of this stanza, to add my modest brick to a palatial pile, but to reflect on possible ways of reading such a text, in which the abundance of coinages makes the simplest attempt at reading problematic. The easiest way to deal with the text is to engage in a systematic linguistic reading, based on the two operations of analysis and synthesis, i.e. on the order of Saussure's *langue*. This impels us to read the text on four levels: phonetics, morphology, syntax and semantics. On the *phonetic* level, we shall note that the text is eminently readable, an excellent choice for public reading. All the words can be pronounced, even the coined ones, because they all conform to the phonotactics of English, i.e. to the licit ways of combining phonemes. 'Hjckrrh!', the Gryphon's exclamation[33] is an unpronounceable illicit combination of phonemes: not so 'slithy toves' or 'borogoves'. In technical parlance, Carroll's coined language is neither *lanternois*, the compulsive repetition of obsessional sounds which have nothing to do with a real tongue, and which one hears, for instance, in glossolalia, nor *baragouin*, the imitation of the sounds of another language, but *charabia*, the imitation of one's own language.[34] At this level, the stanza is a perfectly acceptable, even normal, text. Things are equally normal when we go into *morphology*. The stanza is made up of words, separated by the usual blanks and punctuation signs. And the words are susceptible of an immediate constituent analysis: they can be analysed, every single one of them, into their constituent morphemes: the slith-y tove-s. The analysis is successful, since it is complete. And it is also coherent, a thing it is not always with 'normal' texts: the stanza does not contain actually existing words like 'raspberry', which must be analysed ('berry' is an independent word) and yet cannot ('rasp-' in 'raspberry' has no connection with the word 'rasp'). *Syntax* is equally coherent. We have sentences, easily analysed into syntagmata, and we can ascribe a part of speech to every word: 'slithy' is an adjective, and 'toves' a noun in the plural: they are part of the subject noun phrase, which combines with the verb phrase 'did gyre and gimble in the wabe', to form a sentence. So coherent is the syntax that potential ambiguities are easily resolved. One might analyse 'the mome raths outgrabe' into either a noun phrase followed by a verb in the third person present ('raths') and an adverb ('outgrabe'), or as an article, an adjective and a noun in the plural ('the mome raths'), followed by a verb in the past tense ('outgrabe' is the past form of 'outgribe'). Of course, the second choice is the right one – it is indeed Humpty Dumpty's choice in his explanation of the word. Not only because 'outgrabe' makes a recognisable verb in the past (complete with prefix and vowel change), whereas it makes a rather strange adverb, but because the sequence of tenses requires a verb in the past ('all mimsy *were* the borogoves, and the mome raths *outgrabe*'). Things are not so rosy, however, when we reach the fourth level, *semantics*. There, we draw a blank. We understand grammatical words like articles, prepositions and auxiliary verbs, but the normally meaningful words, nouns, adjectives and verbs, are meaningless. Nor do Humpty Dumpty's explanations really help. The creature is obviously a logophilist, and therefore not to be trusted. All we have is the global coherence of discourse: something is being said, only I do not know exactly what. Which is precisely Alice's reaction to the whole poem:

'It seems very pretty,' she said when she had finished it, 'but it's *rather* hard to understand!' (You see she didn't like to confess, even to herself, that she couldn't make it out at all.) 'Somehow it seems to fill my head with ideas – only I don't exactly know what they are! However, *somebody* killed *something*: that's clear, at any rate – '[35]

This is the best description I know of the experience of reading nonsense. What Alice is dimly aware of is that narrative coherence somehow compensates for semantic incoherence. This appears more clearly in the body of the poem, which deals with the heroic slaying of the Jabberwock – but even in the first stanza events and states of affairs are referred to, which I can rephrase, in true Shandean fashion: A borogove! Very well. Have I ever seen one? Might I ever have seen one? Would I had seen a mome rath (for how can I imagine it?).[36]

The reading I have just proposed is banal. As we saw, it is a commonplace in linguistics textbooks. It shows that grammatical analysis can afford to treat sense as a black box and proceed in blissful ignorance of it. The linguist need not actually understand the language he studies; he may exclaim, like Alice: 'it's all in some language I don't know'.[37] Such a reading comforts the grammatical structure of language by making it manifest. This structuralist practice, however, soon causes unease. One of the structural levels is void: this may preserve the coherence of the reading, but it makes its completeness impossible. The lack of analysis on the semantic level will soon threaten to destabilise the coherent reading I have engaged in, together with the lingustic order on which it is based and which it reveals. The *langue* reading of the text is subverted by the absence of sense, and a second reading is induced.

This new reading starts from the semantic blanks. It does not treat them as a residue, but as the essential aspect of the text. Are they not, after all, the most striking parts of the stanza, what has given 'Jabberwocky' its fame? The orderly character of the poem on the other linguistic levels is seen as a failed attempt to conceal or deny the pervasive attraction of the coinages. And if we look at the poem as a whole, we shall notice two things. The first stanza, which everyone knows by heart, is so memorable because of the sheer abundance of coined words in it; the other stanzas, although they contain a number of coinages, are more 'conventional' in that they narrate a recognisable tale, a tale of quest, ordeal and triumphant return which corresponds to the usual pattern of fairy tales and would be susceptible of a Proppian analysis.[38] And the first stanza is repeated at the end of the poem, like a leitmotiv. Indeed, it has already appeared *before* the text, for it is printed in reverse, together with the title, to let us experience the same puzzlement as Alice when she first opens the looking-glass book, before she thinks of holding it up to the mirror. No doubt this compulsive repetition contributes to the meaninglessness of the stanza: Carroll himself noted the 'curious phenomenon (which the reader can easily test for himself) that if you repeat a word a great many times in succession, however suggestive it may have been when you began, you will end by divesting it of every shred of meaning, and almost wondering you could ever have meant anything by it.'[39] It also contributes to the fascination of the text, by focusing our attention on the semantic blanks. The per-locutionary effect the poem has on Alice, in the passage quoted above, is in fact ambiguous. One can stress either the 'it fills my head with ideas' aspect (forgetting the modal verb, for Alice does say: 'it *seems* to fill my head . . . '), i.e. the coherence of the text, or the 'only I don't know what they are' aspect, i.e. the contagious incoherence induced by the semantic blanks. From this point of view, the portmanteau-words work like a sort of linguistic *punctum*.[40] They fascinate the reader much more efficiently than the snake-like Jabberwock, a rather banal dragon, hardly saved from utter triviality by the fact that, in Tenniel's illustration, he happens to be wearing a waistcoat. The semantic blanks compel us to look

23

at the text in a new way, to read it anew. They are not only duplicated even before the narrative begins, they also replicate the text, i.e. fold it on to itself – because they compel us to go from a visual to a linguistic form of imagination. This is where Humpty Dumpty's explanations are wide of the mark. They try to make us visualise those toves, a thing which is either impossible (if, as is the case with the Snark, the creature's 'unmistakable marks' are paradoxical or contradictory) or trivial (Tenniel does represent a tove, a chimera-like combination of badger, lizard and corkscrew). But the semantic blanks are not meant to be visualised. They are meant to be playfully explored, or exploited, by our linguistic imagination, which is boundless. We do not spontaneously read the poem with an eye to Tenniel's drawings, or like the authors of those linguistics textbooks: the words sing in our ears, unexpected links are established between them, relationships of alliteration, assonance or rhyme, of potential spoonerism (why not 'the rome maths outgrabe'? After all Carroll did teach mathematics at one stage), of leisurely exploration of phonetic similarities ('mimsy' will evoke 'flimsy', 'mime' and 'prim'). The reading is no longer systematic and rational, but desultory and playful. There is no fixed and unique meaning or interpretation, but a proliferation of variously ambiguous partial structures. By focusing on the semantic gaps, this second reading lets language play on its own – it lets language speak. This is no longer a *langue* reading, but, in Lacanian terms, a *lalangue* reading. Or again, to change the terms of reference, if the body of the poem more or less belongs to the category of the marvellous (it does exercise our conventional narrative and visual imagination), the first stanza, with its semantic blanks is characterised by the *Unheimlichkeit* of the fantastic. It does not appeal to our conventional imagination, but rather induces an epiphanic intuition of the real workings of language. *Unheimlich*, we remember, is not only Freud's term, it is also the term Heidegger uses to translate the Greek word *deinon*.[41] Language is both more real and more terrible than the tame dragons of our nightmares.

The poem, therefore, is a balancing act between an orderly and a disorderly reading. It must be read as a locus both for Markov chains (the structure is so coherent that when I know the beginning of a string of words, the end becomes predictable, more and more so as I progress along the chain) and for the romping of a linguistic unconscious. I think we can take 'Jabberwocky' as an emblem of nonsense as a genre: a conservative-revolutionary genre, subverting but also comforting language, given free rein to our linguistic imagination, but also imposing the constraints of a regular language on us with a vengeance. The commonplace view of nonsense is that it presents us with the charming disorder of freedom. Alice is liberated, during her stay in Wonderland, from the constraints of a Victorian education; the text is freed from the usual rules of language. This is not a false, but a partial and therefore a naive conception of nonsense. Countless critics have stressed the uneasy feelings which Wonderland suggests in Alice and the reader alike (Carroll's world is rather unlike Walt Disney's version, and much closer to the Czech film version of *Alice in Wonderland*,[42] in which a whiff of Kafka is perceptible). I would, on the other hand, like to stress the uneasy feeling the reader experiences when the order of *langue* is threatened with subversion or disruption. Nonsense, therefore, is a kind of textual double-bind, or paradox. It is both free and constrained. It tells the reader to abide, and not to abide, by the rules of language. We are back with the already mentioned paradox: I speak language, in other words I am master of the instrument which allows me to communicate with others, and yet it is language that speaks: I am constrained by the language I inhabit to such an extent that I am inhabited, or possessed by it. The grandeur of nonsense, as a literary genre, is that it foregrounds the predicament of every speaker of language: we are torn apart between the two opposite poles of the paradox and yet we must, somehow, hold them together. What I am suggesting is that nonsense itself, if this is the core of it, is a paradoxical object.

CONCLUSION

Coming after my reading of Ettelson, the last section has an appearance of hubris that will not have escaped the reader. Any reading of 'Jabberwocky' is pre-empted by the very excess of Ettelson's reading – it can only appear as a pale copy of it. My only excuse is that I have not offered an interpretation of the poem so much as a method, a series of instructions for use, for reading nonsense texts. I have concentrated not on the results of the interpretation of the poem (be they in terms of existential angst, the classic fairytale or the Talmud) but on the linguistic paths towards interpretation. Ettelson has taught us the madness that lies at the core of nonsense; I have been trying to sketch the method. I shall try, in my reading of nonsense texts, to be faithful to both aspects.

1

THE LINGUISTICS OF NONSENSE

INTRODUCTION

It is a vexed question whether rules of grammar, or linguistic laws, describe properties of a language, or of all languages, which are real, that is which have real existence in language or in the mind-brain (to speak like Chomsky), or whether they are only theoretical constructs. The epistemology of linguistics, as of all other sciences, has its realist, and its constructivist, versions. Thus, whether the four levels at which we have accounted for 'Jabberwocky' – phonology, morphology, syntax and semantics – are natural, or real, levels, or only figments of the linguist's fertile imagination, is a hotly debated point. Although I sympathise with the constructivists, I do not intend to enter the field. What interests me is that nonsense texts treat those levels as natural. The texts can be easily analysed along such levels because they seem spontaneously to conform to them. And the numerous intuitions about language which authors of nonsense express, in their rare moments of reflection or in their abundant practice, confirm this – the texts not only conform to the levels, they play with them, or play one against the others, as if they were natural objects. I shall attempt to show this by reading another nonsense poem.

In the Gloaming

The twilight twiles in the vernal vale,
In adumbration of azure awe,
And I listlessly list in my swallow-tail
To the limpet licking his limber jaw.
And it's O for the sound of the daffodil,
For the dry distillings of prawn and prout,
When hope hops high and a heather hill

27

Is a dear delight and a darksome doubt.
The snagwap sits in the bosky brae
And sings to the gumplet in accents sweet;
The gibwink hasn't a word to say,
But pensively smiles at the fair keeweet
And it's O for the jungles of Boorabul.
For the jingling jungles to jangle in,
With a moony maze of mellado mull,
And a protoplasm for next of kin.
O' sweet is the note of the shagreen shard
And mellow the mew of the mastodon,
When the soboliferous Somminard
Is scenting the shadows at set of sun.
And it's O for the timorous tamarind
In the murky meadows of Maroboo,
For the suave sirocco of Sazerkind,
And the pimpernell pellets of Pangipoo.

James C. Bayles[1]

The most striking aspect of this ballad is that, in spite of its rather banal title, we do not understand much, and feel that its inclusion in an anthology of nonsense verse is entirely justified. There are two obvious reasons for this incapacity to understand – the semantic incoherence of the text, and the presence of coined words. At first sight, coinages seem to be particularly abundant, to the point that the semantic gaps defy interpretation. We shall never know what a snagwap or a gumplet is. But if we look at it more closely, the situation is not as simple as it seems. We must remember that for the meagre 20,000 words that a cultivated English-speaker knows, there are a million and a half in the largest dictionary of the language. As a consequence, not all the apparent coinages – apparent, at least, to this reader – are true inventions. Thus, 'snagwap' is not in the *Oxford English Dictionary* (*OED*), but 'gumplet' is, or at least 'gump', a dolt. The Somminard does not appear to exist, but if it did it might well be soboliferous (from latin *soboles*, bearing shoots). The use of false coinages is traditional in nonsense, from Lear's spurious Indian poem, 'The Cummerbund', where the innocuous silk waistband, rarely seen nowadays except at Cambridge May balls, becomes a damsel-devouring monster, to Mervyn Peake's

Of crags and octoroons,
Of whales and broken bottles

28

Of quicksands cold and grey,
Of ullages and dottles,
I have no more to say.[2]

Even if we disregard the false coinages, truly invented words are numerous in 'In the Gloaming', and they are of two kinds. Some, like 'mellado', are exotic: they boast of their alien origin, they obtrude. Some, like 'gibwink' or even 'prout', are more timid: they make an attempt at integration, they would like to pass for native creatures by conforming to the phonotactics of the English language. In other words, coinages naturally fall into the same categories as actually existing words. Some are simple and English-looking, and modestly conform to the Fowlers' rules ('Prefer the familiar word to the far-fetched. Prefer the Saxon word to the Romance'),[3] while others are linguistic immigrants.

It now appears that my two obvious reasons for our incapacity to understand reduce to one: semantic incoherence. One can never be certain that the 'coined' word one discovers in a text does not have existence, and conventional meaning, in a larger dictionary or a specialised jargon. The frontier between coinages and normal words is uncertain, and it is notoriously difficult to commit a 'barbarism' in English. In the case of our poem, this mixture of true and false coinages, which is more perverse than in 'Jabber-wocky', results in semantic undecidability. We imperceptibly go from metaphors, like 'azure awe', which in spite of their exaggerated nature possess partial coherence and allow for pragmatic calculus, to the semantic void of coinages. Even if the image evoked by the 'limpet licking his limber jaw' is ludicrous (pleasantly so), it does allow me to understand the line. Whereas, when I read about 'the snagwap sitting in the bosky brae' (I have no objection to the brae being 'bosky', but I still do not know what a 'snagwap' is), I find myself like the gibwink, who 'hasn't a word to say'. In fact, the passage from semi-coherent metaphors to downright incoherent nonsense is hardly noticeable. Metaphors in this text are self-destroying because they exaggerate one of the characteristics of all metaphors, their blatant falsity. Awe is not naturally 'azure', nor is the sirocco 'suave'. This exaggeration tends towards paradox, or the random filling of syntactic positions, as embodied in true coinages. The tendential passage from metaphor to semantic void is, I believe, characteristic of the whole genre.

There is another aspect of the text that ought to attract our attention, although it is not as obvious as the first: the syntax is entirely correct. There is no chaos at this level. Not only is the syntax correct, but it is also by no means elementary or childish. The ballad form of the poem might lead us to expect a dominance of paratactic devices. Indeed, the 'And it's O for . . .' leitmotiv belongs to the tradition of oral poetry. But apart from lines 14 to 16 ('For the jingling jungles . . .'), there is little paratax. Grammatical links, words like 'and' and 'when', regularly recur, and the text as a whole tends towards hypotax. The paratactic 'and' is sometimes caught in a network of clauses, and the hypotactic 'when' explicitly introduces subordination. Of course, poems syntactically more complex are not difficult to find, but this incipient attraction to hypotax is interesting, because it illustrates the moment when, or rather the logical point where, nonsense goes from the transcription of oral popular literature to a form of written high literature. We understand why, if such is the evolution of the genre, syntactic regularity, or even conformism, is of the essence.

The poem is not only syntactically, but also prosodically, regular. It is composed of iambic tetrameters, with a rather high proportion of anapaests, as appears in line 4:

$$\text{Tŏ thĕ l\=impĕt l\=ickĭng hĭs l\=imbĕr j\=aw.}$$

This regularity is also an important feature of the poem. All the more so as it is not restricted to prosody, but is increased by the obsessional recourse to alliteration. As appears in the case of the limpet, alliteration paradoxically compensates for semantic incoherence and induces it. It compensates for it because it provides a structure which allows the reader to cling to a formal regularity when he or she is semantically lost. It induces it because the real mode of composition of the line is the semantically random but alliteratively constrained filling of syntactic positions. In other words, the text has adopted Swinburne's method of composition – the poem is an obvious parody of his style – to extreme and excessive lengths, to the point where the metaphors dissolve and sense disappears. Swinburne himself was, of course, perfectly capable of doing the same thing, as appears in his self-parody, *Nephelidia*:

> From the depth of the dreamy decline of the dawn through a
> notable nimbus of nebulous noonshine,
> Pallid and pink as the palm of the flag-flower that flickers with
> fear of the flies as they float.[4]

30

And since intertext compensates for the absent semantic structure, we may also note that the poem's lurid exoticism, as in Lear's 'Cummerbund', mocks the fake local colour of Anglo-Indian poetry. Three lines from Kipling's 'Christmas in India' will suffice:

Dim dawn behind the tamarisks – the sky is saffron yellow –
As the women in the village grind the corn,
And the parrots seek the river-side, each calling to his fellow.

In this analysis of 'In the Gloaming', a principle of composition has emerged, which we shall consider as characteristic of nonsense writing. The lack of structure at one level (here, the semantic level) is amply compensated by an excess of structure at other levels (here, the syntactic and prosodic levels). Lack of sense here is always compensated by excess or proliferation of sense there. This, which is the central paradox, or contradiction, of the genre, we shall explore by methodically going, as announced, from one linguistic level to the next.

PHONETICS

In my analysis of 'Jabberwocky', I have already used a typology of imaginary languages, borrowed – or rather adapted – from the seminal essay by Etienne Souriau, which dates back to 1965, 'Sur l'esthétique des mots et des langages forgés'.[5] *Charabia*, it will be recalled, is the name I give to the coinage of 'regularly' invented words, *baragouin* the playful imitation of a foreign tongue, and *lanternois* the proliferation of obsessional phonemes. *Charabia* concerns *langue* coinages, of which 'In the Gloaming' offers a superb instance in the first line:

The twilight twiles in the vernal vale

The verb 'twile' does not exist – but this sad fact does not prevent us from being aware that it is a verb, and knowing exactly what it means. The coinage conforms not only to the phonotactics, but also to what we might call the morphotactics of English. *Lanternois*, on the other hand, refers to idiosyncratic, or *parole* coinages, in which the speaker's instinctual drives are more directly expressed, and the unconscious returns in the guise of linguistic symptoms. They are not frequent in nonsense, but they are prevalent in the delirium of mental patients or in glossolalia. Their theory is adumbrated in Fónagy's essay on the instinctual

31

basis of speech sounds.[6] Sounds represent – 'embody' might be a better word – instinctual drives. Like drives, which Freud describes as being on the frontier between soma and psyche, they have a somatic aspect, and a psychic one, in that on the one hand they can be made the bearers of intentionality while on the other hand they can cathect affects. Lastly, coming as they do from one of the orifices of the body, from a sphincter, they can easily be eroticised and made, by metonymy or metaphor, to represent various erogenous zones and the pleasures there produced. Thus, Fonagy has fascinating pages on the 'vulgarity' which ordinary speakers ascribe to certain sounds, a vulgarity due to the metonymic association between the position of the organs of speech during their production and that of the other orifices of the body.[7] We understand why we may call the coinages of *lanternois* symptomatic. Here is an instance of *lanternois* in our corpus: the main character in one of Lear's ballads is called the Yonghy-Bonghy-Bò.[8] What I find most interesting in this name is the accent on the last syllable, a typographic sign banal in Italian but exotic in English. That it expresses the exotic nature of the bearer of the name, who lives 'on the coast of Coromandel, where the early pumpkins blow', is certain – but here the exotic becomes personal, as the accent must be taken for what it is, for instance, in Italian, a mark of phonetic stress, giving the name a trochaic rhythm: Yŏnghy̆-Bŏnghy̆- Bò. And, of course, the repetition of the same cluster of phonemes (/gɪ/ and /bɔ/) is a characteristic of the *lanternois* one encounters in child language, with its duplicated syllables as in 'gigi' or 'namby-pamby'. That the name also expresses one speaker's phonic fantasies is made apparent by another coined word, in one of Lear's nonsense letters to his friend Evelyn Baring, 'abbiblebongibo', in which the same phonemes are obsessionally disseminated.[9]

Although it would be of greater interest to the psychoanalyst, *lanternois* is rare in nonsense. So is, for that matter, the deformation of the speaker's language which is a characteristic of comic literature. In *Alice's Adventures in Wonderland*, Pat the lizard, who is employed by the White Rabbit as a gardener, is a character out of a comic novel:

'Now tell me, Pat, what's that in the window?'
'Sure, it's an arm, yer honour!' (He pronounced it 'arrum'.)[10]

As we can see, the distortion is only allowed in parenthesis, as a curiosity, after it has been 'normalised' in the text. Carroll's use here is no different from Dickens's or any other mimetic novelist's, except that it is rather more timid, and more respectful of 'correct' language. It is not even entirely coherent, since 'yer' is allowed within the text. The whole thing does not go beyond a rather limited use of a widely accepted convention. Again, we find that, surprisingly, the author of nonsense is, as far as language is concerned, something of a conformist.

The form of imaginary language that prevails in nonsense is *charabia*. Nonsense does not invent words at random. It exploits the possibilities offered by the phonotactics of English, i.e. the rules governing the possible combinations of phonemes. The meaningful combinations of phonemes, in other words morphemes, do not exhaust the possibilities of lawful combinations, thus leaving room for the nonsensical author's linguistic (i.e. constrained) imagination. To quote one phonetician:

> English does not exploit, in the word and the syllable, all the possible combinations of its phonemes. For instance, long vowels and diphthongs do not precede final /ŋ/; /e, æ, ʌ, ɒ/ do not occur finally; the types of consonant clusters permitted are subject to constraints. *Initially*, /ŋ/ does not occur; no combinations are possible with /tʃ, dʒ, ð, z/; /r, j, w/ can occur in clusters only as the non-initial element; such initial sequence as /fs, mh, stl, spw/ are unknown, etc. *Finally*, only /l/ may occur before non-syllabic /m, n/; ... terminal sequences such as /kʃ, ʃp, lð, ʒbd/ are unknown.[11]

What Gimson is telling us is that, for commonsensical or for obscure reasons, for reasons of ease of articulation or of historical accident, there are constraints on the possible combinations of phonemes. These, nonsense ordinarily respects – all the coinages in 'Jabberwocky', for instance, and most of Lear's coinages are licit. But ordinary language does not actually use all the licit combinations. A simple subtraction will give us the field where the coinages of nonsense grow. Their 'irregularity' is therefore always contingent (the English language has not used this string of phonemes, but it might have done), and dominated by a deeper regularity. This, we have already come to realise, is the centre of the position of nonsense towards language. The irregularity of *charabia* is controlled and tame, it comforts the regularity it seems to exploit; and, within the genre, *charabia* dominates over the true irregularity of *lanternois* (as one talks of 'true madness'), which, however, returns and threatens subversion, as we saw in the case of Lear. This contradiction between a form of hyper-coding, an exaggerated respect for the code, and a form of hypo-coding, the subversion of the code, is what makes nonsense texts what they are. Souriau is aware of this when he contrasts the 'plastic nature of the language of novels and poems' with the 'rigidity of rational and institutional language',[12] and when he celebrates the psychological significance and efficacy of coined language. There is, he claims, a whole aesthetics of the *hapax*, of the unique encounter, a rare experience in the collectivised field of language. In this, the practice of the nonsense writer reflects and enhances that of the poet – his is a controlled misprision of language, like the poet's and unlike the delirious mental patient's. The only difference is that the writer of nonsense is more timid than the poet, whose flights of fancy may take him beyond the code – the former wishes to remain within the pale, the latter is prepared to cross the border.

A nonsense writer, then, is a timid poet, whose attitude towards the linguistic code is one of conformity and, at the same time, exploitation. Provided, of course, that conformity eventually triumphs over the dangers of exploitation. Nonsense is a serious genre – preserving the code is its main task. This is why coinages, which exploit the code, are not always present in nonsense, and the following anonymous poem is as characteristic of the genre as 'In the Gloaming':

'*Tis midnight*

'Tis midnight, and the setting sun
Is slowly rising in the west;
The rapid rivers slowly run,
The frog is on his downy nest.
The pensive goat and sportive cow,
Hilarious, leap from bough to bough.[13]

It is easy to see why the poem belongs, as of right, to nonsense. Semantic incoherence and logical paradoxes are also constitutive of the genre, and we shall deal with them in due course. At this point, however, we can only note that from the point of view of syntax, morphology or phonetics, the poem is totally regular. There is no question of an imaginary language here. In fact, although they are justly famous, instances of *charabia* and *lanternois* are not so frequent in Carroll, and rare in Lear. Or rather, in Lear's case, there appears to be a separation between the published nonsense of the limericks, where the excessive appeal to constraints at all levels precludes the use of imaginary language, and his letters, where Lear's own *lanternois* is rather frequent. Lear was a facetious correspondent, who often spelt 'note' as 'gnoat', 'physical' as 'fizzicle' (modern advertisers of fizzy beverages have remembered this), 'fibs' as 'phibs', and 'an armchair' as a 'a narmchair', which is only the reverse of the folk- segmentation that has given us 'an umpire' out of 'a non-peer'. Here is one of his letters to Evelyn Baring, a young man who seems to have provoked the best, and the worst, nonsense that Lear had in him – for reasons which, no doubt, Fonagy would be prepared to explain:

> deerbaringiphoundacuppelloffotografsthismawningwitchi sendjoo thereiswunofeachsortsoyookankeepbothifyooliketo doosoandwenyoohaveabetterwunöfyourselfletmehaveit.[14]

This, although it is obviously adequate as the expression of Lear's affect(ion), is not nonsense, precisely because it is too direct a form of expression. Nonsense does not seek to express the writer's emotions. Its main interest is in language, in the exploration and preservation of what Husserl calls the *formal* aspect of language. And because the exploration is careful and systematic, nonsense is not merely concerned with language, but also functions as metalanguage – it dwells within the paradoxical necessity and impossibility of a metalanguage for natural languages. The linguist needs a metalanguage in order to talk about language, and yet, in spite of his sometimes feeble and sometimes strong attempts at formalisation, he always has to resort to a natural language in order to talk about it. *Alice's Adventures in Wonderland* is full of potentially metalinguistic episodes, the best known of which is the Cheshire Cat's question: 'Did you say "pig", or "fig"?',[15] in which the crucial structuralist thesis on phonology, the differential value of phonemes, is embodied in the guise of the usual test for differential value, a minimal pair. However, this episode, which once again demonstrates the quality of Carroll's linguistic intuitions, is only one side of the coin. For the paradox is that the metalinguistic intuition has already been implicitly ruined in an earlier episode, when Alice is falling down the rabbit-hole:

> 'But do cats eat bats, I wonder?' And here Alice began to get rather sleepy, and went on saying to herself, in a dreamy sort of way, 'Do cats eat bats? Do cats eat bats?' and sometimes,

'Do bats eat cats?' for, you see, as she couldn't answer either question, it didn't much matter which way she put it.[16]

By inverting the terms of the sentence, Alice turns the 'bat'/'cat' opposition into a minimal pair. But, as so often in Carroll, the context is so peculiar that it prevents the normal application of the rules. If the pair is a 'minimal pair', changing the terms must change the meaning. What enables me to state that 'p' and 'f' in English are distinct phonemes is the fact that the phonemic strings 'pig' and 'fig' do not have the same meaning. But in this case, the meaning does not seem to have significantly changed. Alice, 'in a dreamy sort of way', is playing with the words without paying attention to their differential value, as children and nonsense texts are apt to do. In other words, if the 'pig'/'fig' episode preserves the code by explicitly proposing an example, from which a general rule will be deduced, the 'bat'/'cat' episode subverts the code by describing a possible playful exploitation of the rules. Rules of grammar, in the widest sense, are always stated tongue in cheek in nonsense – but using them paradoxically, or parodically, presupposes that one recognises them first, in both senses of the term.

Nevertheless, this episode has clearly shown that the attitude of nonsense texts towards language is not one of playful imitation or random disorganisation. Comic imitation of the language of children or country bumpkins is not frequent in nonsense, and always disastrous, as in the case of the child Bruno in Carroll's *Sylvie and Bruno*, whose baby-talk is unbearably mawkish. There is no blurring of the code in nonsense – what there is is either description or exploitation. Or both. Exploitation always threatens to subvert the rules, which description reaffirms.

At the level of phonetics, exploitation takes two forms: euphony or dysphony. Euphonic exploitation corresponds to *charabia*. Here is another instance – and another pastiche of 'Jabberwocky', this time by Harriet R. White:

> *Uffia*
> When sporgles spanned the floreate mead
> And cogwogs gleet upon the lea,
> Uffia gopped to meet her love
> Who smeeged upon the equat sea.
>
> Dately she walked aglost the sand;
> The boreal wind seet in her face;

36

The moggling waves yalped at her feet;
Pangwangling was her pace.[17]

The usual features can be noted. The poem can be read aloud, and it is obviously in English. The coined words conform to the rules of phonotactics to the point that they never disturb the prosodic structure of the poem, which is composed of iambic tetrameters. All those new words, like 'sporgle' and 'cogwog' deserve to exist; indeed, 'cog' and 'wog' already exist independently – where it appears that the phrase 'deserving to exist' is no longer a convenient metaphor, but a concept, the extension of which is the class of licit but unused combinations of phonemes. The author enjoys the rare pleasure of being a deliberate *Sprachkünstler*. Not the usual Unknown Coiner, but a self-conscious coiner, whose taste for the music of words takes her into controlled glossolalia. We understand why the nonsense of nursery rhymes is so useful to young children: they learn language by learning to manipulate its sounds. Thus, they learn what no rules can teach them – that there is a music specific to the English tongue. Euphony is the right name for this type of exploitation.

But nonsense sometimes adopts the opposite tactics of dysphony. Uffia was pleasant; the Crankadox is much more reminiscent of the Jabberwock – which is obviously its source:

The Crankadox leaned o'er the edge of the moon,
And wistfully gazed on the sea
Where the Gryxabodill madly whistled a tune
To the air of 'Ti-fol-de-ding-dee'.
The quavering shriek of the Fliupthecreek
Was fitfully wafted afar
To the queen of the Wunks as she powdered her cheeks
With the pulverized rays of a star.[18]

Although the dysphonic nature of the words 'Crankadox' and 'Gryxabodill' should be intuitively obvious, the limits of the attempt must be noted. These words may not be as 'deserving' as the coinages in 'Uffia', but they can still be pronounced without doing undue violence to our linguistic habits. I can ascribe their natural stresses to these inexistent words – Cránkadox, Grýxabodìll (with main stress on the first syllable and secondary on the last), no doubt because I am aware of the anapaestic structure of the poem. Dysphony is never total, not only because unpronounceable words do not always make good poems, but also

37

because exploitation never produces chaos – merely a cosmos that is slightly awry. Homer sometimes nods; nonsense texts often limp, but the limp is affected. The poem is ready to leap when the opportunity comes.

We can take the contrast between dominant euphony and dominated dysphony as our first illustration of the dialectics of excess and lack in nonsense. There is an excess of phonetic rules in nonsense: rules of phonotactics, of accentuation, of prosody and metrics. And there is also exploitation, a threatened but never achieved subversion of these rules – dysphony and *lanternois* are its names. But there is no extremist flouting of rules, no equivalent of Artaud's *cris*. We understand why Artaud disliked Carroll so much, why he accused him of having plagiarised him in advance. The object of nonsense is not the dissolution of all phonetic or phonological rules, but rather the mapping of them. Nonsense seeks to find out exactly what can be said, given the fact that not everything is actually said. We shall see later that such an attitude is deeply concerned with pedagogy.

MORPHOLOGY

The reason why screams are absent from nonsense is that nonsense texts explore articulate language. One way of doing this is to coin new words. We have studied the phonology of coinages – now is the time to consider their morphology.

Not all coinages have a specific morphology. The easiest – one might even be tempted to say, the most inventive – way to coin a word is just to produce a string of phonemes as different from any existing word as one can make them – in other words, to coin a totally unmotivated word in Saussure's sense, a word in which no information can be derived from its constituent parts. 'Five', according to Saussure, is such a word, as opposed to 'thirty-five', which, being the logical combination of two independent constituents, is said to be partially motivated. Global coinages, i.e. unmotivated new words, are rather rare in nonsense. Here is an example, '*l'envoi*' in an anonymous ballad entitled, 'To Marie':

> It is pilly-po-doddle and aligobung
> When the lollypup covers the ground,
> Yet the poldiddle perishes plunkety-pung
> When the heart jimny-coggles around.
> If the soul cannot snoop at the gigglesome cart

THE LINGUISTICS OF NONSENSE

> Seeking surcease in gluggety-glug,
> It is useless to say to the pulsating heart,
> 'Yankee-doodle ker-chuggety-chug!'[19]

The origin of this type of nonsense is clear. It imitates the onomatopoeic jingles of nursery rhymes and Irish ballads. But there is facility in such imitation. Child language – such repetitive words as 'higgledy-piggledy' or 'hoity-toity' – is profoundly satisfactory because of its use of onomatopoeia, but its imitation is pointless, both facile and difficult. In 1726 Henry Carey parodied the sentimental ballads of Ambrose Phillips, and gave the word 'namby-pamby' to the English language:

> Let the verse the subject fit
> Little subject, little wit.
> Namby-Pamby is your guide,
> Albion's joy, Hibernia's pride.
> Namby-Pamby, Pilly–piss,
> Rhimy-pim'd on Missy-Miss;
> Tartaretta Tartaree
> From the navel to the knee.[20]

The object of Carey's satire is the ease with which one produces such words, by a rather simple rule of duplication of vowels and change of consonants. One is reminded of a character in Kingsley Amis's *Ending Up*, who affects child language of this type and utters phrases like 'you noodle-poodles', or 'she's most frighfully sweetle-peetles'.[21] And it is easy to see why success, as opposed to ridiculous failure, is difficult. Imitative harmony, which is aimed at in these coinages, needs subtler methods than the simple repetition of a vowel.

Such coinages are rare in nonsense. The genre prefers regular morphology to imitative harmony. Most of the coinages, therefore, are of the relatively motivated type. Even a word like 'tove' in 'Jabberwocky', which is not easily analysed into meaningful constituents, can be the bearer of suffixes, that is, it can enter into the morphological structure of the sentence. Indeed, in the poem, those toves are definitely plural. And the word 'outgrabe' will under analysis yield three constituent morphemes, 'out', 'gribe' and 'past', thus allowing conjugation. The mome raths were outgribing last night; and what, pray have they outgribben? (No actual occurrence of the last word has been observed so far, except of course for this, but it is a most obvious candidate for existence; Carroll himself uses the present participle, 'outgribing'.) To unmanageable units like 'pilly-po-doddle' or 'aligobung', which I would hardly call words were it not for typographic signs like spaces and hyphens, nonsense will prefer Lear's 'runcible' spoon, the bearer of a well-known adjectival suffix, and obviously cognate with the adjective 'runcinate', from the specialised language of botany (where it designates a leaf whose shape is 'irregularly saw-toothed').

The speciality of nonsense, therefore, is not merely word creation, but *regular* word formation. I am using the latter term to show that nonsense only does, on the individual level, what language does all the time on the social level. As usual, the linguistic imagination of nonsense is highly constrained. It does not invent in a vacuum, but by imitating and exploiting rules. It does not, for instance, imitate all the techniques of regular word creation. There are no acronyms, like 'nylon', in nonsense, unless we decide that 'tove' is an acronym which we can no longer interpret. What is chiefly imitated is the regular derivation of words from existing suffixes or prefixes, the borrowing of foreign words, or the conversion of a word from its habitual part of speech to another.

If we look at Lear's coinages, we shall find them as regular as possible. The 'great Gromboolian plain' uses the normal suffix. Even the Pobble's action, when he 'tinkledy-binkledy-winkled a bell'[22] is produced by regular techniques of composition and derivation, and the word can be analysed into its immediate constituents, as shown in Figure 1.1.

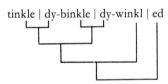

Figure 1.1

This is a striking phrase, since it combines imitative harmony (repetition of the vowel in the onomatopoeic verb 'tinkle', and change of consonant) with regular suffixes (derivation) and marks of concatenation (composition). Nonsense often plays with sounds; but what it really likes to play with is rules. I should, however, add that my immediate constitutent analysis normalises a construction which is ambiguous. I have separated 'tinkle-' and

'-dy' because of the verb that is the obvious origin of the phrase – one *can* hear a bell tinkle. But the phrase offers another possible structure, morphologically incoherent but nevertheless somehow regular, (tinkled)y-(binkled)y-(winkled), where the final past form is anticipated, illegally so, in the first two constituents. This subversion, however, is not chaotic – it substitutes another regularity for the expected one. As we can see, subversion in nonsense does not result in the dissolution of all rules, but in the creation of new ones.

Playing with language in nonsense texts is very similar to what Judith Milner calls 'linguistic jokes'.[23] Those, she claims, presuppose a certain knowledge about language, which, even if it does not reach the level of metalinguistic explicitness, goes some way beyond mere knowledge *of* language. Thus, Lear's coined verb implies an intuitive knowledge of the immediate constituents of a complex word and of their hierarchy, even if it also subverts them. Such knowledge is indeed implicit when those hierarchies are mocked or exploited, as is the case with many of Carroll's coined words. Thus, the Mock Turtle embodies a mistake in immediate constituent analysis, which presupposes the possibility of a correct analysis (Figure 1.2).

Figure 1.2

The hyphen in the first phrase is the mark of the wrong segmentation, and it creates the creature. Carroll's portmanteau-words can usually be analysed along the same lines (see Figure 1.3).

Figure 1.3

As the figure shows, the analysis is not so much wrong as paradoxical: Carroll practises a form of syntactic Brissetising,[24] that type of compulsive analysis which compels us to re-analyse what has already been analysed once, with the result that the visual monster, or chimera, that results from Tenniel's attempt at representing the Rocking-horse-fly is in reality the best representation of a *linguistic* monster, an impossible double analysis. Of course, nonsense only practises what language normally practises. The morphological monsters of false composition are the mirror-images of the analytic monsters of folk etymology. When I analyse 'hamburger' into 'ham' and 'burger', I am analysing the same string *a second time*, since the correct analysis, 'Hamburg' and '-er' logically precedes the incorrect one. Linguists have described the practice under the name 'metanalysis': the Snap-dragon-fly is an embodied metanalysis.

Nonsense also imitates, and mocks, the borrowing of foreign words, which is one of the quickest ways of increasing the lexicon of a language. The practice is rife with potential mistakes and misunderstandings. Jerusalem artichokes are so called not because they come from Jerusalem, but because their name in Italian is *girasole* (sunflower), the plant that rotates with the sun. 'Cravats' were first worn by Croatians, and so on. If ordinary language indulges in provocation in this way, we understand the mischievous pleasure with which Lear must have written his 'Cummerbund':

> She sate upon her Dobie,
> To watch the evening star,
> And all the Punkahs as they passed,
> Cried, 'My! how fair you are!'
> Around her bower, with quivering leaves,
> The tall Kamsamahs grew,
> And Kitmutgars in wild festoons
> Hung down from Tchokis blue.[25]

A lexicon of Anglo-Indian terms will tell us that a dobie is a washerman, a punkah a fan, a kamsamah a cook, a kitmutgar a butler, and a tchoki a shed or a chair. And we also understand the strategic importance of botany for Lear, who wrote some 'nonsense botany'. His *monstres de langue*, when they are not banal dragons like the Cummerbund, are plants. For botany is a rich and specialised lexical field, both in scientific discourse (the Linnean taxonomy) and in local dialect and lore – a lexical field that is usually opaque to the layman, and as a result particularly apt to harbour false coinages. We must also note that, in this poem, as usual, the Indian words are morphologically Anglicised (some bear the plural morpheme), and inserted into correct syntactic slots – in my quotation, they are all nouns. This is no different from 'Jabberwocky', of which 'The Cummerbund' is probably an imitation. Lear has marked his difference by shifting from true to false coinages.

The third type of nonsense coinage is produced by conversion. Two examples will be better than any explanation:

> Across the moorlands of the Not
> We chase the gruesome When;
> And hunt the Itness of the What
> Through forests of the Then . . . [26]
>
> Why and Wherefore set out one day
> To hunt for a wild Negation.
> They agreed to meet at a cool retreat
> On the Point of Interrogation . . . [27]

The second poem turns the linguistic play into mere witticism. Its title, 'Metaphysics', makes the satirical point of such undertaking explicit. But conversion is not the only means of satirising the obscure jargon of philosophers, lawyers and theologians, it is also an essential aspect of the workings of the English language, the plastic character of which it illustrates and celebrates. Here, nonsense is not only imitating an age-old tradition which goes back to Shakespeare ('Grace me no grace, nor uncle me no uncle', *Richard II*, II. iii. 85), it is exploiting one of the richest devices for word formation in contemporary English: the nominalisation of almost any word, in order to produce what Lakoff and Johnson call an ontological metaphor.[28] Our lives as philosophers or social scientists are spent among such linguistic monsters. We are daily trafficking with the Ego and the Id, and the When and the What (or indeed the Whatnot) are not unknown to us. Nonsense, in resorting to this type of conversion, rather than to the more productive adjectivalisation of nouns, as in 'a film buff' or 'a taxi driver', is not only exploiting a rule of the English language, but also reflecting on our attitude to grammar. As Nietzsche said, how can we hope to get rid of God, so long as we insist on believing in grammar? Nonsense is the enactment of this belief. By mocking the capacity that grammar possesses to create entities destined for Occam's razor, it does not just show us how language constrains thought, it also demonstrates the power that grammatical rules derive from their very regularity. The nonsense poems quoted above seem to deride the excesses of metaphysicians – they end up exalting the regularity of language. Behind the author of nonsense who exploits the loopholes of grammar, there is a linguistic realist lurking, who believes in the positive (even the positivist) thesis that grammatical practice reaches objective characteristics of the language it describes.

The type of word that nonsense is famed for is not simply coinage, but a specific type of coinage: portmanteau-words. Not so much because they first appeared in a nonsense text, as because they were named in one:

> Well, '*slithy*' means 'lithe and slimy'. 'Lithe' is the same as 'active'. You see it's like a portmanteau – there are two meanings packed up into one word.[29]

The phrase, which is of course Humpty Dumpty's, has now found its way into most dictionaries. The name may be new, but the thing is not. Again, language does it all the time. A number of words in our everyday vocabulary are concealed portmanteau-words. 'Knoll', I am told, comes from the fusion of 'knell' and 'toll', and French '*intendance*' from '*intention*' and '*tendance*'. And the device is extremely productive, especially in the fields of advertising and journalese, as witnesses the following list, which I borrow from A. Grésillon's study of portmanteau-words: Air Farce, alcoholidays, beducation, cabarazy, chaosmos (this one comes from Joyce himself), refujews, sexploitation, soliloquacity. Grésillon's complete list, which does not claim to be more than a sample, is three pages long.[30]

In the dream-work of language, ordinary coinages are instances of displacement. Carroll's verb 'gyre' will evoke, on the one hand, 'gyroscope', and on the other hand the series 'bire', 'mire', 'dire'. Portmanteau-words are instances of condensation. Such, at least, is Humpty Dumpty's theory. The only trouble with it is that it is obviously false. Humpty Dumpty's explanations are semantic, whereas the rules for the formation of portmanteau-words are morphological. In fact, Carroll's coinages, which are rather difficult to understand without help, are marginal cases. They do not conform to what for Grésillon is the *sine qua non* for the formation of a portmanteau word, the presence of a string of phonemes common to the two words that have merged into one. She calls this the 'homophonous string'. Thus, the presence of 'hol' makes 'alcoholidays' immediately understandable. There is no such string in 'slithy'. And if we look at Humpty Dumpty's explanations of the difficult words in 'Jabberwocky', we shall note that they are inconsistent. I can, at a push, agree with his analysis of 'slithy', or with the usual analysis of 'snark' as the fusion of 'snail' and 'shark' (which has produced the rather pleasant French monster, the *escarquin*). But I cannot accept his explanation for 'the mome raths outgrabe' as anything but an exercise in arbitrary definition:

> 'Well, a *"rath"* is a sort of green pig: but *"mome"* I'm not certain about. I think it's short for "from home" – meaning that they'd lost their way, you know.'
> 'And what does *"outgrabe"* mean?'
> 'Well, *"outgribing"* is something between bellowing and whistling, with a kind of sneeze in the middle: however, you'll hear it done, maybe – down in the wood yonder – and, when you've once heard it, you'll be *quite* content. Who's been repeating all that hard stuff to you?'[31]

It must be said that although Humpty Dumpty's definitions are arbitrary, they are also, in this case, tentative. Those are 'hard' words, the meanings of which are difficult to understand. An ostensive definition is better when it is available, although it is suggested that when Alice finally knows what outgribing means, she may not like it. But Humpty Dumpty *is* inconsistent, as much as Ettelson. His methods for ascribing meaning to words are as diverse as they are numerous. 'Mome', for instance, is not accounted for by linguistic condensation, but by corruption or linguistic erosion, a case of what etymologists call aphaeresis, or the clipping of initial sounds. But the most striking aspect is the sheer difficulty of inventing entirely new words. My *Annotated Alice*[32] tells me that ' "mome" has a number of obsolete meanings, such as mother, a blockhead, a carping critic, none of which, judging from Humpty Dumpty's interpretation, Carroll had in mind', and the same applies to 'rath' or even 'gimble' ('According to the O.E.D., "gimble" is a variant spelling of "gimbal". Gimbals are pivoted rings used for various purposes, such as suspending a ship's compass so that it remains horizontal while the ship rolls. Humpty Dumpty makes clear, however, that the verb "gimble" is here used in a different sense.'[33]) The nonsensical coiner is in a position of belatedness. He lives in a linguistic world where Aristotle's views about the scarcity of words in relation to potential referents (in *De Sophisticis Elenchis*, 1, 615a, 11) is true, and it is no longer possible to invent truly new words (this, of course, is gross exaggeration), so that the coiner is reduced to coining new meanings, through catachresis or metaphor.

The morphological account of portmanteau-words, which is the only coherent one, is constantly avoided, one perhaps should say repressed, in Carroll. It is replaced by a number of different accounts, as Carroll himself plays a second Humpty Dumpty for the benefit of the readers. The first account can be found as early as the preface to *Through the Looking-Glass*. Apparently, it is not so much a theory of the formation of portmanteau-words as a series of phonetic instructions for use:

> The new words, in the poem 'Jabberwocky', have given rise to some differences of opinion as to their pronunciation: so it may be well to give instructions on *that* point also. Pronounce 'slithy' as if it were the two words 'sly, the': make the 'g' *hard* in 'gyre' and 'gimble': and pronounce 'rath' to rhyme with 'bath.'[34]

There is a certain amount of flippancy in this indirect account. The use of 'also' and of the underlined 'that' seems to leave the task of explanation to Humpty Dumpty. But at the same time, Carroll suggests a *different* explanation for the word 'slithy', under the disguise of phonetic analysis. Indeed, if 'slithy' is to be a portmanteau-word, is it not natural that it should contain 'sly' and perhaps 'the' or, why not, 'thee'? As a result, Humpty Dumpty's semantic account is, in anticipation, undermined by a phonetic account. All the more so as the rest of the paragraph suggests an analysis for coined words other than the condensation of portmanteau-words – displacement, as in the phonetic series 'rath'/ 'bath'. Not that Carroll was really hostile to a semantic analysis of coinages. The portmanteau-words of 'Jabberwocky' first appear in 'Stanza of Anglo-Saxon Poetry', a juvenile poem which he wrote for *Misch-Masch*, the journal he produced for his brothers and sisters. The stanza, which is the same as the leitmotiv stanza in 'Jabberwocky', is glossed by a lexicon, where we find the following definitions:

> SLITHY (compounded of SLIMY and LITHE). 'Smooth and active.'
> TOVE. A species of Badger. They had smooth white hair, long hind legs, and short horns like a stag; lived chiefly on cheese.[35]

We know where Humpty Dumpty derives his explanations from, and why Carroll appears to have full confidence in him. The second example, 'tove', is mentioned to show that portmanteau coining does not account for all coinages.

We now have two accounts, which are not entirely coherent, one phonetic, and one semantic. In order to help us out, no doubt, Carroll suggests a third, psychological, explanation. It occurs in the preface to *The Hunting of the Snark*, where Carroll gives an analysis of the word 'frumious', which is used in 'Jabberwocky' as a qualifier for the Bandersnatch, and in *The Hunting of the Snark* to describe that creature's jaws:

> For instance, take the two words 'fuming' and 'furious'. Make up your mind that you will say both words, but leave it unsettled which you will say first. Now open your mouth and speak. If your thoughts incline ever so little towards 'fuming', you will say 'fuming-furious'; if they turn, by even a hair's breadth, towards 'furious', you will say 'furious-fuming'; but if you have that rarest of gifts, a perfectly balanced mind, you will say 'frumious.'[36]

This we might call the stuttering theory of portmanteau-words – and we must remember that Carroll was afflicted with a stammer, which is one of the main reasons why he gave up teaching and failed to take full orders.

The abundance of accounts for portmanteau-words in Carroll, together with his careful avoidance of the most likely explanation, which is morphological, indicate that we must interpret his coinages as symptoms. They are closest to the expression of affect. Indeed, outside Carroll, some of the best-known portmanteau-words are to be found in Freud's book on jokes,[37] like the celebrated *familionär*, which originally comes from Heine. This is why portmanteau-words are so important. Because they are 'points of poetry', to use Milner's term,[38] they not only allow the repressed side of language, the remainder, to play its tricks on the surface of discourse, they also embody the contradiction which is central to nonsense. On the one hand, they conform to structural or formal regularity, belonging as they do to identifiable parts of speech and filling the correct syntactic slots. On the other hand they are also the bearers of semantic excess, of two meanings packed up into one word, and of formal irregularity, which ends up producing a semantic void, since, not conforming to the structural necessity of a homophonous string, their structure is impossible to determine without the help of an authorised commentary. Such words, for all their seeming regularity, tend towards private language, of which Humpty Dumpty appears to be a practitioner. They are truly *monstres de langue*, as Grésillon calls them. Her account, which is the best on the subject, and which goes far beyond the study of a corpus of coinages in Heine, is fully aware of the paradox, which she expresses thus: portmanteau coinages are an instance of linguistic *creativity*, as they exploit potentialities allowed by the linguistic system; they are also instances of *otherness* within language, being irregular linguistic monsters, which it is impossible to assimilate within the system. In other words, they are both within and without *langue*, on the uncertain frontier between *langue* and the other side of language, the remainder – they are the emblems of nonsense.

The term 'exploitation' is a good description of what nonsense does on that frontier where it dwells: it crosses the border back and forth, in a constant shuttle movement, which threatens to subvert but eventually supports the law. I shall end on two instances of such regular–irregular playing with the rules of language: declension and conjugation. This is an example of conjugation:

> I said, 'This horse, sir, will you shoe?'
> And soon the horse was shod.
> I said, 'This deed, sir, will you do?'
> And soon the deed was dod!³⁹

This is typical of the tactics of nonsense. The poem notes a correspondence between verbs and nouns: 'shoe'/'shoe'; 'deed'/ 'do'. It also notes another correspondence, which has nothing to do with the first, between the root form of the verb and its past participle. This, it takes to the letter: if 'shoe' → 'shod', then 'do' → 'dod'. The implicit, and erroneous, rule is: verbs ending in the same phonemes have the same past participles. Nonsense breaks rules not by forgetting about them, but by following them to the letter, in a deliberately blind fashion, thus illegally extending their scope. Nonsense as a kind of writing has its own metalinguistic rules. We could formulate the first two thus: (1) a grammatical rule can always be transgressed or defeated in a nonsense text, providing the transgression introduces a new rule, which must be at least as visible as the old one (the term 'visible' is deliberately vague, but its meaning is intuitively clear); (2) the transgression does not cancel the old rule, it maintains it in the background, so that the new rule is limited in its scope, and temporary. The conjugation 'do'/'dod' conforms to both these principles.

And here is an example of declension, the first two stanzas of an anonymous poem:

> I might not, if I could;
> I should not, if I might;
> Yet if I should I would;
> And, shoulding, I should quite!
>
> I must not, yet I may;
> I can, and still I must;
> But ah! I cannot – nay,
> To must I may not, just![40]

The text packs as many modal auxiliaries as it can into a stanza – it attempts to exhaust a paradigm, modal auxiliaries being mutually substitutable, but notoriously unable to combine (this is why I have extended the range of the term 'declension', which normally applies to nominal paradigms). This constraint generates a series *within the rules*, which, however, the last line of each stanza flouts. Line 4 gives us an impossible (although apparently regular) participle; line 8 produces an impossible infinitive and a forbidden combination of modals – again, we may note that such syntactic impossibility is not semantic incoherence, witness the existence of semi-modals like 'be able to' or 'be allowed to', which the English language uses to bypass this syntactic constraint. Such bypassing the poem also indulges in, only more flippantly. The last line of each stanza is the locus for a release of the tension caused by the hyper-regular recourse to declension. But since the transgression is repeated, the poem is not only an illustration of our second rule as formulated above, it also enables us to formulate the third rule of nonsense: (3) no transgression can be isolated; transgressions must always come as a series. As we shall see again and again, the series, what Elizabeth Sewell calls the rule of 'one and one and one',[41] is an essential element of nonsense. And our three rules are coherent, for the series is the main cause of the visibility of the new, transgressive, rule.

We can conclude on this point. Morphological rules are deeply respected in nonsense and, contradictorily, subverted or exploited, often by being understood literally, that is extended beyond their actual (but contingent) scope, for false (but logical) reasons. Thus, a portmanteau-word is the playful inverse of an immediate constituent analysis. The only coinages in Carroll that conform to Grésillon's 'homophonous string' condition are words like

'Rocking-horse-fly' or 'Snap-dragon-fly', which, we saw, are the results of constituent analysis mistakes. By coining such words, Carroll Wolfsonises language, i.e. indulges in the most dubious forms of linguistic synthesis, but only because the English language itself Brissetises,[42] i.e. indulges in the most dubious forms of analysis and metanalysis. The transgressions of nonsense are in a way always 'authorised' ones, because they merely follow the transgressions of language itself. Thus, language posits morphological rules (a verb root gives a participle through the addition of a suffix), and it breaks them, by allowing exceptions ('shall' has no participle). Nonsense pretends to reject the possibility of exceptions and follows the rule to the bitter end: the transgression uses and abuses the authority of the rule. This is the main characteristic of the linguistics of nonsense. The dominant aspect of our contradiction is the respect for rules. The rule both precedes and dominates its temporary subversion. But subverted it is nevertheless by the return of the repressed linguistic free play, which I call the remainder.[43] This dominated aspect, which is secondary in nonsense, becomes essential in the linguistic production of mental patients. Portmanteau-words are to be found not only in Lewis Carroll, but also in the case histories of psychoanalysts. Thus Leclaire gives us the case of Philippe, whose deepest fantasy revolves around the 'secret noun' *pordjeli*.[44] Analysis shows that this key word, to which interpretation always returns, is the portmanteau condensation of several phrases: the patient's name (*Georges Philippe*), the expression of self-pity ('*pauvre Philippe*', poor Philip) and of his desires ('*joli corps de Lili*', Lili's beautiful body). This secret unconscious name is both the product and the source of a multiplicity of meanings. It has links with the patient's body, with its movements, with its erogenous zones, with the instinctual drives that turn it into *this* body, a human body – we understand why it embodies the subject's fundamental fantasy. In the same vein, Leclaire shows that a dream often contains a key word which is the locus for the direct fulfilment of desire – what he calls a *mot-carrefour*, a crossing of ways, where the condensation and displacement that organise the dream become linguistic devices, and where the linguistic concentration reflects the intensity of the affect. The portmanteau-words of nonsense have the same origin – this is why they embody the return of the remainder within *langue*. But because they are linguistically regular, they also serve to repress the returning remainder and reaffirm the rule of law. They are symptoms only because they are first instances of a linguistic rule; conversely, they confess that there is no linguistic rule that is not also the expression of a symptom. On this troubled frontier nonsense dwells.

SYNTAX

In structural analysis, all the levels recognised by theory have the same importance. At least in theory, for in practice some are more equal than others. Phonological studies by structural linguists have been notoriously more successful than, for instance, studies of syntax. It is Chomsky's merit to have realised that this imbalance was structural, and to have turned the equivalence of levels, which, in the usual metaphor, were simply piled up, into a hierarchy. Grammar now has a central component, syntax, in relation to which other levels are either ancillary subparts (morphology is syntax on a smaller scale) or interpretative filters (phonology and semantics interpret the output of syntax). We have come to accept, or reject, the thesis of the centrality of syntax.

The practice of writers of nonsense, and especially Carroll, who had the keenest linguistic intuitions, anticipates this theory. Literary nonsense is a Chomskyan game. With generative grammar, it shares a number of intuitions about the importance of syntax. In nonsense, these do not appear as epistemological theories, but in the shape of a practice of syntax, marked by strict correctness, or even hyper-correctness, and by syntactic intuitions, mostly in the work of Carroll, which are of the utmost interest to today's linguist because they are well in advance of the knowledge of language possessed by his Victorian colleagues. It is striking that syntactic incoherence is extremely rare in nonsense texts and that, when it is present, it is clearly indicated, through irony or explicit disapproval. One might expect nonsense to indulge in syntactic chaos – although, from what we have seen at other levels, *we* no longer expect it. In fact, nonsense texts do not indulge in solecism, let alone the total dissolution of syntax. One can even go further. Because the genre finds its origins in children's or folk literature, because of its frequent use of series, one might expect the texts to have simple syntax, that is to prefer paratax to hypotax. Nursery rhymes are not supposed to require complicated parsing. Not so Lear's limericks or Carroll's tales. This is in fact the great difference between folk nonsense, the nonsense of the oral tradition, and literary nonsense.

51

One is reminded of Heidegger's view on paratax.[45] The commonplace idea, he says, is that paratax is the symptom of a lack of linguistic sophistication. It lacks linguistic architecture and it is, as a result, the proper syntax for primitive people and children. The example of such infantile paratax he gives is: 'Bow-wow. Nasty. Bite.' He then proceeds to overturn this commonplace by analysing paratactic effects in a few lines by Parmenides – a writer whose antique diction is not a sign of primitiveness, but of closeness to Being. Paratax, he says, is the language of thought. A paratactic sentence speaks in its interstices. I am not interested here in the philosophical value of this rehabilitation of paratax – I will not even wonder whether it is not itself mythical, embodying the Romantic commonplace of a spontaneous language of thought, free at last from the constraints of syntax. What I am interested in is the fact that nonsense upholds the commonplace view, that it tends to privilege hypotax as a way of 'saving syntax', which is also, incidentally, a way of teaching it. There is no attempt at grammatical simplicity in nonsense – quite the contrary. I shall demonstrate this point by producing examples of two kinds: negative instances of syntactic mistakes that embody grammatical intuitions, and cases of exaggerated syntax.

The Duck's 'it' in *Alice's Adventures in Wonderland* is well known.[46] I have shown elsewhere that when the Mouse, who is telling the driest story he knows, uses the sentence 'and even Stigand, the patriotic archbishop of Canterbury, found it advisable –', he uses an 'it' which is not an anaphora for a noun phrase, but the trace of a movement of extraposition.[47] The Duck's intervention, when he asks 'found *what?*' and then proceeds to say that when *he* finds a thing, it is usually a frog or a worm, deeply upsets the Mouse, as it would have upset a contemporary linguist, whose grammatical theories would not have allowed him to answer the Duck's question. Carroll's intuitive knowledge of language is far in advance of the contemporary grammarian's. He is intuitively aware that the 'it' in the Mouse's sentence has a different syntactic function from the common or garden variety. As a result, we can expect him, when he commits a solecism, to do it for similar reasons, as the embodiment of an intuition about language in advance of systematic understanding.

There is only one solecism in *Alice's Adventure in Wonderland*. It occurs at the beginning of Chapter 2, when Alice is growing at an alarming rate. No doubt its position in the opening sentence of the chapter is meant to draw the reader's attention to it:

> 'Curiouser and curiouser!' cried Alice (she was so much surprised, that for the moment she quite forgot how to speak good English). 'Now I'm opening out like the longest telescope that ever was! Good-bye, feet!' (for when she looked down at her feet, they seemed to be almost out of sight, they were getting so far off).[48]

We can note straight away that the setting of the solecism is carefully thought out. It is important that the transgression should be conspicuous, or, as I said earlier, 'visible'. It is also important that it should fall under the narrator's judgement – a narrator who is usually more discreet than this, but who obviously can tell the difference between good and bad English. We must also note that, in Alice's speech, such a mistake is uncommon, and that she can use more complex and more correct syntax, as the rest of the sentence shows.

The narrator's concern is justified – there lies Carroll's intuition. This grammatical mistake is not unprovoked. The rule that governs the comparative of adjectives is vague and treacherous. Nor will its formulation in the Victorian grammar I have consulted help. 'If adjectives are of more than two syllables, comparatives and superlatives are formed by placing "more" and "most" before the positive degree. Even words of two syllables often take this form, and occasionally words of one, as "more manly", "more true". Our older writers, however, never scrupled to affix "er" and "est" to words of any length.'[49] The first thing that ought to strike us is that the formulation is vague: words like 'often' and 'occasionally' are of unfortunate occurrence in a rule of grammar, which, *pace* the dogma of descriptivism, always has a normative aspect. And the ambiguous reference to 'our older writers' tends to dissolve the rule. Are they admirable in their practice, a worthy source of imitation, or archaic and *passé*? Worse still, as it is formulated, the rule is incorrect. It states that one may, not that one must, say 'more curious', and therefore allows Alice's 'curiouser'. Alice's exclamation is not even an exception. Since 'curious' has two syllables, she has conformed to the general case as described by the rule, the generality of which is therefore in serious doubt. But perhaps there is more to it than a simple mistake in the formulation of the rule, for my demonstration is based on the fact that 'curious' has two syllables. But has it? The presence of a schwa in the middle of the word, /kjuəriəs/ might allow us (for instance in a poem) to treat it as a three-syllable word. Carroll is, once more, crossing a frontier back and forth. His keenest intuition is perhaps that rules of grammar are not so much injunctions as the delineation of frontiers on a map, a partition between what can and what cannot be said that is arbitrary and ultimately unpredictable.

Alice's solecism is a solution to the difficulties caused by the vagueness of the rule – a solution, not a dissolution. Her linguistic invention is in no way chaotic. She explores the rule, points out a loophole in its formulation by Victorian linguistics, and simplifies it – makes it both more general and easier to learn. Her implicit new rule could be stated thus: the comparative of an adjective of any length is formed by adding the suffix '-er'. In so doing, not only does she follow the practice of 'our older writers', but she takes the principles of analogy and economy, which govern grammar but, unfortunately, not natural languages (at least, not to the same extent), to extremes. This may have some unfortunate consequences, such as the derivation 'good' – 'gooder', but the price is modest when compared to the advantages this offers to learners of the language. Her attitude is in fact the normal attitude of the child learner, who systematises the rules she learns, and derives 'goed' from 'go' by analogy, until she is made to realise the unfortunate existence of exceptions. Alice's is an infantile linguistic theory, as one talks of infantile sexual theories.

There is an element of the child in Lewis Carroll. Although in this passage he seems to condemn Alice's solecism, he secretly condones it. The idea that when usage is not logical it ought to be corrected is as dear to the logician as to the little girl. What she does to morphology or syntax, he does to spelling. The following comes from the preface to *Sylvie and Bruno Concluded*:

> Other critics have objected to certain innovations in spelling, such as 'ca'n't', 'wo'n't', 'traveler'. In reply, I can only plead my firm conviction that the popular usage is *wrong*. As to 'ca'n't', it will not be disputed that, in all *other* words ending in 'n't', these letters are an abbreviation of 'not'; and it is surely absurd to suppose that, in this solitary instance, 'not' is represented by ' 't'! In fact, 'can't' is the *proper* abbreviation for 'can it' just as 'is't is for 'is it'. Again, in 'wo'n't', the first apostrophe is needed, because the word 'would' is here

abridged into 'wo': but I hold it proper to spell 'don't' with only *one* apostrophe, because the word 'do' is here *complete*. As to such words as 'traveler', I hold the correct principle to be, to *double* the consonant when the accent falls on that syllable; otherwise to leave it *single*. This rule is observed in most cases (e.g. we double the 'r' in 'preferred', but leave it single in 'offered'), so that I am only extending, to other cases, an existing rule. I admit, however, that I do not spell 'parallel', as the rule would have it; but here we are constrained by the etymology, to insert the double 'l'.[50]

This is the theory of Alice's practice in our passage. Carroll explicitly recognises that where a rule has exceptions one must 'extend it to other cases' in order to make it truly general. It is not enough that the rule should be 'observed in most cases'. This is the rationale behind Carroll's rather exaggerated prescriptivism. There is no way his suggestions can be adopted, for they complicate usage, and produce some rather strange analyses, such as this 'wo' in 'won't', which he claims corresponds to 'would' rather than 'will'. But they do make English spelling more regular, so that the complication of the surface is compensated by the deeper simplicity of the rule. But the remainder is lying in wait, and will trip even the most enthusiastic and systematic linguistic logician. By confessing that he is not willing to alter the spelling of 'parallel' (a word for which, as a mathematician, he must feel some partiality), and by introducing a new principle or rule for spelling, etymology, Carroll ruins his attempts at clarification. For etymology will, of course, justify the most exotic quirks of usage. When diachrony returns within synchrony, as indeed it does, the systematicity of the synchronic *état de langue* gives way. So that Carroll's desire for extreme regularity is merely the expression of a fantasy, the cardinal linguistic fantasy of the speaker's total control over his language, the best embodiment of which is Carroll's immortal creation, Humpty Dumpty. Like character, like author. Both dream of imposing *their* rule on language, and both will have a fall.

To go back to Alice's solecism, we must note another element. Carroll's syntactic intuition that the rule is vague and the practice riddled with exceptions is also a pragmatic intuition. The contents of this intuition suggest that when rules give way, as they are apt to do in extraordinary or emotionally harrowing circumstances, communication is in no way affected. When you cross the frontiers of grammar, you are still within language – this is indeed what the concept of the remainder attempts to account for. So our passage shows a contradictory attitude to syntax, which I believe is characteristic of the genre. On the one hand, the centrality of syntax is upheld, and rules are deemed so important that the only possible attitude to language is one of strong prescriptivism. On the other hand, it appears that, in practice, communication can be established – can always be established – beyond grammar. This we shall call the paradox of Lucretius, as a tribute to the passage in the *De Natura Rerum* where Lucretius wonders what would happen if, having reached the end of the world, I threw my javelin beyond the edge of the saucer. Two things, he claims, could happen. Either my javelin would cross into something else, or it would rebound against something.[51] There is always something beyond the limit, if only the limit itself. Nonsense both explores and embodies the paradox of Lucretius, for nonsensical words either rebound into grammaticality or else cross into a type of a-grammaticality that turns out to be no chaos.

I shall illustrate this last point by quoting what is perhaps the only instance of chaotic syntax in Carroll – this time, we go beyond even solecism. The passage occurs in Chapter 9 of *Alice's Adventures in Wonderland*, and is known under the name of 'the Duchess's sentence'. The ugly Duchess, who has designs upon Alice, enthusiastically agrees to whatever Alice says. Alice has just suggested that mustard is a mineral (to which the Duchess has agreed), but she changes her mind:

'Oh, I know!' exclaimed Alice, who had not attended to this last remark, 'it's a vegetable. It doesn't look like one, but it is.'

'I quite agree with you,' said the Duchess; 'and the moral of that is – "Be what you would seem to be" – or, if you'd like it put more simply – "Never imagine yourself not to be otherwise than what it might appear to others that what you were or might have been was not otherwise than what you had been would have appeared to them to be otherwise." '

'I think I should understand that better,' Alice said very politely, 'if I had it written down: but I can't quite follow it as you say it.'

'That's nothing to what I could say if I chose,' the Duchess replied, in a pleased tone.[52]

The first thing to note is the elaborate context, which leaves us even more baffled than Alice, so that the joke is on us. The sentence ís presented as a paraphrasis, and also a clarification ('if you'd like it put more simply'), of a sentence which is syntactically perspicuous, and semantically not quite so. For the contents of the maxim 'Be what you would seem to be' are not entirely clear. How can I, by a mere effort of will, make my essence correspond to my desired appearance? The sentence that follows this, of course, is neither semantically nor syntactically coherent, which Alice attributes to its oral transmission. This is where the joke is on us. As we read 'I think I should understand that better . . . if I had it written down', we are bitterly reminded that *we* have it written down, and that we cannot follow it at all. As for the syntax of the sentence itself, I must confess it still produces the same dizzying bafflement in me as it did when I first read it years ago. The sources of this bafflement are clear. They are semantic, an abundance of negations which cancel, or fail to cancel, each other, and, more importantly, syntactic. Carroll uses all the devices one can resort to in order to make a sentence complex: repeated embedding, extraposition, not to forget 'pseudo cleft' clauses of the 'what S_2 VP' type (where an embedded sentence S_2 is inserted after the relative and before the main verb phrase: 'what you were or might have been was not otherwise . . . '). One is strongly reminded of Chomsky's remark on the fact that there are psychological (not linguistic) limits to the length of sentences, especially in the case of multiple embedding. But here it is not a question of the readers' memory being inadequate to the length of the sentence, but rather of their powers of linguistic analysis failing them because a syntactic trick is being played on them, the exact nature or location of which they (this reader at least) cannot pinpoint. There may be a psychological explanation for this after all – I can take any amount of semantic incoherence in my stride, but syntactic chaos, because of the centrality of syntax, provokes the deepest unease. And, truly, the sentence is incomprehensible for syntactic, not semantic, reasons. Syntax has logical precedence over semantics – the construction of coherent meaning presupposes the coherence of the syntactic organisation of the utterance. We are not even in the situation of Husserl's rather elementary instance of *Unsinn*, ' a square and or', where the reader's need for meaning is such that 'some sort' of interpretation, however tenuous and fleeting, will be constructed. In Carroll's more complex example – the increased complexity is due to the complex syntax – no interpretation whatsoever crosses the reader's mind. Syntax is the core of language. Indeed, the passage ends on the Duchess's idiosyncratic formulation of Chomsky's principle of linguistic creativity. Not 'I constantly produce or understand sentences that have never been heard before', but, 'That's nothing to what I could say if I chose'. There is a threatening aspect to this. But, on the other hand, it illustrates what we said about the tendential drift from paratax to hypotax. This is hypotax with a vengeance, taken to its self-destroying extremity.

Nonsense texts strictly conform to the rules of syntax – we may even go further, and note that they relish their syntax. I have called this hypersyntaxism. Even paradoxes are expressed through canonic sentence structures. When Alice confesses 'I'm not myself, you see',[53] she states this impossibility in correct English, where the reflexive pronoun has its normal use. We can compare this to the choice made by the poets, from Whitman's 'one's self I sing', which is syntactically rather inventive, to Rimbaud's '*je est un autre*', where verb concord is grossly flouted – Alice would have said '*je suis une autre*', i.e. she would have preferred metaphor to solecism. Not that her conformity really helps her, for the linguistic purist will always meet someone who is even more of a stickler for convention – the Caterpillar duly answers 'I don't see', showing that correct syntax is not enough, and must be combined with the most literal interpretation.

My last example of exaggerated concern for syntax comes from Lear's longest prose text, 'The Story of the Four Little Children Who Went Round the World', where we can read the following sentence:

So they all climbed up the single high tree to discover, if possible, if there were any people; but having remained on the top of a tree for a week, and not seeing anybody, they naturally concluded that there were no inhabitants, and accordingly when they came down, they loaded the boat with two thousand veal-cutlets and a million of chocolate drops, and these afforded them sustenance for more than a month, during which time they pursued their voyage with the utmost delight and apathy.[54]

This is a parody of Robinson Crusoe exoticism, and of the rather pompously written travellers' tales of which the British reading public was inordinately fond in the nineteenth century. But one can also feel Lear's delight (which is no apathy) in supporting the flattest platitudes by a complex syntactic construction, where participle clauses, 'that' nominalisations and clauses of time surround an innocuous main clause, and turn the sentence into a labyrinth. Although, unlike the Duchess's sentence, this sentence is entirely coherent and susceptible of analysis, it plays a similar trick on the reader. The kind of trick which, in an incipient way, the rhetorical trope called zeugma also plays on us. In the famous leitmotiv line in *The Hunting of the Snark*, 'they pursued it with forks and hope', the joyful semantic incoherence is supported by an excessive respect for the letter of the syntactic rules of coordination: a coordinated prepositional phrase is obtained by placing the common preposition before the two noun phrases joined by 'and'. Minor constraints, that is selection restrictions, not being entirely syntactic in nature, are disregarded. To go back to Lear's sentence, his rather heavy insistence on the trivialities of tautological *Sinn*, with its emphasis on total respect for the formal aspect of language at the expense of its material aspect, is so close to Husserl's *Widersinn* that we have no difficulty in understanding why this is an archetypal instance of a nonsense text. Exaggerated correctness is on the frontier of incorrectness, where, as we know, nonsense is to be found. But the point here, which is different from the conclusion we reached earlier, in spite of the similarity in formulation, is that nonsense does not even cross the frontier of syntax, that it is a *syntactic genre*. True, hypercorrection is close to transgression, it is a form of transgression *par le haut*, even as hyperrealism is sometimes close to the uncanny. The main contradiction, however, is not within the level of syntax, but between this and the next level. In nonsense, syntax plays with semantics. It compensates and exposes semantic incoherence.

SEMANTICS

In her analysis of *mots-valises*, of portmanteau-words in Heine, A. Grésillon reaches the following paradox.[55] On the one hand portmanteau-words are a linguistic scandal – they flout the principle of the linearity of signifiers, since the homophonous string is the locus for the superposition, not the concatenation, of the two words that make up the portmanteau. On the other hand, they strictly conform, with the exception of the homophonous string, to internal principles of order and linearity, 'as if to remind us that it is not possible to flout order for ever, or without having to suffer for it'. This could be a description of the relationships between syntax and semantics in nonsense. The formal excess of syntax compensates for a semantic (material) lack, or incoherence. Here is an instance of this incoherence, which comes from *Punch* (I quote only the first stanza):

> *Ballad of Bedlam*
> Oh, lady, wake! the azure moon
> Is rippling in the verdant skies,
> The owl is warbling his soft tune,
> Awaiting but thy snowy eyes.
> The joys of future years are past,
> To-morrow's hopes have fled away;
> Still let us love, and e'en at last
> We shall be happy yesterday.[56]

We understand why this was first published in a comic journal. That this is a parody of a love ballad, through the quoting of clichés out of their natural context, is obvious. The result is a contrast between the strict correctness of the prosodic and syntactic structures, and the semantic incoherence of the text. It contains semantic anomalies like 'verdant skies', logical contradictions in lines 5, 6 and 8, and referential impossibilities like that 'rippling moon' (the next stanza introduces a huntsman who 'winds his mad guitar'). Personification is exaggerated, as in the last lines of the poem:

> Then, lady, wake! my brigantine
> Pants, neighs, and prances to be free;
> Till the creation I am thine,
> To some rich desert fly with me.

In spite of the fascinating activities of this brigantine, the poem gives an impression of extreme regularity behind its apparent incoherence. Not only because the formal structure is right, but also because the use of clichés, even inverted ones like 'rich desert' (which puns on the other sense of 'desert': 'he richly deserves this') strictly limits the impression of semantic chaos. Wit dominates over true madness. This is the literary representation of madness, not madness itself. It is generated by semantic rules: a rule of inversion ('we shall be happy yesterday'), a rule of pastiche ('the

60

azure moon' mocks a poetic cliché of the tritest kind), a rule of exploration of the dictionary (the best instance of which is the play on 'desert'). This regular irregularity has of course nothing to do with the incoherence of delirium, to be found in what the French call a *texte brut*. Here is an extract from a text by an early nineteenth-century lunatic, James Tilley Matthews:

> James, Absolute, Sole, & Supreme Sacred Omni Imperious Arch Grand Arch Sovereign. Omni Imperious Arch Grand Arch Proprietor Omni Imperious Arch-Grand-Arch-Emperor-Supreme etc. March the Twentieth One Thousand Eight hundred & four.
>
> The following are the Rewards by Me offered so long ago Issued for the putting to Death the Infamous Usurping Murderers and their Families & Races, agreeable to the Just Sentence by Me pronounced against them and their Agents & Adherents, Under the Special Conditions That Neither Machines or Art, Air-Looms, Magnets, Magnet or other Fluid-Effluvias whether of Poisons or otherways are made Use of: Nor any Poisons or any Dastardly, Secret, or Cowardly Act be used –.[57]

This is real linguistic chaos, both semantic and syntactic. In the first paragraph the compulsive repetition of the same titles, which has nothing to do with a regular nonsensical series, precludes any structure in the list. In the second paragraph, although a semblance of order is preserved, which might make us think that we are in the same universe as that of Lear's sentence, the syntax is not hypercorrect but vague, the construction of the clauses governed by 'agreeable' being uncertain. This apparently minor gap in the syntactic hierarchy threatens the whole construction. All the more so as, towards the end of the sentence, paratax (in this case lists of nouns and adjectives) seems to replace hypotax. The lack of semantic coherence is increased by the vagueness of the syntax, whereas in the *Ballad of Bedlam* the apparent incoherence is compensated by the semantic series of clichés *and* the hypercorrect syntax.

A simple representation of what I have called the semantic incoherence of nonsense could be given using Husserl's terms. We might call this the principle of *Widersinn*, where the formal slots, each in its lawful position, are randomly filled, without concern for material adequacy. Thus are 'square circles' produced. We shall find examples of such randomness in Surrealist poetry, for instance in Breton's line '*Il y a ce soir un crime vert à commettre*' (tonight a green murder is to be committed). The best instance, of course, is Chomsky's sentence, 'colourless green ideas sleep furiously'. Such illicit combinations can be found in nonsense texts, like the 'azure moon' or 'verdant skies' of our ballad. But, contrary to expectations, they are not frequent in Victorian nonsense. The genre seems to prefer paradox and tautology to potential metaphors, for the natural interpretation of a phrase like 'verdant skies' is metaphorical.

This raises the problem of the attitude of nonsense towards metaphor. As we have suggested, the normal procedure for dealing with semantic incongruity is to produce a metaphorical interpretation. The calculus takes the form of classic Gricean implicature (see p. 73),[58] and indeed metaphor is one of the indirect speech acts studied by Searle in *Expression and Meaning*.[59] Since Richard is obviously not a lion, but the speaker is cooperating, i.e. meaning something by this unusual proposition, another, metaphorical, meaning must be computed. There are maxims or precepts that will guide this computation and ensure that it is transmissible. Thus, in Lear's 'nonsense alphabets', we encounter a 'perpendicular purple polly'. Now, parrots cannot by any stretch of imagination be 'perpendicular'. But imagination can always be stretched a little further, and a metaphorical account of this perpendicularity will eventually be produced. Since the metaphor is not at all conventional, since it is as alive as the parrot itself (there are also, of course, countless stuffed metaphors), the result is a little uncertain, but a similarity is bound to emerge. All we have to do is wait for the intuition that will yield it.

This is the stuff that poetry is made of. I read the phrase 'scented herbage of my breast', and the little grey cells start working. I will eventually remember that the metaphor occurs in a book entitled *Leaves of Grass*, and I shall start making connections. But that is the poetic, or serious, interpretation of the phrase, not the nonsensical one. A nonsensical interpretation will evoke the ludicrous picture of Walt with perfumed grass growing out of his chest – it will interpret the metaphor literally, it will reject the semantic creativity the new metaphor unleashes. In nonsense, a blind wall is not a wall devoid of apertures, but a wall wearing dark glasses and carrying a white stick, groping its way around. In other words, for nonsense a blind wall is like the wall in the play within the play in *A*

Midsummer Night's Dream, a comically personified wall ('Wall. "Thus have I, Wall, my part discharged so; And being done, thus Wall away doth go." [*exit Wall*]' V. i. 203–4). Personification, as so often in nonsense, destroys metaphor. This rejection of metaphor is another characteristic of the genre. Or, rather, it is the logical consequence of the avoidance of semantic anomaly. Indeed, nonsense texts seem to deploy complex and ingenious strategies in order to avoid metaphors. I shall evoke four. The first, and easiest, is strict literalism, or matter-of-factness. If you wish to avoid the semantic pitfalls of metaphor, the safest way is to restrict yourself to tautology. Nonsense is deliberately down to earth. It relishes interminable descriptions, especially if they take the form of lists. It enjoys providing the reader with useless details, of the most precise type, especially if they have nothing to do with the matter in hand. This is Lear:

After a time they saw some land at a distance; and when they came to it, they found it was an island made of water quite surrounded by earth. Besides that, it was bordered by evanescent isthmusses with a great Gulf-stream running about all over it, so that it was perfectly beautiful, and contained only a single tree, 503 feet high.[60]

Platitudes are always welcome, for they have the solid obviousness that allows easy recognition and avoids mental stress (computation is often uncertain, always difficult). Humpty Dumpty needs Alice to do the subtraction 365 minus 1 on her memorandum book before he will concede that the result *seems* to be 364.[61] And the King of Hearts is full of sound advice for the White Rabbit:

The White Rabbit put on his spectacles. 'Where shall I begin, please your Majesty?' he asked.
'Begin at the beginning,' the King said, very gravely, 'and go on till you come to the end: then stop.'[62]

We sympathise with the King's gravity (which has its source in Aristotle's famous definition of the 'complete story' as having a beginning, a middle and an end). It is important to conform to all the rules of language, even the simplest ones, to the letter. The price to pay for even the slightest transgression is the threat of chaos. No wonder *lapalissade*, i.e. tautology turned into literature, is a subgenre of nonsense. Oliver Goldsmith is the author of several of these, the best known of which is 'An Elegy on the Glory of her Sex, Mrs Mary Blaize'. I quote the first two stanzas:

> Good people all, with one accord,
>   Lament for Madam Blaize,
> Who never wanted a good word –
>   From those who spoke her praise.
>
> The needy seldom pass'd her door,
>   And always found her kind;
> She freely lent to all the poor –
>   Who left a pledge behind.[63]

With *lapalissades* (the name comes from the French nursery rhyme hero, M. de la Palisse, who is famous for having remained alive till the day he died), nonsense seems to make the fantasy of the speaker's absolute control over his language, and, through his language, over the world of referents, come true. What is so attractive in tautology is that it is necessarily true. What is so dangerous about metaphor is that it is always obviously false.

The second strategy of avoidance of metaphor goes through coinage. If tautology is hypo-metaphor, the *degré zéro* of metaphorical creativity, coinages are hyper- metaphors, a rejection of the dangers of metaphor through excessive indulgence. As we saw earlier, we shall never be able to decide whether 'runcible', in 'runcible raven' (there is also, in 'The Owl and the Pussycat' a 'runcible spoon'), is highly metaphorical – what can a raven and a spoon have in common? – or strictly literal. Here, language has decided for us. 'Runcible', a word coined by Lear, is now in the dictionary. In the *OED* a 'runcible spoon' denotes a three-pronged fork for pickles. As a *langue* coinage, the word was always a candidate for adoption. This, however, does not solve our problem, for it certainly does not turn the phrase 'a runcible raven' into a metaphor. There is one striking difference between Heine's portmanteau-words and Carroll's. Heine's words are easily, and immediately, interpreted; Carroll's are not. Nor should they be, for the process of interpretation would require the same qualities of inventiveness as the computation of a metaphorical interpretation. The only explanation of a portmanteau-word must be entirely arbitrary, or at least extremely far-fetched so as to be beyond the ordinary reader's reach. So Humpty Dumpty is right after all, for his account hesitates between these two extremes. And, as the French say, *les extrêmes se touchent*. Hyper-metaphor has the same consequence as hypo-metaphor: it precludes the semantic creativity of metaphorical interpretation.

The third strategy consists in kicking incongruity upstairs. This is achieved by using sentences without any logical link between them, so that no metaphorical interpretation (which must rely on contextual meaning) can develop, and the only interpretation of each sentence is literal. Nonsense here is global, as the sentences or syntagmata constituting the text are down to earth and trivial. There are innumerable instances of this in nonsense, but the best is still Samuel Foote's 'The Grand Panjandrum', which he wrote as a text no actor could memorise:

> So she went into the garden to cut a cabbage-leaf to make an apple pie, and at the same time a great she-bear, coming down the street, pops its head into the shop. What! no soap? so he died. She imprudently married the barber, and there were present the Pickaninnies, the Joblilies, the Garyulies, and the Grand Panjandrum himself with the little round button on top, and they all fell to playing catch-as-catch-can till the gunpowder ran out at the heels of their boots.[64]

The irony of this is that not only did the text become so memorable as to be compulsory material for anthologies of nonsense, but that, again, the word 'Panjandrum' has found its way into the dictionary: a 'Panjandrum', the *OED* states, is 'a mock title for a mysterious or exalted personage; a local magnate of great airs; a pompous pretender'. Each syntagma, however, taken in isolation, is easily understandable; if we take it in combination with its neighbours we cannot make head or tail of the sequence. At no point can a metaphorical interpretation arise: it would have to be supported, or at least allowed, by the absent logical connections.

The fourth strategy consists of circumscribing metaphor and replacing it with puns. The advantage of a pun is the same as that of an ambiguous phrase or sentence in grammar. True, it lets meaning begin to proliferate, since it allows more than one meaning. But this proliferation is strictly limited, since ambiguities have a limited number of possible meanings: in most cases two, rarely three or more. When I read the following sentence: 'They fed her dog biscuits', the ambiguity of the syntax (who did they feed?) does not produce existential angst. Puns belong to the same category. They offer two meanings at the same time, but only two, and those are conventional, so that interpretation, once I have noticed that a pun has been made, is immediate and certain. If tautology is the zero degree of metaphor, puns are only the first degree. They are the very beginning of metaphor. The first feathers are here, but the bird is not allowed to become fully-fledged and take to the wing. True metaphor is never entirely decidable, it offers a multiplicity of potential meanings, between which I cannot always choose.

Nevertheless, there is the beginning of danger in puns. Puns *are* close to metaphors. Authors of nonsense are sometimes aware of this. Carroll certainly was, for his fondness for puns was, on the face of it, of a strange kind. First, his puns are notoriously awful – they are so facile that one wonders why he bothered to make them. But the strange thing is that, the more facile they are, the more we enjoy them. In technical parlance, paronomasia, or the play on similarity ('uglification'/'multiplication') is preferable to antana-clasis, or the play on identity, phonic if not graphic (as in 'tail'/ 'tale'). Carroll's intuition is right. In paronomasia there is no danger of confusion, no disorder threatening, for the difference is too great. It would take a very stupid person, or a practitioner of nonsense such as Mrs Malaprop, to confuse 'subtraction' with 'distraction'. We can only *pretend* to take one for the other. Whereas in antanaclasis, confusion is real, and a mistake always possible. I can misinterpret a whole sentence, or rather text, because I believe the sole that has been mentioned is a fish rather than part of a shoe. The danger of misinterpretation is only the extreme instance of the dangers of proliferation of meaning that metaphors involve. For my meaning to be wrong, the condition is that there should be more than one meaning. Paronomasia does not let meaning proliferate – we know that ambition is not addition.

But Carroll uses another form of protection. His puns rarely come on their own: usually they come in pairs, or in series. As my examples show, the subject of the pun is not simply one branch of arithmetic, but all four. Arithmetic, in turn, is only one of the subjects the Mock Turtle was taught at school, and the others are also punned upon. In Chapter 9 of *Alice's Adventures in Wonderland*, Alice is asking what the regular course was:

> 'Reeling and Writhing, of course, to begin with,' the Mock Turtle replied; 'and then the different branches of Arithmetic – Ambition, Distraction, Uglification and Derision.'[65]

Later, other subjects are mentioned: Mystery, Seaography (not a very impressive effort), Drawling and Fainting in Coils, Laughing and Grief (this is much better, as the semantic proximity of Latin to Greek is inverted in the quasi-antonymy of the puns). In the meantime, the dangerous potential of one of the puns has been defused – the Gryphon has explained to Alice that uglification is the action of uglifying, even as beautification is the action of beautifying. A rule has been found, which makes the whole thing regular – danger is behind us at last. The passage I have just quoted is the one in which the serial nature of punning in Carroll is most apparent. But in countless other instances, puns come in pairs. Thus, in Chapter 2 of *Through the Looking-Glass*, the pun on 'bark' (of a tree/of a dog) is accompanied by a laboured paranomasia on bough-wough/bow-wow. And in Chapter 3 of *Alice's Adventures in Wonderland*, the pun on not/knot comes with the well-known, and rather facile pun on tale/tail.

It is time to reflect on this complex strategy. The value judgements in which I have indulged about Carroll's puns must not be taken literally. I have described a strategy, which is entirely justified. Carroll *wanted* his puns not to be 'good', that is clever. And the justification of the strategy should now be clear. There is semantic creativity in metaphors, which involves a potential disruption of order. The strategy of avoidance aims at restoring semantic order by limiting creativity. With paradox or tautology, but also with paronomasia, we know where we are. With metaphor, we do not – to this extent, I share Elizabeth Sewell's intuition that nonsense is concerned with order.[66] However, at this stage, and this is where we must go beyond Sewell, we ought to feel slightly uneasy. By choosing semantic void against semantic proliferation, non-sense against metaphor, nonsense runs the risk of reintroducing the danger it deprecates. Semantic void is the locus either of no creativity or of maximal creativity. That 'runcible' spoon can be nothing, have no meaning, or it can be everything, i.e. have whatever meaning I wish to impose upon it – an infinity of potential meanings. One of those meanings happens to have won the struggle for survival and to have wormed its way into the dictionary.

Here lies the semantic contradiction of nonsense. Semantic non-sense illustrates the plasticity of meaning, the impossibility to limit it, to fix it, as one applies chemical substances to 'fix' colour on a photographic film. To the contradiction between semantic void and hypercorrect syntax we must add an internal semantic contradiction between semantic void and the proliferation of semantic constraints (clichés, tautologies, lists and series). This is why, in spite of appearances, a portmanteau-word is not an instance of Freudian condensation: it is both, contradictorily, entirely meaningless and infinitely meaningful.

CONCLUSION

In this chapter I have sought to demonstrate three points. The first is that nonsense as a genre believes in the *centrality of language*. The world of Wonderland is not mainly about little girls and Jabberwocks, it is about little girls as apprentice speakers and Jabberwocks as coinages, that is, as words. The second is that nonsense texts spontaneously treat language as a hierarchy of levels, the most important among which is syntax – take care of the syntax and the rest of language will take care of itself. Before Chomsky, practitioners of nonsense had an intuitive awareness of the *centrality of syntax*. Third, the essence of the attitude of nonsense texts towards language lies in the fact that they play one level against the other, so that a law of compensation operates. Excess always counterbalances lack, and semantic incoherence is cancelled by either semantic series, or syntactic hypercorrectness, or both. I have used two words to describe this situation: paradox, and contradiction. Nonsense texts do indulge in paradoxes on a grand scale – Lewis Carroll is a notorious offender. They will run the risk of chaos without abandoning their yearning for cosmic order. So that perhaps the better word for this type of structure is *contradiction*, for the concept does distinguish between a primary or essential, and a secondary aspect. And there lies the essence of the game nonsense plays with language. Both aspects are present, and seem to form a paradox, but one aspect, the orderly or cosmic aspect, is always in the end revealed to be dominant, so that the risk of disorder is strictly limited. Freedom there is in language, but order comes first. This is the lesson which, after Alice, we must learn from our journey through nonsense.

2

THE PRAGMATICS OF NONSENSE

INTRODUCTION

In certain dialects of Italian, people whose manners are not quite what they ought to be are described by the phrase *non conosce il Galateo*, meaning that had they read the famous sixteenth-century treatise on good manners and politeness, Della Casa's *Galateo*, their behaviour would have considerably improved. They would, for instance, have read numerous passages such as the following:

> Those people who dispute every statement by questioning or contradicting show that they have little understanding of human nature, because everyone likes to have the upper hand and hates to be worsted no less in argument than in practice. Besides, it is the part of an enemy rather than a friend to take the opposite side. It follows that anyone who wants to be friendly and pleasant to talk to must not be too ready to say, 'It was not at all like that' or 'Let me just give you the true facts', nor should he stake a wager on the matter. Instead, if the question is of little importance, he should make an effort to submit to the opinions of the others, because a point gained in cases of this sort will turn to his own disadvantage. This is because we often love our friends through outwitting them on small points and making ourselves so tiresome to them that they dare not have anything to do with us for fear of a continual bout of controversy. Then they give us the nickname of Fire-eater, Crosspatch, Wise Bird, or Know-all.[1]

There is a philosophy implicit in this passage, not only of manners, but of language. Politeness, especially in conversation, is what a gentleman must strive for, thus distinguishing himself from the rabble, who indulge in the natural tendency to contradict and generally aggravate one another. In other words, peace and cooperation are attained by an effort of will, as a result of a civilising process, against a background of strife and violence. The same would apply to table manners, which is the other main area where the rules of polite behaviour apply. The quality daintily use their knives and forks, while the rabble greedily gobble up their food, clean their teeth with their napkins, and spit out in public the wine with which they have rinsed their mouths.[2]

Such a philosophy is of some interest to us, because characters in nonsense texts, with the exception of Alice – nonsensical characters, that is – might one and all be called Fire-eater, Wise Bird or Know-all. Beneath these outlandish nicknames, we recognise Tweedledum and Tweedledee, Humpty Dumpty and the Caterpillar. As the Mad Tea-Party testifies, characters in nonsense are not notorious for the excellence of their table manners;

> The March Hare took the watch and looked at it gloomily: then he dipped it into his cup of tea, and looked at it again: but he could think of nothing better to say than his first remark, 'It was the *best* butter, you know.'[3]

Bad as this is, it is nothing to their conversational manners, and Alice has a rough time of it, being subjected to constant verbal aggression and unpleasantness of all description. Nor is this a feature of the idiosyncratic world of Carroll's Wonderland, for in the rare cases when speech is mentioned in Lear's limericks, the same difficulties occur:

> There was an Old Man of Thermopylae,
> Who never did anything properly;
> But they said: 'If you choose
> To boil eggs in your shoes,
> You shall never remain in Thermopylae.'[4]

Crosspatch and Know-all are obviously at work here. Instead of gently submitting to the mild eccentricity of the Old Man – no one will deny that the question of where one is to boil one's eggs is 'of little importance' – they enter into acrimonious controversy and seek to gain the upper hand by threatening violence. Again, there is a philosophy of linguistic behaviour, of pragmatics, implicit here.

The first point to be noted is a focusing on language itself, here in the guise of a quotation of the characters' words. This is mild enough, but nonsense very often goes much further. In limericks or elsewhere in nonsense, *verba dicendi* ('But they said . . .') are abundant. Characters like to listen to the sound of their own voices, and also to reflect on what they say and how they say it. This propensity is by no means restricted to Humpty Dumpty; witness the portentous statement of the Bellman in *The Hunting of the Snark*: 'What I tell you three times is true.'

The result is that nonsense, not a mimetic genre, does not construct characters, but rather presents eccentricities, more often than not quirks of language. What the texts construct are speech situations, usually ones in which something goes wrong, and the phrase 'rules of exchange' must be taken in its military acceptation. Thus, the *Alice* books are not so much about a little girl as about conversations, or about the verbal exchanges at trials – the vast number of trial scenes in nonsense has often been noted by critics. Not the presentation of characters, but the staging of speech acts, is the aim of the text: illocution and perlocution rather than psychological analysis.

This means that nonsense is not merely a linguistic genre, one which is highly preoccupied with language, but also a pragmatic genre, in which pragmatic intuitions in advance of Searle and Grice will be expressed, even as we saw that Carroll had syntactic intuitions that anticipated the work of Chomsky. But if nonsense is a pragmatic genre, this is not due simply to the empirical fact that we do encounter such intuitions in our corpus. There is also a theoretical reason for this, which, following an essay by F. Recanati,[5] I shall express in deliberately anachronistic terms. Recanati distinguishes between two periods in analytic philosophy, the older analytic (roughly, up to Austin), and ordinary language philosophy. In the older analytic, the reason why ordinary language is disregarded is that it is an endless source of nonsensical utterances, utterances which do not confine themselves to the expression of sense impressions and are not verifiable. As a result, 'nonsense' is an essential concept for the older analytic. With the newer analytic, however, ordinary language comes to the foreground, and is no longer an object of pity mingled with contempt, but one of attention and interest. This is obtained by the replacement of the concept 'nonsense' by such concepts as speech acts (in all their variety), implicature or language-game. Apparent nonsense is merely the locus for pragmatic calculus, for instance the computation of implicatures. It can be argued that by exaggerating the nonsensical aspects of

71

ordinary language, literary nonsense anticipates the need for pragmatic analysis. The passage which the philosophy of language achieved in the 1950s had already been effected in practice by Carroll and Lear a hundred years before.

Yet this is not all, for in spite of its pragmatic intuitions, a nonsense text is not a particularly Austinian or Searlian sight. The pragmatic intuitions in fact go even further than this – they also indicate, in anticipation, the limitations of ordinary language philosophy and of contemporary pragmatics. Instead of following the irenic principles of a philosophy of cooperative conversation, such as one finds in Searle and Grice, nonsense texts seem to prefer the violence of *agon*. Two intuitions will provide us with a starting point for this chapter. The most superficial reading of our corpus is enough to convince us that (a) in nonsense, as in the plays of Harold Pinter, dialogue is mostly agonistic, that it is not a cooperative undertaking for mutually rewarding ends, but a verbal battle, where the speaker's linguistic survival is always at stake; and that (b) speech is always threatening to give way to brute force, for, being reduced to the function of a weapon, it may always be discarded if or when a more powerful weapon is available – this is the essence of the Queen of Hearts's philosophy, when she exclaims, as she is apt to do, 'Off with his head!'.

However, these two intuitions, which explain why nonsense as a genre is so interested in trials – there is a sense in which the legal institutions can be defined as the channelling and limitation of authorised violence[6] – will be found to be somewhat superficial. Nonsense is never that simple. We shall see, in this and the next chapter, that if an Anglo-Saxon conception of pragmatics is proleptically convoked only to be refuted, the typically continental themes of the violence of language, of language as power, will not offer an entirely adequate account of our texts either. On the level of pragmatics as on other levels, the dialectics of subversion and support will be seen to be at work. If nonsense insists on depicting the violence of conversation, it is in order to deprecate it.

THE PRAGMATICS OF CONVERSATION

In the opening lines of *Alice's Adventures in Wonderland*, Alice is feeling rather bored:

> Alice was beginning to get very tired of sitting by her sister
> on the bank, and of having nothing to do: once or twice she

had peeped into the book her sister was reading, but it had no pictures or conversations in it, 'and what is the use of a book,' thought Alice, 'without pictures or conversations'[7]

Alice would have every reason to be proud of the book of which she is the heroine. Not only does it contain a good many pictures, by Carroll himself in the manuscript version, or by Tenniel in the published version, but it is also full of conversations. Nonsense characters may not always look like real persons, but they certainly sound like them. They indulge, and sometimes overindulge, in the gentle, and often not so gentle, art of conversation. We recall the episode in which Tweedledum and Tweedledee insist on reciting the *longest* poem they know, in spite of Alice's discreet protest (' "If it's *very* long," she said, as politely as she could, "would you please tell me first which road — " ')[8] and we may also note that the characters Alice encounters are always prepared either to converse, or, in the case of the grumpier ones, to expostulate with her. And since, in spite of Alice's attempts at being polite, or sometimes because of her conversational *faux pas*, the flow of conversation is usually rather chaotic, the dialogues in the *Alice* books are a rich ground for the study of implicatures and indirect speech acts. I shall therefore read the *Alice* books in the light of the tradition of speech act theory and pragmatic calculus, to be found in the works of Searle and Grice.

Briefly, the tradition accounts for conversation in terms of an exchange of information, aiming towards a discursive goal common to all participants in the game. The game itself is governed by a general *Cooperative Principle* (CP) and a few essential commonsense rules, such as (a) a rule of fair play – one speaks only in one's turn, and one does not interrupt the speaker; (b) a rule of compromise – one does not seek to impose one's point of view upon others by using threatening behaviour or verbal terrorism; and (c) a rule of transparence – one must be sincere in one's utterance and avoid Moore's paradox. This may tentatively be expressed in Carroll's own terms (about which more in the next chapter): 'you must say what you mean and mean what you say.'

The two best-known versions of the theory are to be found in H.P. Grice's 'Logic and Conversation'[9] and J. Habermas's theory of communicative action.[10] Grice's Cooperative Principle provides a framework for the conversational game. It is supplemented by four maxims, the Kantian origin of which betrays their transcendental function: *quantity* (your contribution must contain the requisite quantity of information for the common conversational goal, neither more nor less); *quality* (your contribution must be truthful); *relation* (it must be relevant); and *manner* (a rag-bag of precepts: be perspicuous, be brief, be methodical – here Grice is beginning to sound like the Fowlers' *King's English*). If those maxims are respected in actual conversation, it is all to the good. If they are not, and we shall quickly come to suspect that they are rarely followed, then their flouting, provided it is obvious and deliberate, that is provided it is practised within the framework of the game as defined by the cooperative principle, gives rise to the computation of implicit meanings, called *implicatures*. The reason for the introduction of this new concept is the necessity to distinguish a linguistic implicit from the conversational implicit. The first type, the best instance of which is presupposition ('he is tall for a Frenchman'), depends on the grammar of the words concerned, not on the context. Conversational implicature depends entirely on the context and is (almost) indifferent to the words used. If, to quote Grice's canonic example, I provide one of my philosophy students with the following recommendation: 'John Doe regularly comes to my classes, and his shoes are always meticulously polished', the colleague who reads the note will understand the perfidious hint. The maxims of quantity and relation are clearly breached, yet the note conforms to the cooperative principle, since it is sent as a recommendation. The implicature is, of course, that John Doe is no good at philosophy. But we must note that in order to convey the same implicature, I might have used almost any words, except the truthful statement of John Doe's lack of ability, or its ironic inverse (which would run the risk of being interpreted literally). 'He regularly comes to my classes and always wears a bright red tie' provides the same implicit meaning. The following diagram sums up the difference between the two types of implicit meaning:

Linguistic implicit	*Implicature (conversational implicit)*
Implicit meaning remains the same when context changes	Implicit meaning remains the same when the words change
Implicit meaning changes when words change	Implicit meaning changes when context changes

Habermas's theory of 'communicative action' derives from this a much more ambitious philosophy of language, which he calls 'universal pragmatics'. It starts from a concept of truth defined as neither adequacy nor coherence, but consensus. This concept is constructed from the following three theses: (1) truth is a 'validity claim' typically associated with constative speech acts; (2) questions about truth arise when commonly accepted validity claims become problematic; in other words the question of truth typically arises in a discussion; (3) in such a discussion, the point debated is the adequacy of the arguments put forward to the facts of the matter. 'Truth' is the name for the manner in which, in the course of the discussion, validity claims are 'honoured', i.e. fulfilled. This, of course, firmly places a theory of truth within a broader theory of communication, of which it is a subpart – here lie the interest and originality of Habermas's attempt. Truth, according to this, is one of the four validity claims that must be honoured in the process of communicative action, in other words for speech acts to be successful. Here are the four validity claims. The speakers must:

1 make the propositional contents of their utterances and their pragmatic relations to other speakers clear;
2 be committed to the truth of their utterances;
3 recognise the norms within which their speech acts are produced;
4 abstain from questioning the sincerity of other speakers.

These validity claims describe an ideal speech situation in which participants in the discussion (a) all have the same right to initiate or pursue the verbal exchange; (b) are all given the same opportunity to produce whichever speech acts they choose, be they assertion, interpretation or justification; (c) are all offered the same opportunity to express their feelings, wishes and opinions; and (d) all have the same right to issue orders, warnings, promises and even threats. In conditions (b) to (d) one recognises a typology of speech acts, or of functions of language (language, for Habermas, has three main functions: to establish interpersonal relationships; to express lived experience; to present events and states of affair). In the four validity claims, together with the four conditions of the ideal speech situation, one recognises the cooperative construction, by the participants in the discussion, of a common 'public space', a shared *Lebenswelt*, in which true assertions can be produced and recognised as such. On the horizon of more or less vague common convictions, which are felt to be unproblematic, the subjects engage in communicative action, as opposed to strategic action (where the validity claim to sincerity is suspended) and symbolic action (where the validity claim to truth is suspended), reach an understanding and share a lived world, which draws on a tradition of accepted commonplace knowledge or beliefs, and is a locus for the production of new ones.

Both Grice and Habermas offer us an *ideal* view of language. There is no need to be unduly troubled about this. Grice's attitude, as we have seen, is transcendental – it would be no use exclaiming: an actual verbal exchange does not work along such optimistic lines. Both Grice and Habermas are interested in the conditions of possibility of verbal exchange, not in its superficially chaotic practice. Grice, I am sure, was fully aware that actual conversations are not always cooperative, that even in the most cooperative an element of strife can be felt. This is why the concept of exploitation, of the explicit and deliberate flouting of maxims, is crucial to his theory, the centre of which is, after all, his account of implicature. Even in Grice one has the feeling that cooperative conversation is a custom more honoured in the breach than in the observance. Because the maxims are exploitable, and therefore exploited, the computation of implicatures becomes necessary. There is room, however, for a critique of this transcendental position. A simple question will provide a starting point. Since, more often than not, the surface of conversation is agonistic rather than ironic, why did Grice and Habermas choose a deep structure which is irenic? Why can we not replace the Cooperative Principle by a principle of verbal struggle, from which we could derive a number of agonistic maxims (I shall formulate a few in a moment)? Since both sets of maxims would have the same transcendental value, the reason for the choice must be sought elsewhere. Nor do we have far to go in order to find it. Both Grice and Habermas (in Habermas, this is entirely explicit) seek to provide a foundation for scientific discussion, the cooperative exchange of information and ideas for the advancement of learning. Their ideal conversation is an ideal discussion between scientists. We know that in daily life conversations may be a little aggressive ('ARGUMENT is WAR' is Lakoff and Johnson's cardinal metaphor[11]), but there is, or at least there ought to be, an area where this does not apply: in order for scientific knowledge to progress, the results of research must be publicly submitted and discussed. That this is a somewhat idealistic view of scientific discussion is not our concern here (see the work of B. Latour).[12]

Our concern is with nonsense, and the type of dialogue or conversation one finds in nonsense texts. Needless to say, they will be of the everyday type, and will contradict the ideal views of Grice and Habermas to a disturbing extent. What nonsense shows us in practice – and this is where pragmatic intuitions begin to emerge – is that polite conversation is a fragile conquest, which needs constant protection and propping up. A nonsense conversation is an anti-Gricean sight – which does not mean that it is not susceptible of analysis in terms of maxims and implicatures.

I shall seek my first illustration outside nonsense, in order to show that nonsense conversations only make more manifest general features of ordinary conversations. The following discussion between two schoolboys, Ryan and Bell, occurs in Patrick Hamilton's *The West Pier*. Bell, who is an intellectual child, always ready to show off his knowledge or, more to the point, to use it to the detriment of others, has just made an apparently derogatory remark about Ryan's nose:

> Ryan now had to do some quick thinking. He had not understood what had been said: but he was certain that whatever had been said was unfavourable to himself. 'Proboscis', he at any rate knew, was long-languagese for nose: so presumably something nasty had been said about his nose. But what? Had it been called red, long, dirty, ugly? He floundered about in doubt (as Bell had intended he should) for a matter of ten seconds, and then, unable to make a retort in kind, rather shamefacedly took the easiest way out.
> 'So's yours', he said, and a moment later added, 'Only worse . . .'
> 'That *happens* to be a *tu quoque*,' said Bell without hesitation, and Ryan, having been recently taught in class what a *tu quoque* was, this time did not hesitate.
> 'You're a *tu* silly ass,' he said. 'And I should say you've got a bit *tu* above yourself.'
> This was definitely witty and clever, and it was Bell's turn to be momentarily dumbfounded. He paused for as long as he had previously made Ryan pause, and at last was only able to manage:
> 'Really . . . Your *brain* . . .'
> 'Really,' said Ryan, '*yours* . . .'[13]

This 'conversation', which goes on for another half-page, has two eminent characteristics. It is, explicitly and emphatically so, a verbal battle. And it imposes itself on the participants, who would like to stop, to find a way out of their predicament, but are unable to, being caught in what the French language aptly calls a process of *fuite en avant*. The conversation has taken over the speakers, who are tumbling headlong in an endless spiral of verbal aggression. The only possible end is an arbitrary one. After our text, Bell adopts one last tactic, negation. To 'Bell is the silliest fool in Rodney House', he retorts 'Bell is *not* the silliest fool at Rodney House.' This, of course, like the rest of the exchange, may go on for ever. Such is the double bind of verbal deadlock: I wish to leave the game, but I cannot quit, even if my opponent apparently wishes to do the same, because he who first expresses the desire to quit loses all. This is the kind of dilemma that game theory is interested in, and the only conceivable solution is of the cooperative type – agreement through negotiation, or recognition of an already existing convention, in the sense of David Lewis,[14] which would provide an end move for the game. Neither is applicable here, since cooperation is out of the question, and there is no conventional closure. The only possibility open is the attempt to win the game, which ends in stalemate, by using language as a dialogic weapon. Seen from this point of view, the dialogue is rich in rhetorical invention. Bell uses the authority of jargon and metalinguistic learning (words like 'proboscis' or 'tu quoque' are bound to impress the opponent, especially if he does not know them). Ryan counters this by witty paranomasia, where Latin 'tu' is reinterpreted as an English word, 'you've got a bit *tu* above yourself', and the authority of jargon and learning is deflated by the classic recourse to 'plain English'. And after our text, the battle becomes more and more moronic, as Bell resorts to psittacine duplication, which engages the interminable process of repetition:

> Ryan thought for a moment.
> 'Are you trying to imitate me?' he then said.
> ' "*Are you trying to imitate me?*" ' said Bell.
> 'Don't be a fool,' said Ryan. 'Anybody can do that.'
> ' "*Don't be a fool,*" ' said Bell. ' "*Anybody can do that.*" '[15]

All this, of course, is susceptible of a Gricean interpretation. It is a case of *video meliora proboque, deteriora sequor*. Both boys recognise the advantage of verbal cooperation, but they cannot go back to it without losing face (an important concept in conversation analysis). The result is a breach in cooperation, the best example of which is the episode of psittacic repetition. Yet this exchange is also susceptible to another, anti-Gricean, account, one which we may find, on this occasion at least, more convincing. Rather than a divided text, beginning in conversation and ending in chaos, we might wish to treat this as a unitary text, conforming from beginning to end to another principle, the principle of verbal struggle, and another set of maxims. Here is a tentative formulation. Although our verbal exchanges are not collections of desultory remarks, and can therefore be said to conform to a rational plan, this is not due to the fact that we make efforts towards verbal cooperation, but that each speaker has his or her own strategy and goal. So that a Principle of Struggle (PS) can be formulated, as a first approximation, in the following manner – and like the CP it will be a general principle, which we can expect all participants to abide by: make your conversational contribution such as is required by your strategy, at the stage at which it occurs, and by the goal towards which you are moving, which is to defeat your opponent and drive him or her off the verbal battlefield. The PS would be accompanied by the usual four maxims. *Quantity* first: adapt your verbal production to your strategy and tactics. Speak as much, or as little, as is necessary to make your opponent uncomfortable. Sometimes logorrhoea, and sometimes silence will do the trick. Since this is an agonistic, not a cooperative, account, we might expect profusion (of threats or insults) to win the day. But it is not always so; far from it. The retorts in the passage from *The West Pier* are as short as can be, and the most superficial reading of Pinter's plays will produce this unexpected version of the quantity maxim: they who talk most, lose, because they expose themselves, and their opponents consequently gain the upper hand since, being silent, they remain inscrutable. The essential aspect of the maxim, however, is not so much the quantity of information produced, as the dissymmetry of the opponents. The situation described is one of unequal exchange and excessive behaviour, not of symmetry and fair dealing, as in Gricean cooperation. We shall also have a maxim of *Quality*: you can state anything, provided it hurts, that is provided it gains you a status, a place in the verbal hierarchy, which you can force your opponent to recognise. Lying or stating without proof are perfectly legitimate devices – often they are the only adequate ones. There is no question of sincerity here. If stating the truth helps your position, be truthful; if not, you may lie with an easy conscience – the only 'morality' of your

79

speech is its efficacy as a verbal attack or defence. (This is not, of course, a defence of lying as one of the fine arts, or an account of ordinary conversations – *encore que* . . ., as the French say: my new maxims are, in their way, as ideal as Grice's.) The third maxim is *Relation*: every speech act is dependent on the constraints of the speaker's strategy. The question of relevance is to be raised only in connection with the aim of the game. Agonistic conversation is as rational as its cooperative counterpart: it calls for rational choices, the adaptation of means to ends, on the part of the speaker. The last maxim is *Manner*. Again, you may be brief or digressive, obscure or perspicuous, according to the context of struggle. But it is always better to be ambiguous and not let the opponent see your game. In this framework, any instance of verbal cooperation – there are such things in life, as when I ask you the time of day, and elicit a correct answer – will be attributed to an exploitation of the maxims, the meaning of which is to be pragmatically computed.

The principle of struggle – do not expose your position; adapt your verbal weapons to your strategy and to the context; never forget that your goal is to achieve recognition, to place yourself – is the mirror image of the cooperative principle. It has the same transcendental value, and the picture of conversation it suggests is as idealised, a dystopia rather than a utopia. The question of course arises naturally: if there is no transcendental difference, why not keep to cooperation? There are two answers to this. The first is that there is a structural difference between the two principles. Although they are both transcendental, the CP implies a symmetrical relationship between the participants in the conversation, and therefore a stability in each maxim: brevity and method are always in order, because they are in the best interests of everyone, since all participants have the same interests; while the PS implies an asymmetrical relationship between participants, what the French call *rapport de force*, which establishes a hierarchy of places – something like a dialectics of master and slave rather than peaceful cooperation. As a result, the maxims of *agon* are deeply unstable – their contents, as we have seen, may vary with the context. It is not always in the best interest of the speaker to remain silent – the speaker's best interest being determined by her current position in the verbal struggle. The second answer is simply that our texts appear to prefer the non-cooperative version of conversation, and to represent the asymmetrical aspects of *agon*. Nonsense texts focus on the wild spiral of argument described by Patrick Hamilton.

Dialogues are almost always antagonistic. Even the obvious exception in *Alice's Adventures in Wonderland*, the conversations between Alice and the Cheshire Cat, involve an element of fear under their friendly surface:

> The Cat only grinned when it saw Alice. It looked good-natured, she thought: still it had *very* long claws and a great many teeth, so she felt that it ought to be treated with respect. 'Cheshire Puss,' she began, rather timidly. . .[16]

Friendliness here is causally related to fear, that is to the hierarchic places, based on relations of power, which the speaker ascribes to herself and to the other participant, to be called an opponent, even if the game turns out to be what one sometimes calls 'a friendly'.

As usual, if nonsense appears to subvert the commonsensical view of conversation as exchange of information, there is an element of protection or support involved. Alice is learning the rules of the game the hard way. It is not irrelevant that *agon*, not *irene*, should be the beginning, and also the end, of what Alice is taught in Wonderland – she will be better equipped to deal with everyday situations in real life. But *agon* and *irene* have one aspect in common, which distinguishes Carroll's nonsense from the deeper, more chaotic nonsense of, for instance, Samuel Beckett. They both involve strategy, i.e. rational choice. Both the CP and the PS imply that conversations have meaning, that the participants have goals and know what they are doing – whether they are of the same mind or at odds is of secondary importance. In this, both the CP and the PS are subsumed under what Sperber and Wilson call the Principle of Relevance.[17] The main point is that the speakers are in control of the conversation, and not the reverse. All we have to do in order to understand this is to compare the dialogues in the *Alice* books to the verbal exchange in *Waiting for Godot*, which very often hesitates between struggle and cooperation, and can hardly ever be described in terms of the speakers' intentions or strategies. This is why Patrick Hamilton's text is not nonsense. Such a *fuite en avant* is too dangerous. Nonsense, on the contrary, entertains a fantasy of exaggerated or total control of the speakers over their exchange, which is embodied in Humpty Dumpty.

I shall give two illustrations of this. The first occurs in Chapter 4 of *Through the Looking-Glass*, when Alice meets Tweedledum and Tweedledee, those rather nasty schoolboys. And nasty they are to Alice. They lead her to the place where the Red King is happily snoring away:

'Isn't he a *lovely* sight?' said Tweedledum.

Alice couldn't say honestly that he was. He had a tall red night-cap on, with a tassel, and he was lying crumpled up into a sort of untidy heap, and snoring loud – 'fit to snore his head off!' as Tweedledum remarked.

'I'm afraid he'll catch cold with lying on the damp grass,' said Alice, who was a very thoughtful little girl.

'He's dreaming now,' said Tweedledee: 'and what do you think he's dreaming about?'

Alice said 'Nobody can guess that.'

'Why, about *you*!' Tweedledee exclaimed, clapping his hands triumphantly. 'And if he left off dreaming about you, where do you suppose you'd be?'

'Where I am now, of course,' said Alice.

'Not you!' Tweedledee retorted contemptuously. 'You'd be nowhere. Why, you're only a sort of thing in his dream!'

'If that there King was to wake,' added Tweedledum, 'you'd go out – bang! – just like a candle!'

'I shouldn't!' Alice exclaimed indignantly. 'Besides, if *I'm* only a sort of thing in his dream, what are *you*, I should like to know?'

'Ditto,' said Tweedledum.

'Ditto, ditto!' cried Tweedledee.

He shouted this so loud that Alice couldn't help saying 'Hush! You'll be waking him, I'm afraid, if you make so much noise.'

'Well, it's no use *your* talking about waking him,' said Tweedledum, 'when you're only one of the things in his dream. You know very well you're not real.'

'I *am* real!' said Alice, and began to cry.

'You won't make yourself a bit realler by crying,' Tweedledee remarked: 'there's nothing to cry about.'

'If I wasn't real,' Alice said – half-laughing through her tears, it all seemed so ridiculous – 'I shouldn't be able to cry.'

'I hope you don't suppose those are *real* tears?' Tweedledum interrupted in a tone of great contempt.

'I know they're talking nonsense,' Alice thought to herself: 'and it's foolish to cry about it.' So she brushed away her tears, and went on, as cheerfully as she could, 'At any rate I'd better be getting out of the wood, for really it's coming on very dark. Do you think it's going to rain?'[18]

The passage is famous, a *locus classicus* for a philosophical question which seems to have much preoccupied the British mind since Bishop Berkeley. Are we nothing but figments of God's dreams? Are the cows still in the field even if nobody is looking at them? Can I prove that I am real by kicking a large stone? Not to forget the abysmal thought that if Alice is a creature of the King's dream, he, in turn, is nothing but a creature of Alice's dream, since the whole tale is a dream, and his fate on the last but one page of the book is to be the fate predicted to Alice by Tweedledum and Tweedledee: when she wakes up from her dream, he will be simply nowhere. Even as on the *last* page of the tale, the same fate will overcome Alice, a creation, her reality as the daughter of an Oxford don notwithstanding, of Carroll's literary musings.

This, although fascinating, is not what interests me now, at least at first sight – the verbal exchange is my object. And it is violent. Alice cries, even if she laughs through her tears, and the two boys scream (' "Ditto, ditto!" cried Tweedledee. He shouted this so loud that Alice couldn't help saying "Hush! You'll be waking him, I'm afraid, if you make such noise." '). But the real violence of the exchange is more perverse than downright insults or threats. It is the violence of interpellation, where the opponent is destroyed by being denied her place, any place, in the conversational game. 'You know very well you're not real' is the ultimate aggression, which reduces Alice to tears. The conversation is also of interest because it evinces one of the main characteristics of nonsensical, and especially Carrollian, *agon* – the use of logic, of sophistry I should say, as conversational tactics. The two schoolboys are sophists. Their argument is based on a verbal sleight of hand, which conflates and confuses the two sentences: 'The king is dreaming about you' and 'The king is dreaming you'. Even as the real Alice can be the object of Carroll's tale without detriment to her solid Oxford reality, the fictional Alice, who is dreaming a character, can be the object of that character's dream without her fictional existence being threatened. The sophistry is helped by the fact that it is combined with straightforward logic – Tweedledum and Tweedledee are also adept at eristics. If Alice is not real, then of course her tears are not real tears. Tweedledum can say this 'in a tone of great contempt' because the conclusion is flawless. He is, in fact, an embodiment of the classic figure of the Sophist, and his paradox is typical of the Sophists' paradoxes about language, to a refutation of which Aristotle devoted a large part of his energy.

And yet he may be even worse than this. Perhaps the most worrying aspect is that, in spite of what I suggested earlier, there does not appear to be any strategy behind this aggressiveness (as there is in the trial scene, for instance). The two schoolboys are just being nasty for the pleasure of it, almost automatically, as if their words carried them away, or rather carried hostile affects independent of any subject. Words trap you, even without the help of a conscious trapping speaker, of a Sophist. They construct paradoxes, and catch you in their linguistic meshes. This is the real function of the pseudo-paradox of dreaming. It is not so much a reflection on the ambivalence of dreamer and dreamt as the framework for a linguistic nightmare. Tweedledum and Tweedledee are trying to make Alice as mad as they are (since, as the Cheshire Cat tells Alice, 'We're all mad here. I'm mad. You're mad').[19]

But 'trying' is the wrong word, as the characters cannot help themselves – language impels them so to act. If Alice is threatened by madness, it is because she is caught in one of Bateson's linguistic double binds.[20] As a result, she has only two solutions: helpless defeat, that is bursting into tears, which will not help her escape the trap (but one of the characteristics of a situation of double bind, according to Bateson, is that the subject cannot leave the game), or rebellion, that is using words to counterattack and conceal the nefarious effect of those paradoxical schizogenic words. This she does in two steps. First, she recognises the schoolboys' words for what they are, weapons of aggression, screams. When she tries to hush Tweedledee, it is because he has been screaming 'Ditto, ditto!' to Alice's 'Besides, if *I'm* only a sort of thing in his dream, what are *you*, I should like to know?' Here, she is learning the art of interpellation, and of questioning as a form of counterattack. The answer she gets is fascinating, for by using this Italian-sounding word, 'ditto', 'the same', Tweedledum and Tweedledee seem to be confessing that they, too, are creatures of the King's dream (in which case Alice is right to hush them), although they do not behave as if they were, and do not appear to be unduly preoccupied by the situation. So that 'ditto', the original meaning of which is 'said' in Italian, must be interpreted as a purely nonsensical interruption, where the word 'said' does not have an *en abyme* metalinguistic function (ranging from 'as you said' to 'that's what you said!'), but rather a 'counter-phatic' function, to distort

Jakobson's concept, which is not to establish contact but to break the opponent's chain of words.

The second step Alice takes at the end of the exchange: ' "I know they're talking nonsense," Alice thought to herself: "and it's foolish to cry about it." ' And she closes the exchange with that archetypically British phatic question: 'Do you think it is going to rain?' Again, the closure is arbitrary. But it is made possible by Alice's metadiscursive move, when she calls the whole exchange 'nonsense'. As we have seen, Alice is far from powerless, and she is learning, more and more efficiently, to hold her own. By exclaiming 'nonsense!', which she has already done at the end of *Alice's Adventures in Wonderland* when she greets the Queen of Hearts's infamous 'Sentence first – verdict afterwards' with a vigorous 'Stuff and nonsense!',[21] Alice finds the usually forbidden way out of the conversational double bind. This is a use of the word 'nonsense' that is straightforwardly pragmatic, i.e. in which the illocutionary force is much more important than the semantic contents. Pragmatic, but not cooperative: it is one of the typical weapons of verbal *agon* (which explains why a nonsense tale will naturally choose the agonistic version of the principle of relevance), or of philosophical polemic, for that matter. For the exclamation is not only used on various occasions in the *Alice* books, but also in the language of philosophers. A careful reading of A. J. Ayer's *Language, Truth and Logic* will yield at least twenty-five occurrences of the words 'nonsense', 'nonsensical' or 'senseless', of which some are notorious, like 'all utterances about the nature of God are nonsensical'.[22]

The Tweedledum passage suggests reasons why a cooperative analysis will not do. My second passage, the trial scene in *Alice's Adventures in Wonderland*, shows that Habermas's ethics of interpersonal communication will not do either. His ideal, as we have seen, is a type of scientific discussion which is free of external interests and constraints (that is in which positions are not determined in advance by previous positions or extra-discursive interests), and takes the form of dispassionate controversy (dispassionate in the sense that positions can change as the discussion progresses: conviction and admission of error are possible). While this is an ethical ideal to which I, like most of us, subscribe, and which is indeed worth fighting for, I must nevertheless note that there is another possible model for discussion and communication: judicial debate, which can only be described as a verbal battle between contestants, between prosecutor and defendant, in which sometimes life is at stake. In this case, the end of the debate decides who shall be master and who slave, who wins and who loses – truth is less important than verisimilitude, sincerity is not a value, and the equality of the participants is constitutively impossible (the prosecution and the defence are on an equal footing, but the judge, the jury and the defendant are not in an equal position – the whole situation of the trial is based on a hierarchy of places). In such a dystopic ideal (where the shadowy figure of the ancient Sophist creeps back to the centre of the stage), certainly less pleasant a model than disinterested scientific discussion, but as close to our daily experience of discussion as the irenic version, Habermas's validity claims and conditions for the ideal speech situation are obviously not all fulfilled, but more often than not vigorously denied or inverted. Thus, in a trial, the authors of speech acts (1) do not always make the propositional meaning of their utterance and their pragmatic relation to other speakers clear. Imagine Perry Mason dealing with a prosecution witness. The propositional meaning of each question is clear, but the general drift of the questioning is far from being so; the hope is to elicit a dangerous admission from the witness; (2) although all the participants are 'committed to the truth of their utterances' – there is such a thing as perjury – the situation paradoxically admits that two incompatible narratives of the same facts can be proposed, one of which, since they are sometimes contradictory, will of necessity be false. In a trial, the prosecution and the defence cannot both make true contentions, but the structure of the speech situation allows, constitutively so, for an untruth to be defended, sometimes successfully. (One could of course object that the truth of the matter is what the jury decides – this, although undoubtedly correct at a certain level, does not protect us from the possibility of miscarriages of justice, the list of which would be too long); (3) they must recognise the norms within which their speech acts are produced. In this, the speech situation is highly constrained – there is such a thing as contempt of court; (4) but, on the other hand, it is the duty of some of the participants to question the sincerity of at least some of the other speakers. If we were to believe, out of principle, in the sincerity of the defendant's denials, there would be no trial. And this applies not only to, 'I didn't do it', but even to 'I did not intend to do it' – whereas in a normal speech situation, intentions, like statements of bodily pain, cannot easily be called into question. This has induced the distinction, which can be found in the philosophy of law, between *intended* actions, which are the objects of explicit intentions on the part of the agent, and *intentional* ones, in which the responsibility of the agent is determined by computation, after the event, of 'intentions' the agent may never have consciously entertained, but which are derived from the predictable consequences of his action. If you set fire to a house without intending to kill the residents, in the case where they actually die in the fire, you are guilty of an intentional crime, and the charge will be murder rather than manslaughter.[23] To go back to our milder situation of conversation, the conditions for the participants in the discussion are denied or inverted to an even greater extent. Not all participants have the same right to initiate or pursue the verbal exchange – a master of ceremonies assigns turn-taking. Not all participants are given the same opportunity to produce the type of speech act they wish – the witness winces under the lawyer's insinuations but cannot answer back. They are not given the same opportunity to express wishes, emotions or opinions, not the same right to issue orders, warnings and threats – only the judge can normally do this.

Even if such a speech situation is known to most of us only through detective stories and Perry Mason films, they are common fare in Carroll. Alice's linguistic learning if acquired through one such scene, the trial scene in *Alice's Adventures in Wonderland*, and in conversations which have similar structures. And, as I hinted earlier, this is not such a pessimistic view of ordinary dialogue as it seems. Perhaps going up for trial is as satisfactory a way to learn the rules of intersubjective communication as indulging in polite drawing-room conversation. In fact, we encounter the dialectics of subversion and support again. *Alice's Adventures in Wonderland* is part of the satirical tradition of the critique of a corrupt judicial system (one of the best instances of which is Godwin's *Caleb Williams*), and as such is also an *a contrario* defence of an ideal of judicial fairness and the correct administration of justice. But Carroll goes further than *Caleb Williams*. In Godwin's novel, the class bias of the judiciary and the powerlessness of the innocent to protect himself against the false accusations of the powerful are at the centre of a bitter critique. In Carroll's tale, the emphasis is on the link between the machinery of justice and the use of language – an argumentative, or rhetorical use of language, which can easily be generalised to all speech situations.[24] The interest in trial scenes that we find in nonsense texts, therefore, is not due only to the notorious fondness of the judicial profession for the most abstruse – and, to the layman, nonsensical – jargon, but also to metalinguistic and pedagogic aims. Intuitions about language are often produced by encounters with the judiciary.

The trial scene in *Alice* takes up the last two chapters of the tale. I shall concentrate on the last chapter, 'Alice's Evidence', and more particularly on two moments of it, the interrogation of Alice and the interpretation of the poem which the Knave of Hearts is supposed to have written.

The beginning of the trial has been a rather unruly and messy affair. The jurors are all busy writing their own names on their slates, the King has asked them to consider their verdict even before the first witness has been heard, and the witnesses, when they do appear, are not particularly helpful. Nor do the admonitions of the King, who presides, improve matters. ' "Give your evidence," said the King; "and don't be nervous, or I'll have you executed on the spot." '[25] – a neat instance of double bind, this, where the perlocutionary effect is bound to ruin the illocutionary force of the utterance. Lastly, the Dormouse has been 'suppressed' in a surprisingly forceful manner. In this disorderly context, Alice, who is feeling a little uneasy because she is beginning to grow again, is called as a witness and testifies:

'What do you know about this business?' the King said to Alice.

'Nothing,' said Alice.

'Nothing *whatever*?' persisted the King.

'Nothing whatever,' said Alice.

'That's very important,' the King said, turning to the jury. They were just beginning to write this down on their slates, when the White Rabbit interrupted: '*Un*important, your Majesty means of course,' he said, in a very respectful tone, but frowning and making faces at him as he spoke.

'*Un*important, of course, I meant,' the King hastily said, and went on to himself in an undertone, 'important – unimportant – unimportant – important –' as if he were trying which word sounded best.

Some of the jury wrote it down 'important,' and some 'unimportant.' Alice could see this, as she was near enough to look over their slates; 'but it doesn't matter a bit,' she thought to herself.

At this moment the King, who had been for some time busily writing in his note-book, called out 'Silence!' and read out from his book, 'Rule Forty-two. *All persons more than a mile high to leave the court.*'

Everybody looked at Alice.

'*I'm* not a mile high,' said Alice.

'You are,' said the King.

'Nearly two miles high,' added the Queen.

'Well, I shan't go, at any rate,' said Alice; 'besides, that's not a regular rule: you invented it just now.'

'It's the oldest rule in the book,' said the King.

'Then it ought to be Number One,' said Alice.

The King turned pale, and shut his notebook hastily. 'Consider your verdict,' he said to the jury, in a low trembling voice.

'There's more evidence to come yet, please your Majesty,' said the White Rabbit, jumping up in a great hurry: 'this paper has just been picked up.'

'What's in it?' said the Queen.

'I haven't opened it yet,' said the White Rabbit; 'but it seems to be a letter, written by the prisoner to – to somebody.'

'It must have been that,' said the King, 'unless it was written to nobody, which isn't usual, you know.'

'Who is it directed to?' said one of the jurymen.

'It isn't directed at all,' said the White Rabbit: 'in fact, there's nothing written on the *outside.*' He unfolded the paper as he spoke, and added, 'It isn't a letter, after all: it's a set of verses.'

'Are they in the prisoner's handwriting?' asked another of the jurymen.

'No, they're not,' said the White Rabbit, 'and that's the queerest thing about it.' (The jury all looked puzzled.)

'He must have imitated somebody else's hand,' said the King. (The jury all brightened up again.)

'Please, your Majesty,' said the Knave, 'I didn't write it, and they can't prove that I did: there's no name signed at the end.'

'If you didn't sign it,' said the King, 'that only makes the matter worse. You *must* have meant some mischief, or else you'd have signed your name like an honest man.'

There was a general clapping of hands at this: it was the first really clever thing the King had said that day.

'That *proves* his guilt, of course,' said the Queen: 'so, off with —'.

'It doesn't prove anything of the sort!' said Alice. 'Why, you don't even know what they're about!'

'Read them,' said the King.

The White Rabbit put on his spectacles. 'Where shall I begin, please your Majesty?' he asked.

'Begin at the beginning,' the King said, very gravely, 'and go on till you come to the end: then stop.'[26]

It is clear that this text is far more than a piece of satire. It has, to my mind, two objects. First, it is an account of the institutional violence of language, of the power of rhetoric and sophistry, and of the necessity of agonistic retort if one does not wish to be made the victim of arbitrariness. One of the most striking aspects of the scene is that Alice not only holds her own, but is capable of thwarting the King's strategy – this is the end of the tale, she has learnt much, and, besides, she is growing much taller than the rest of the characters and can afford to patronise or despise them. Second, it insidiously provides a context for the text which will be produced as evidence against the Knave of Hearts. And this is where Alice has not learnt enough yet, for in this, which is an instance of rhetorical cunning and covert aggression, she is defeated. Not having been able to prevent the poem from being produced as evidence and becoming the object of a necessarily distorted interpretation, she will have to escape from the game by an act of arbitrary violence, by exclaiming, 'You're nothing but a pack of cards' and waking up.

But a battle there is, the pretexts for which are the failure of language to describe the facts accurately and the arbitrariness of rules. It is not only a verbal battle between two opponents – it is also, *en abyme*, a debate about the nature of language. First, language is seen to be hopelessly vague, to the point that it fails to convey distinct meanings. True, the King has a singularly muddled mind, since he cannot tell the difference between 'important' and 'unimportant'. But this is partly the fault of the

English language, as there are cases when merely adding an apparently negative prefix to an adjective fails to alter its meaning: from 'flammable' to 'inflammable', or from 'habitable' to 'inhabitable', there is no semantic difference, because of the etymological ambiguity of the prefix 'in-'. The King, therefore, may be forgiven if his linguistic intuitions are no longer reliable. And he does what we all do when we are not sure of a word – we repeat it to ourselves to try and find out whether it sounds right: ' "important – unimportant – unimportant – important – " as if he were trying which word sounded best.' No wonder the jury are confused and write different words on their slates. Second, language is a source of arbitrary power, the power of naming. The King has just invented a rule, 'All persons more than a mile high to leave the court', an obviously *ad hoc* rule, the only function of which is to exclude Alice. But he gives it authority by providing it with a name, or rather a number, 'Rule Forty-two'. We are in fact witnessing an act of primal baptism, in the sense of Kripke,[27] which fixes the reference of a rigid designator and initiates the causal chain of its transmission. The King has placed himself in the mythical position of the *nomothetes*, he who, like Adam, gives their referents to names. And it appears that this anti-descriptivist process is liable to two kinds of infelicity. First, the performative act of baptism is open to denial. It is possible for a witness to claim that the circumstances are not right. Rules of law cannot be invented on the spur of the moment; they must always already have been in the Statute Book. You cannot make up new rules in the middle of a game without ruining all rules: 'that's not a regular rule [Alice says to the King]: you invented it just now.' Second, the anti-descriptivist position is sometimes let down by the relatively motivated nature of language. Unfortunately for the King, 'Rule Forty-two' *means* something, it entails, if not necessarily a cluster of descriptions, at least one: the rule situated between Rules Forty-one and Forty-three in the Statute Book. As a result of this it cannot be the oldest rule in the Book, as Alice logically argues. The designator cannot be rigid because two members of the cluster of descriptions inevitably associated with it, 'Rule Forty-two' and 'the oldest rule in the Book' are incompatible. I am not offering this as a serious argument against Kripke's theory, but I may note that Alice's position has considerable illocutionary force and perlocutionary effect, and consequently great agonistic value:

The King turned pale, and shut his notebook hastily. 'Consider your verdict,' he said to the jury, in a low trembling voice.

Third, even tautology, that apparently innocuous and vacuous form of repetition, can be used in the agonistic game. It allows the King to recover face by laying down the law beyond any possibility of debate, as he does at the end of our text: 'Begin at the beginning . . .' More importantly, he does the same just after being verbally defeated by Alice:

'What's in it?' said the Queen.

'I haven't opened it yet,' said the White Rabbit; 'but it seems to be a letter, written by the prisoner to – to somebody.'

'It must have been that,' said the King, 'unless it was written to nobody, which isn't usual, you know.'[28]

Apparently, the King and the White Rabbit keep to safe ground, in order to avoid being the victims of Alice's logical skill. It is, in virtue of the definition of the term, necessarily true that a letter is written by someone to someone. But in fact, behind the innocuous analytic statement we can sense a pragmatic counterattack, an aggressive move in the verbal game. It is not necessary to read Derrida to know that not all texts are letters, and that a letter that has been withdrawn from the original act of communication in which it was addressed by x to z reverts to the status of a text with unknown or implicit author and dubious addressee, a linguistic machine working autonomously, the origin of which is no longer a particular subject, but a universe of discourse, a language. What the White Rabbit and the King are insidiously doing is creating a context that will pre-empt the future reading of the poem. The Rabbit appears to be cautious at first – 'it seems to be a letter . . .', but by naming the object 'a letter', it imposes on whoever will talk about it from then on a number of descriptions: it is written by someone, it is written to someone, it has a point, and as such is susceptible of interpretation, and so on. He himself provides the first two of these descriptions straight away: '. . . written by the prisoner to – to somebody.' Again, he seems to hesitate, to wish to hedge his words – like a serious and reliable witness, who does not wish to mislead the court. But if this vague 'somebody' testifies to his scruples, it also conceals (and sharply contrasts with) the unfounded ascription of authorship which he makes in the very same sentence: 'by the prisoner'. As the Knave of Hearts will commonsensically argue, the poem is not a letter, and there are no indications of either addressee or author. The Rabbit's sleight of hand is a form of *petitio principii*: he conceals within the premisses what should be the conclusion of his proof, that the defendant is the author of the letter/of the crime. But there is, of course, no cause for moralistic grumblings. As an agonistic move, in the course of a prosecution or a defence, this is entirely licit. Of course, in a real trial no member of the legal profession would be taken in by such an elementary piece of deceit – this is where Alice is still naive.

The Rabbit has an ally in the King, who uses this exchange to gain the upper hand again. By making a remark worthy of M. de la Palisse, 'unless it was written to nobody, which isn't usual, you know' (come to think of it, not so unusual as that, at least if we interpret 'nobody' as 'nobody in particular' rather than 'nobody at all': an 'open letter' falls within this category, or a poetic 'epistle' – our text is, after all, a poem), the King is sustaining the implicit statements of the Rabbit. He fails to question the ascription of authorship which from now on will be taken for granted, even by Alice, and deflects the attention towards the Rabbit's apparent hesitation, not about the existence of an addressee, but about his identity. This enables the King to proceed with the piece of sophistry that immediately follows, when he interprets the fact that the poem is not in the prisoner's handwriting and that he did not sign his name to it as proofs of an intention to deceive – an improbable explanation, but the only possible one once we have granted the Rabbit's illicit premiss. No wonder that when the King exclaims: 'You *must* have meant some mischief, or else you'd have signed your name like an honest man', the audience start clapping. They are right in thinking that this is a 'clever' thing for the King to say. No wonder too that the Queen adds: 'That *proves* his guilt, of course.'

The Queen is interrupted by Alice, who, like us, is shocked at the unfairness of the proceedings: 'It doesn't prove anything of the sort! Why, you don't even know what they are about!' She is, of course, right. The Knave is being tried on the charge of stealing some tarts, and his so-called dishonest refusal to sign his own letters can have only indirect bearing on the charge. But in saying this, Alice concedes far too much. She fails to question the Rabbit's premiss. Worse even, by suggesting that the judgment should be withdrawn till the text has been read, she implicitly accepts that the Knave is the author of the 'letter'. By letting the poem be read as evidence (and indeed this is how the Rabbit's *petitio principii* began: 'There's more evidence to come yet, please your majesty'), she accepts it as evidence, and therefore authorises the subsequent commentary by the King, a commentary guided by the context he and the Rabbit have successfully constructed. Such is the insidious violence of sophistry, which Alice will be able to avoid only by an act of direct violence, when she 'tries to beat off' the cards – an admission of verbal defeat. The poem is, therefore, duly read and interpreted:

> There was dead silence in the court, whilst the White Rabbit
> read out these verses: –
> 'They told me you had been to her,
>   And mentioned me to him:
> She gave me a good character,
>   But said I could not swim.
> He sent them word I had not gone
>   (We know it to be true):
> If she should push the matter on,
>   What would become of you?
> I gave her one, they gave him two,
>   You gave us three or more;
> They all returned from him to you,
>   Though they were mine before.
> If I or she should chance to be
>   Involved in this affair,
> He trusts to you to set them free,
>   Exactly as we were.
> My notion was that you have been
>   (Before she had this fit)
> An obstacle that came between
>   Him, and ourselves, and it.
> Don't let him know she liked them best,
>   For this must ever be
> A secret, kept from all the rest,
>   Between yourself and me.'
> 'That's the most important piece of evidence we've heard
> yet,' said the King, rubbing his hands; 'so now let the jury —'
> 'If any one of them can explain it,' said Alice, (she had
> grown so large in the last few minutes that she wasn't a bit

afraid of interrupting him), 'I'll give him sixpence. *I* don't believe there's an atom of meaning in it.'

The jury all wrote down on their slates, '*She* doesn't believe there's an atom of meaning in it,' but none of them attempted to explain the paper.

'If there's no meaning in it,' said the King, 'that saves a world of trouble, you know, as we needn't try to find any. And yet I don't know,' he went on, spreading out the verses on his knee, and looking at them with one eye; 'I seem to see some meaning in them, after all. " *– said I could not swim –* " you can't swim, can you?' he added, turning to the Knave.

The Knave shook his head sadly. 'Do I look like it?' he said. (Which he certainly did *not*, being made entirely of cardboard.)

'All right, so far,' said the King; and he went on muttering over the verses to himself: ' "*We know it to be true –* " that's the jury, of course – "*If she should push the matter on*" – that must be the Queen – "*What would become of you?*" – What, indeed! – "*I gave her one, they gave him two –* " why, that must be what he did with the tarts, you know —

'But it goes on "*they all returned from him to you*" ' said Alice.

'Why, there they are!' said the King triumphantly, pointing to the tarts on the table. 'Nothing can be clearer than *that*. Then again – "*before she had this fit –* " you never had fits, my dear, I think?' he said to the Queen.

'Never!' said the Queen, furiously, throwing an inkstand at the Lizard as she spoke. (The unfortunate little Bill had left off writing on his slate with one finger, as he found it made no mark; but he now hastily began again, using the ink, that was trickling down his face, as long as it lasted.)

'Then the words don't *fit* you,' said the King, looking round the court with a smile. There was a dead silence.

'It's a pun!' the King added in an angry tone, and everybody laughed. 'Let the jury consider their verdict,' the King said, for about the twentieth time that day.

'No, no!' said the Queen. 'Sentence first – verdict afterwards.'

'Stuff and nonsense!' said Alice loudly. 'The idea of having the sentence first!'

'Hold your tongue!' said the Queen, turning purple.

'I won't!' said Alice.

'Off with her head!' the Queen shouted at the top of her voice. Nobody moved.

'Who cares for *you*?' said Alice (she had grown to her full size by this time). 'You're nothing but a pack of cards!'

At this the whole pack rose up into the air, and came flying down upon her.[29]

When we read this famous poem, we recognise how fitting it is that it should have appeared in this context, or rather that a context should have been provided for it in advance. The poem is the best justification I know for the fact that utterance meaning is not enough, that it must be supplemented by utterer's meaning. We must provide an utterer in order to decipher the occasion meaning of those shifters, whose shifting leaves us in the dark. This, at least, is what the King is trying to do. By providing an author for the text, he has identified a situation, a set of individuals, states of affairs and events, which can provide referents for the uncertain words of the poem. Once the words have picked out their referents, the text becomes fully intelligible. It is fitting, therefore, that the interpretation should end on a pun on 'fit' – it is all a question of how the situation will fit the words.

But there is something wrong here. In saying this, I seem to indicate that the text, to speak like Searle,[30] has a world-to-word direction of fit, which makes it a series of performative utterances. Surely, this cannot be the case. If the poem is to be admitted as *evidence*, we must take it for granted that it has a word-to-world direction of fit, that the words of the poem adequately fit the situation it describes, so that we can draw conclusions as to the Knave's guilt or innocence. The King, in his interpretation, is reversing the normal order of things. Instead of using the text as a source of information about the situation, he is using the situation in order to inject meaning into the text – in other words the *petitio principii* is going on at a deeper level. If the King can do this, however, it is because the text, because language, allows him to do it. The text does possess utterance meaning. Even if I cannot pick out their referents, I can understand those words, and I am aware that they are inserted in correct sentences. I can paraphrase the text, to which the systematic recourse to the whole paradigm of personal pronouns gives an aspect of narrative logic. Fictions are created by the text, even at the moment when it becomes clear that communication has broken down, fictions which are merely waiting for referents – characters and events – to come and fill them. This is, of course, what happens at the beginning of any poem or novel. Thus, the first paragraph of Harper Lee's *To Kill a Mocking-Bird* tells us of an accident that befell the narrator's brother, Jem. And this is the second paragraph:

When enough years had gone by to enable us to look back on them, we sometimes discussed the events leading to this accident. I maintain that the Ewells started it all, but Jem, who was four years my senior, said it started long before that. He said it began the summer Dill came to us, when Dill first gave us the idea of making Boo Radley come out.[31]

The reader understands the words, and the sentences, but little else. He or she will have to wait till the very end of the novel in order to understand them completely, by picking out the right referents for those proper names and allusions to events yet unknown. Carroll plays the same trick on us, except that he withdraws the disclosure for ever, and even laughs at us in the last line. Since we have failed to understand anything, how can we keep the *secret* (or *not* keep the secret)?

There is an important *abyme* element in the text. By using *verba dicendi* in every stanza, it focuses on the telling of a tale, on the process of giving evidence. As such, it must be, as the King says, 'the most important piece of evidence we've heard yet'. And yet, of course, as evidence, it is entirely useless. So that the poem is a strange piece of language. It has meaning – Alice is wrong to exclaim: '*I* don't believe there is an atom of meaning in it', and the King right to retort: 'I seem to see some meaning in [the words], after all' – for utterance meaning is what it has. And yet it is also meaningless, and Alice is right. In other words, the text has all the characteristics of a piece of *écriture* in Derrida's sense.[32] Although it is pragmatically void, it is semantically coherent, and as such ready for a multiplicity of interpretations. Because it has meaning, but no specified occasion meaning, it is open to any occasion meaning with which it can be made to fit. This is what the King does – he plays the part, if not of a judge, at least of a literary critic, or rather of a mixture of the two: of a literary critic bent on a literal interpretation of the text, of the was-it-Shakespeare-or-Bacon-who-wrote-it, or the Ettelson, type. His detailed interpretations are irreproachable: the words can be made to mean what he claims they mean, and the network of interpretations ends up making coherent meaning, a meaning so coherent that it leaves Alice speechless. Comparisons, Davidson says, are endlessly and trivially true;[33] interpretations are endlessly and trivially possible.

This does not merely mean that Baker and Hacker's critique of the dogma that 'the distinction between sense and nonsense is absolute and independent of the circumstances surrounding an utterance' is correct.[34] It also means that it is a characteristic of the workings of language that texts, *qua* texts, are open to all the interpretations that can be made to cohere with the utterance meaning, i.e. almost *any* interpretation. There is no nonsense that is not capable of being turned into sense. There is no piece of language that cannot be made the pretext for a pragmatic manipulation which is part of an agonistic strategy. This judicial interpretation by the King is an emblem of all interpretation; and it is constructed not through cooperation, but along the principles of *agon*, by the manipulation of affects of violence and desire, a manipulation that the structure of language fully allows. That this is no abstraction is shown by what I believe is the historical origin, the intertextual source, of the whole scene – what is known as the 'Peacham affair'. We still remember it today because of the infamous part Francis Bacon played in it, and, perhaps even more, because of a passage in Macaulay's essay, 'Francis Bacon'.

> Unhappily he was at that very time employed in perverting those laws to the vilest purposes of tyranny. When Oliver St John was brought before the Star Chamber for maintaining that the King had no right to levy Benevolences, and was for his manly and constitutional conduct sentenced to imprisonment during the royal pleasure and to a fine of five thousand pounds, Bacon appeared as counsel for the prosecution. About the same time, he was deeply engaged in a still more disgraceful transaction. An aged clergyman, of the name of Peacham, was accused of treason on account of some passages of a sermon which was found in his study. The sermon, whether written by him or not, had never been preached. It did not appear that he had any intention of preaching it. The most servile lawyers of those servile times were forced to admit that there were great difficulties both as to the facts and as to the law. Bacon was employed to remove those difficulties. He was employed to settle the question of law by tampering with the judges, and the question of fact by torturing the prisoner.[35]

The cast are all there. Bacon is played by the White Rabbit, the corrupt judges by the King of Hearts, and James I, of course, by the Queen of Hearts, whose exclamation, 'Off with his/her head', uncovers the violent truth that lies beneath the verbal exchanges. And truly, from this point of view, a trial scene deserves to provide a model for the speech situation conceived as a locus for violence and *agon* – it is the speech situation where, *par excellence*, the speaker's life may depend on someone's verbal strategy. This version of the Peacham affair, by the way, is Macaulay's, which suggests that Carroll had read his essay. Modern historians do not seem to be in any doubt that Peacham, a testy old Somerset parson with seditious proclivities, had actually written the sermon. It is Macaulay, whose own verbal strategy is to paint Bacon in as unfavourable a light as he can, who adds the important clause, 'whether written by him or not' – this is the centre of the scene in *Alice's Adventures in Wonderland*.

Let us note one last thing. Alice is by no means powerless. She is defeated by an insidious trick, but she gives almost as good as she gets, and her increased position of independence and power is symbolised by her growing, and rather fast at that: 'she had grown so large in the last few minutes that she wasn't a bit afraid of interrupting him'. Her power is no longer merely verbal, it is also physical – the concealed basis of verbal power. Behind the verbal game of interrogation, there is the threat of torture. Behind the conformity to the conversational rules of turn-taking, there lies the possibility of imposing one's 'turn' on the other by physical violence. That there is ambiguity in this recourse to physical as opposed to verbal violence – fists are a poor compensation for lack of wit – we have seen in the success cum failure of Alice's final *coup de force*, which brings about the end of the game.

It might appear, therefore, that the pragmatics of *agon* are historically motivated – mankind has learnt to replace the sword with the word at a fairly late stage in its history (this, of course, is nothing but a convenient agonistic myth of origins). And it does appear that *agon* corresponds, at least in part, to our daily experience of verbal exchange. So there is a rationale behind the choice, made by nonsense writers, of *agon* as a model for conversation. Institutional mediatised *agon* (the great Bush v. Clinton show, etc.) is part of our political experience. And if we go a little further, we shall realise – this is what the trial scene in *Alice's Adventures in Wonderland* teaches us – that it also provides a model for our practice as readers of texts. The French language has an apt phrase for this. An interpretation may *faire violence au texte*: it may read things *into* rather than out of a text, thus 'offering violence to the text'. This can be generalised to a theory of interpretation as misprision, where the ephebe is trying to get rid of the anxiety of influence.[36] Perhaps *agon* reaches parts of language that other models cannot reach. We shall take up this intuition in the next chapter.

POLITENESS AND IDLE TALK

The preoccupation with *agon* which we have perceived in nonsense texts is too exaggerated to be entirely sincere. There is a hint of deprecation in such unlimited indulgence. The map of *agon a contrario* reveals a map of *irene*, and it will appear that Grice's Cooperative Principle is not so much wrong as in need of a supplement. An attempt to supplement it has been made by Leech in his *Principles of Pragmatics*,[37] where he introduces, next to the Cooperative Principle, a Politeness Principle (PP).

The starting point is a distinction between two types of rhetoric, the interpersonal and the textual. Each rhetoric consists of a number of principles – there is undoubted inflation in Leech, when compared to the modest proposals of Grice. Thus, textual rhetoric has four principles which Leech, following Slobin, formulates in the following manner:

1 Be humanly processible in ongoing time.
2 Be clear.
3 Be quick and easy.
4 Be expressive.[38]

If textual rhetoric corresponds to Halliday's textual function of language, i.e. to the capacity to construct texts, the least that can be said is that nonsense texts refuse to conform to those principles to an extent which betrays some awareness of them or of their commonsense equivalents. Behind the jargon of the first principle lies the idea that a text is linear and time-bound, which raises problems of segmentation into units, of subordination, of order of presentation.[39] Nonsense demonstrates either an exaggerated reverence for such organisation, as with the King of Hearts's 'Begin at the beginning' (there is an element of self-parody in this tautology, since this is the very advice Carroll gives the reader in

100

Symbolic Logic),[40] or a quiet pleasure in subverting them, as shown in the preference for hypotax over paratax, as in the Duchess's sentence. On the whole, however, this first principle is not deeply subverted. The other three are. Nonsense texts are emphatically not clear; nonsense characters relish reciting not the most beautiful but the longest poem they know; and if the expressive principle blocks the other principles to allow for the speaker's expressive needs and purposes, nonsense is both the most expressive of genres – since the other principles are disregarded – and the least so, as no speakers are trying to express themselves.

The rhetoric which is closest to our concern here, however, is what Leech calls the interpersonal rhetoric. Not the rhetoric of text, but the rhetoric of discourse – within which Grice's theory of conversation finds its natural place. The Cooperative Principle, then, is the first principle of the Interpersonal Rhetoric. But Leech adds two others, the Irony Principle and the Politeness Principle. The three principles complement one another, or rather they clash with one another in a way that induces the computation of implicatures. This is how Leech formulates the Politeness Principle: 'Minimize (other things being equal) the expression of impolite beliefs.' And this is the Irony Principle: 'If you must cause offence, at least do so in a way which doesn't overtly conflict with the Politeness Principle, but allows the hearer to arrive at the offensive point of your remark indirectly, by way of implicature.'[41] This implicitly creates a hierarchy between the three principles. The Cooperative Principle applies first, with the usual four maxims. If it seems to be breached by the speaker, the hearer must wonder whether the speaker has not done so in conformity with the Politeness Principle. And if this, in turn, is breached, the hearer will wonder whether the speaker was not being ironic. Thus, a white lie breaches the maxim of quality, but for reasons of politeness. An ironic inversion (Leech's example is: A: Geoff has just borrowed your car. B: Well, I like THAT!)[42] apparently breaches the CP (in this case the maxim of quality again) and appears to conform to the PP only to express impolite thoughts (Leech's gloss of his example is 'What B says is polite to Geoff and clearly not true. Therefore, what B really means is impolite to Geoff and true.') In other words, ironic inversion cancels the apparent breach of the CP and actually breaches the PP. The two cases are represented in Figures 2.1 and 2.2.[43]

101

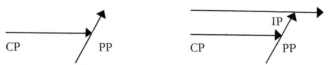

Figure 2.1 Telling 'white lies'   *Figure 2.2* Ironic 'truthfulness'

The Politeness Principle is developed into six maxims:

1 *Tact maxim*: minimize cost and maximize benefit to other.
2 *Generosity maxim*: minimize benefit and maximize cost to self.
3 *Approbation maxim*: minimize dispraise and maximise praise of other.
4 *Modesty maxim*: minimize praise and maximize dispraise of self.
5 *Agreement maxim*: minimize disagreement and maximize agreement between self and other.
6 *Sympathy maxim*: minimize antipathy and maximize sympathy between self and other.

There are constraints on the type of speech acts to which the maxims apply. Thus, the tact maxim applies to impositives (i.e. speech acts which, whatever the grammatical form of the sentence, have the same illocutionary force as an imperative utterance) and assertives, whereas the agreement and the sympathy maxims apply to assertives. It is also clear that the number of the maxims might be cut down as tact is the mirror image of generosity, and approbation of modesty.

The question I wish to ask – and this is why the Politeness Principle is of particular interest – is: does nonsense (by which I mean the narrators of nonsense texts or the characters that speak in them) recognise the Politeness Principle? In the *Alice* books, this is an important question, as the rules of politeness are part of what the Victorian little girl must learn, and characters in Wonderland constantly appeal to them and remind Alice that she must be on her politest behaviour when in conversation with others, although they themselves are rarely polite to her and often infuriate her:

> 'It's really dreadful,' she muttered to herself, 'the way all the creatures argue. It's enough to drive one crazy!'[45] Alice said nothing: she had never been so much contradicted in all her life before, and she felt that she was losing her temper.[46]

The second passage comes from the scene where Alice receives advice from the Caterpillar. And truly, although she always addresses it 'very politely', all she obtains is curt answers and

102

derogatory remarks: ' "You!" said the Caterpillar contemp-tuously. "Who are *you*?" ' No wonder Alice concludes from this exchange that the Caterpillar seems to be 'in a very unpleasant state of mind'.[47] The situation is asymmetrical. The characters expect Alice to conform to the maxims of tact and so on, and the Mouse, quite rightly, takes exception to her repeated allusions to cats and dogs. And it is not enough for Alice to claim that there was no malice intended – she should show more empathy, for the general form of the politeness maxims, which are all constructed according to the same syntactic pattern, is: let the other speaker's advantage override yours. Linguists sometimes talk of a Me-First Orientation:[48] linguistic elements referring to the speaker tend to occur before those referring to the other participants. The Politeness Principle operates on the basis of a linguistic and pragmatic You-First Orientation: 'My husband and I . . .', as the Queen says. In short, Alice is constantly expected to demonstrate pragmatic generosity, modesty and sympathy, and she does. When she forgets to do so, the characters remind her in no uncertain terms:

' – But you make no remark?'
'I – I didn't know I had to make one – just then,' Alice faltered out.
'You *should* have said,' the Queen went on in a tone of grave reproof, ' "It's extremely kind of you to tell me all this" – however, we'll suppose it said.'[49]

But the characters themselves hardly ever conform to the maxims of politeness. They seem to follow a Selfishness Principle, which is the mirror image of its polite counterpart. Its six maxims are obtained by substituting 'self' for 'other' and 'other' for 'self' in Leech's maxims. Its linguistic representation is the Me-First Orientation. In other words, they attempt to live in an agonistic dream, where the unjust expect the just to follow rules which they themselves ignore, as in the old rhyme attributed to Charles, Baron Bowen:

> The rain it raineth on the just
> And also on the unjust fella:
> But chiefly on the just, because
> The unjust steals the just's umbrella.[50]

Politeness is a constraint the characters impose on Alice, while they themselves recognise no discursive constraints and can be as insulting as they please. Even Alice's conventional formulae of politeness are turned against her. When she says 'I beg your pardon', the Red King answers: 'It isn't respectable to beg',[51] while Humpty Dumpty's answer is milder: 'I'm not offended'.[52] When she tries to impose rules of politeness on other characters, as when she tells the Hatter 'You should learn not to make personal remarks. . . . It's very rude', she at first causes bewilderment, as if the idea of rudeness, that is of the breaching of a rule of politeness, was entirely alien to Wonderland ('The Hatter opened his eyes very wide on hearing this'),[53] only to find her own rule used against her, as an agonistic weapon, a few pages later: ' "Who's making personal remarks now?" the Hatter asked triumphantly.'[54]

But in most cases the characters do not even engage in such quibbling. They simply follow their own selfish maxims: minimise damage to self, maximise damage to other. In other words, self-centredness and aggression. Aggression first. The mildest form is insinuation. Alice's weakest point appears to be her face, which is criticised by Humpty Dumpty as being too ordinary: she is so exactly like other people that he will not know her again if they meet. He advises her to make herself more remarkable by having 'the two eyes on the same side of the nose, for instance – or the mouth at the top',[55] thus anticipating the practice of modern painters. He is of course unconcernedly breaking Alice's rule about not making personal remarks. So does the Rose, when she thinks aloud, in Alice's hearing: 'Said I to myself, "Her face has got *some* sense in it, though it's not a clever one!" Still, you're the right colour, and that goes a long way.'[56] The two maxims are, of course, closely linked. It is difficult to decide whether, in this passage, the Rose in insinuatingly insulting, or merely self-centred, i.e. lacking in empathy (as Alice herself is towards the Mouse), by failing to realise that Alice, not being a flower, has a physical appearance which must be judged according to other criteria than hers. On many occasions, however, insinuation gives way to downright insult, the climax of which is, of course, the Queen of Hearts's 'Off with her head!', where brute force replaces verbal violence. The list of what Alice has to suffer is long. 'You're a little goose', says the Sheep,[57] and the Rose: 'It's *my* opinion that you never think *at all*',[58] which the Duchess echoes with: 'You don't know much, . . . and that's a fact.'[59] The object of these insults is always the same: to reduce Alice to silence, and to force her to leave the field. This is how the Mad Tea-Party ends:

'Really, now you ask me,' said Alice, very much confused, 'I don't think —'

'Then you shouldn't talk,' said the Hatter.

This piece of rudeness was more than Alice could bear: she got up in great disgust, and walked off.[60]

If the strategic goal is Alice's departure – this is the tale's death drive, the Thanatos that accompanies the narrative Eros: the characters seem to yearn for the last page, when Alice goes away for good, and the tale, and Wonderland, end – the tactics consist in reducing her to the position of the third person in a dialogue, she who is talked about but has no right to speak, which is the position of the child in the dialogues between adults, or of the fabulous monster in fairy tales. This is how the Unicorn, who is merely abiding by the universal law of reversal in *Through the Looking-Glass*, addresses Alice:

'It didn't hurt him,' the Unicorn said carelessly, and he was going on, when his eye happened to fall upon Alice: he turned round instantly, and stood for some time looking at her with an air of the deepest disgust.

'What – is – this?' he said at last.

'This is a child!' Haigha replied eagerly, coming in front of Alice to introduce her, and spreading out both his hands towards her in an Anglo-Saxon attitude. 'We only found it to-day. It's as large as life and twice as natural!'

'I always thought they were fabulous monsters!' said the Unicorn. 'Is it alive?'

'It can talk,' said Haigha, solemnly.

The Unicorn looked dreamily at Alice, and said 'Talk, child.'[61]

This could be an illustration of our second maxim, self-centredness, or 'Minimize damage to self.' The Unicorn is unable to see the world from Alice's point of view. The same happens with Tweedledum and Tweedledee, in the scene of the King's dream. Superciliousness, indifference, even delusions of grandeur in the case of Humpty Dumpty are the common lot of the characters in the *Alice* books – this is in fact what they derive their appeal, nay their charm, from. In the teddy-bear contests in which the most enthusiastic of the soft toy fans indulge there is always a category for the gruffest bear, an obviously endearing trait. The characters in the *Alice* books would all be *hors concours* in such a contest. And this is what we enjoy in them. We enjoy the constant flouting of conventions of politeness which we all observe, but cannot help finding constraining at times – they dare what we do not dare to do, and give us the vicarious thrill that fantasy is supposed to provide.

This must induce us to reinterpret our analysis of the flouting of politeness maxims in nonsense. Or at least to make it dialectical. On the one hand, nonsense shows us that politeness is a veneer protecting us from the violence of *agon* which is always threatening to erupt. The Queen's interjection spells out the deeper truth behind this civilised surface – the speaker's verbal contract is always in danger of being dissolved; there is always a risk of returning to the discursive state of nature, where the speaker is a wolf to the speaker. The croquet scene, where rules are no longer valid, is a good emblem of this. And we understand why trial scenes and evocations of prisons or executions are so frequent in the *Alice* books. This is not a nice world at all. It is crying out for an account in terms of existential angst, which has duly been provided.[62]

On the other hand, such exaggerated *agon* becomes, because of its very exaggeration, innocuous. From the ruins of this discursive catastrophe a new linguistic cosmos will soon emerge. Such pervading violence can only have a cathartic effect. We identify with Alice, who still believes in the rules of cooperation, and the pathos of her experience purges our agonistic passions, so that politeness will appear not as an unattainable ideal, but as a reasonable proposition. The myth of the state of nature and the war of all against all is always expounded in order to show the necessity of the social contract. This is exactly what happens with Alice and the Unicorn. I have ended my quotation too soon:

> Alice could not help her lips curling up into a smile as she began: 'Do you know, I always thought Unicorns were fabulous monsters, too! I never saw one alive before!'
> 'Well, now that we *have* seen each other,' said the Unicorn, 'if you'll believe in me, I'll believe in you. Is that a bargain?'
> 'Yes, if you like,' said Alice.[63]

This goes to show both the quality of Carroll's intuitions and the kind of compromise nonsense seeks to achieve. Out of the chaos of *agon*, or against the chaos of *agon*, we must preserve the possibility of cooperation. One wishes to save *irene* as the philosopher wishes to save truth. However, not all nonsense texts reach this stage. If Carroll manages this (and I must stress that in his work such a cooperative passage is a rare occurrence), it is in part because he is writing a prose tale, in which the question of conversation is bound to be of importance – this is a problem he shares with the mimetic novelist. But nonsense texts are commonly shorter than this, and written in verse, so their attitude to language will tend to be dominated by angst, and an awareness of the violence of language. If we use Lear's limericks as a corpus, and wonder what happens when the heroes attempt to talk, we will quickly realise that the act of speaking is indeed fraught with violence. Talking is difficult, and indulged in parsimoniously:

> There was an old person of Wick,
> Who said, 'Tick-a-Tick, Tick-a-Tick;
> Chickabee, Chickabaw,' And he said nothing more,
> That laconic old person of Wick.[64]

Nor is it encouraged by the audience:

> There was an old man of Ibreem,
> Who suddenly threaten'd to scream;
> But they said, 'If you do, we will thump you quite blue,
> You disgusting old man of Ibreem!'[65]

When another, at a station, attempts to make a 'promiscuous oration', the reaction is similarly unencouraging. They say: 'Take some snuff! – You have talk'd quite enough/You afflicting old man at a Station!'[66] Apart from the fact that those candidate speakers do not seem to make much sense (the old man of Spithead only says 'Fil-jomble, fil-jumble, Fil-rumble-come-tumble!')[67] their utterances are always threatened by, and sometimes met with, physical violence. There is no time to lose in the four lines of a limerick, and the reaction is always extreme.

In spite of the fact that few characters do speak, such reactions are important, because typical of the ill will that 'they' bear towards the hero, that 'old person of ——— ' or 'young person of ——— ', who is mildly eccentric and always in a position of weakness. Naturally, interpretations of this 'they' in terms of a hostile collective entity, the mob, the sticklers for convention and dogma, are not lacking. I shall offer a philosophical interpretation, which has the advantage of explaining the relationship 'they' have with language. For 'they' in Lear, contrary to the popular wisdom embodied in horror films, does not refer to aliens, a collective other (I am thinking of a rather remarkable American film, entitled *Them*, in which 'they' are giant ants), but to the common people, the silent majority, with their solid common sense and established prejudice. As is well known, 'they' is not only an important collective character in Lear's limericks, it is also the English translation of Heidegger's 'das Man' in *Sein und Zeit*. This 'they' is a threat to the authenticity of *Dasein*. Its dictatorship dissolves *Dasein* within the mass, to the point that the self of everyday *Dasein* becomes a 'they-self':

> In this inconspicuousness and unascertainability, the real dictatorship of the 'they' is unfolded. We take pleasure and enjoy ourselves as *they* take pleasure; we read, see, and judge about literature and art as *they* see and judge; likewise, we shrink back from the 'great mass' as *they* shrink back; we find 'shocking' what *they* find shocking. The 'they', which is nothing definite, and which all are, though not as the sum, prescribes the kind of Being of everydayness.[68]

The way of Being of the 'they' is 'publicness' (*Öffentlichkeit*), a publicness which controls interpretation, levels differences, and obscures so as to make familiar. Thus, 'the "they" which supplies the answer to the question of the "who" of everyday Dasein, is the "nobody" to whom everyday Dasein has already surrendered itself in Being-among-one-another (*Untereinandersein*)'.[69]

From this 'they', the eccentric heroes of Lear's limericks seek to distinguish themselves. One 'divides his jugular artery', another 'suddenly marries a Quaker', a third 'embellishes his nose with a ring'.[70] Such eccentricities in behaviour provoke the same reaction as verbal eccentricities; witness the fate of the Old Man of Whitehaven:

> There was an Old Man of Whitehaven,
> Who danced a quadrille with a Raven;
> But they said – 'It's absurd, to encourage this bird!'
> So they smashed that Old Man of Whitehaven.[71]

A facile interpretation of Heidegger's concept would contrast the need for expression of the 'I' with the violence of the 'they', who invariably thwart any attempt at behaving differently. This elitist reading ignores the fact that being captured by the 'they' is an unavoidable part of every Dasein's being. Even when I seek to express myself by saying 'I', I am only expressing a 'him', part of the 'they'. And, truly, Lear's eccentrics are as alienated as the 'they' that smash them. Their being alienated in and by their eccentricity or madness is the mirror image of the stupid common sense of the 'they'.

This has consequences for language, for it will appear that the nonsense that the eccentrics often talk, and the articulate language of the reproofs of the 'they', are two versions of the same aspect of language, *Gerede* or idle talk, inauthentic language, which Heidegger opposes to authentic discourse, or *Rede*. As Heidegger writes, this 'idle talk' must not be understood in a disparaging sense – it is the inevitable core of *Dasein*'s experience of language, that which allows communication with others. Yet this communication, which relies heavily on linguistic common sense, i.e. on already constituted and formulated meanings, condemns *Dasein*, who transmits and repeats an already uttered message, to linguistic servitude – repetition, made unavoidable by the use of public language, fails to disclose Being, and precludes *Dasein*'s mastery of his language:

> Discourse, which belongs to the essential state of Dasein's Being and has a share in constituting Dasein's disclosedness, has the possibility of becoming idle talk. And when it does so, it serves not so much to keep Being-in-the-World open for us in an articulated understanding, as rather to close it off, and cover up the entities within-the-world. To do this, one need not aim to deceive. Idle talk does not have the kind of Being which belongs to *consciously passing off* something as something else. The fact that something has been said groundlessly, and then gets passed along in further retelling, amounts to perverting the act of disclosing into an act of closing off. For what is said is always understood proximally as 'saying' something – that is, as uncovering something. Thus, by its very nature, idle talk is a closing-off, since to go back to the ground of what is talked about is something which it *leaves undone*.[72]

There is no question of lying in this, only false communication, which precludes communion. The nonsense uttered by the eccentric characters of Lear's limericks is, therefore, the essence of idle talk, its highest degree, which is also the point of its self-destruction. Such nonsense makes it manifest that idle talk, far from disclosing anything in 'communication', is semantic closure, the absence, or even active prevention, of real communication. And, paradoxically, the heroes being forcibly silenced by the others can be understood as the only way to put an end to the interminable garrulousness which is one of the characteristics of idle talk. Not, of course, that the discourse of the others, when it is mentioned, is any more authentic, being the kind of 'ready-spoken' one might expect, and the best embodiment of which is to be found in Virginia Woolf's 'Kew Gardens', where she reports a conversation between two old working-class women:

'Nell, Bert, Lot, Cess, Phil, Pa, he says, I says, she says, I says,
  I says –'
'My Bert, Sis, Bill, Grandad, the old man, sugar,
   Sugar, flour, kippers, greens,
   Sugar, sugar, sugar.'[73]

The French language has an apt phrase to name idle rumour, the garrulously repeated nonsense of commonsensical insinuation: it talks of '*on-dit*', that which is said so widely that it is not really assumed by any subject. The linguistic world of Lear's limericks hesitates between two versions of idle talk: the garrulousness of the *on-dit*, and its translation into action by the lynch mob; and the empty nonsense of the eccentrics, which is only the *on-dit* taken to its extreme, whereby its truth is revealed. There is no place for authentic utterance in such a world. Even laconicism or silence must be ascribed to stupidity rather than reticence. For, as Heidegger points out, he who never says anything cannot keep silent, 'keeping silent authentically is possible only in genuine discoursing'.[74] To be able to keep silent one must have something to say, and laconic characters in Lear do not:

There was a Young Lady of Parma,
Whose conduct grew calmer and calmer;
When they said, 'Are you dumb?' she merely said, 'Hum!'
That provoking Young Lady of Parma.[75]

This is not reticence, this is torpor – merely the inverse of garrulousness.

The choice of *agon* or *irene* in nonsense can be understood as a choice of inauthenticity which is no mere indulgence, but an exploration of its limits, the object and effect of which is exposure. Even as nonsense is either beyond metaphor (in coinages) or on the trivial side of it (in tautology), it is beyond cooperation in violent *agon*, or on the safe side of it in laconic torpor, the torpor of a hyperbolic use of the phatic function of language, where conversation is short, and exclusively about the weather. The reason why linguistic alienation dominates in nonsense is that it provides a foundation for a linguistic cosmos. This is what Alice learns from Wonderland; this is what the child reader learns from Lear's limericks.

CONCLUSION

The last chapter focused on the quality of the phonological, morphological and syntactic intuitions to be found in nonsense texts, especially Carroll's. This chapter has tried to demonstrate that the same applies to the level of pragmatics. The *Alice* books, to my mind, provide the best critical illustration, I should almost say the best discussion, of conceptions formulated by Habermas, Grice and Leech more than a century later. The cumulative weight of such intuitions ought to be food for thought. Beneath the veneer of child's play and the enjoyment of language, a philosophy of language has been emerging, which I shall discuss in my next chapter.

Before turning the page, however, I should like to pause and reflect on the rationality of the genre of nonsense. It is by now clear that there is nothing arbitrary or incoherent in those texts – that they conform to a strategy. This strategy I have called the dialectics of subversion and support. This chapter has shown that this applied to the pragmatic level as to the others. *Agon* is not chosen for the fun of disruption, but in order to comfort cooperation by staging the disasters that its absence entails – which means that the strategy has a pedagogic aim. But, at the same time, staging the lack of cooperation in dialogue draws our attention to the empirical fact of its frequent absence, and to the theoretical possibility of an account of language which would do without it. Alice must learn that the world of conversation is cruel, and the life of dialogues short and nasty, in order to be prepared for future trials (metaphorical ones this time), and to realise that cooperation is a conversational value, to be cherished and sought. But also, contradictorily, in order to learn how to hold her own in verbal exchange and enjoy the violence of language as a creative game, in which the tame virtues of unblemished politeness are happily

111

forgotten and replaced by the sparkling felicities of wit, insinuation, irony and insult – all the possible forms of verbal aggression. This is the Satanic version of angelic cooperation: we may conceive and approve of the best of irenic cooperation, and yet follow the agonistic worst.

We might sum up the dialectics of subversion and support according to the following moments, or stages.

The first stage consists in the realisation that in Wonderland, conversationally and otherwise, all is not well – all is not as the governess says it should be. As we know, 'is' has a sad tendency to part ways with 'ought' at an early stage. Alice always remains polite and cooperative, she does as she is bid and is willing to help – the characters do not conform to this irreproachable mode of behaviour. They are gruff, argumentative, insulting and generally unjust. Like Alice, we are shocked at their sophistry and their recourse to eristics. Like her, we realise that these people take advantage of certain *perversions* of language. For this is not simply the unpleasant idiosyncrasies of a mere pack of cards, to be forgotten when we all wake up – these are perversions of *language*, which threaten us with the same pitfalls in our waking state. There is no escaping them, except perhaps by proceeding to the second stage of the dialectics.

Language is an immoral universe. Those perversions seem to bring success to whoever indulges in them. More often than not Alice remains speechless, for she who believes in the maxims of good breeding and grammar is always surprised at the actions that breach them. There is violence in such perverse deviations: characters are liable to be 'suppressed', like the Dormouse in the trial scene in *Alice's Adventures in Wonderland*, deprived of the use of their heads, or destroyed in various ways, like the mild eccentrics of Lear's limericks. The fabric of social life, and the fabric of language, are torn, and *subversion* triumphs. There are no rules left in this social and linguistic chaos, the best emblems of which are the game of croquet and the poem 'They told me you had been to her' in *Alice's Adventures in Wonderland*. All we can do is watch Alice drift aimlessly, and drift ourselves, as all rules and regularities of language and behaviour dissolve. The characters in Wonderland are not even like the villains in Dickens, who know what they are about and will get their comeuppance – they are not evil, but characterised by an arbitrary and thoughtless general acrimony, the linguistic equivalent of the state of nature.

This, however, is only a superficial, or temporary, description of the world of nonsense, which is destined to be cancelled when we reach the third stage of our dialectics. To the interpretation of Wonderland in terms of existential angst, there will always be an answer accusing Alice, that prim Victorian miss, of invading the Eden of Wonderland and spoiling it with her silly and mean rules and conventions.[76] It might be argued that when she states that it is rude to make personal remarks, she brings guilt and therefore chaos into a natural state of interpersonal freedom where the concept 'rude' does not even exist. Both versions, however, are inadequate: Wonderland is neither totally chaotic nor totally blissful and free. In fact, rather than by chaos, Wonderland is characterised by the emergence of another order, one which is less constraining and more surprising perhaps, but which is nevertheless fairly orderly. The society of Wonderland has its own order – albeit partial and apparently incoherent: one takes turns at deciding the subject of the conversation, as Humpty Dumpty points out; one changes places around the tea table, when the Mad Hatter says that the time has come. And the world of nonsense is itself fairly regular: as we have seen, language is not at all dissolved, but exploited. The rule of exploitation is provided in the preface to *Through the Looking-Glass*. It is a rule of *inversion*, not subversion. The game of nonsense, and the Wonderland it calls into being are the negative moment in the pedagogic dialectics of the acquisition by the child of good manners, in society as in conversation. Once Alice has perceived this negative inverted order she learns to conform to the new rules and to use them for her own purposes. She then becomes a formidable opponent and sometimes triumphs over characters who are, after all, merely cards and chess pieces.

This is the dialectics of the transformation of the pragmatically *infans* into the conversationally skilful speaker. As a result, inversion leads to the fourth stage, *conversion*, when Alice, who has learnt the rules the hard way, comes to accept them; not as painful impositions, but as freely accepted necessities. The linguistic social contract is signed; the importance of linguistic and polite conventions (the definition of which entails their reciprocal recognition by the agents) is firmly impressed on the child's mind. Wonderland is, as far as the rules of politeness and conversation are concerned, the equivalent of the initial situation in Rawls,[77] when the principles of justice and fairness are inevitably chosen.

The mention of Rawls's fictitious, or fictional, 'initial situation' is deliberate. If conversion were to be the climax of my dialectics, we would end up with a cooperative view of conversation and dialogue, and support would overshadow subversion. Since this is obviously not the case, we need a fifth stage, which I propose to call, if you will pardon the nonsensical coinage, *transversion*. The *Aufhebung* of subversion into conversion, which is the global pedagogic aim pursued by nonsense texts, leaves a trace. Alice is, and is not, a conventional speaker. She will always remember, as the closing words of *Alice's Adventures in Wonderland* state, 'the happy summer days',[78] not because they will be banal memories of childhood, but because she has undergone an experience which has changed her for good. This ambivalent stage is the true climax of my dialectics. Alice's acceptance of the conventions of linguistic behaviour is no blind adherence, but rather a show of limited and displaced confidence – literally displaced by her journey through Wonderland, that is across the rules and their subversion. This is the moral of nonsense. Rules of language and conventions there are, but one can only conform to them if one has transformed them, if one still transgresses them, or, to borrow a famous phrase, if one supports them, but only under erasure.

3

NONSENSE AND THE PHILOSOPHY OF LANGUAGE

INTRODUCTION

There is a phrase in French which says: *'n'est pas fou qui veut'* – it takes some talent to be a lunatic. It takes some philosophical talent to write nonsense texts, which accounts for the fascination they have always held for philosophers. It is easy to understand why – there is a philosophy of language implicit in the very word 'nonsense'; the choice of which to name a brand new literary genre cannot have been entirely innocent.

That such a philosophy should be a philosophy of *language* is obvious from what we have seen in the preceding chapters. Writing outside sense proves to be surprisingly difficult, for meaning puts up a fight. The nonsense writer must be wily – he must possess intuitions about the workings of language that are of the most acute type. In other words he must, at least implicitly, consider the question 'What is language?' For one author at least, in at least one of his texts, this question is raised explicitly – the Humpty Dumpty chapter in *Through the Looking-Glass* is justly famous, and I shall attempt a close philosophical reading of it. Indeed, it can be argued that the philosophical programme of twentieth-century Anglo-Saxon philosophy of language is already present, *in nuce*, in Victorian nonsense.

The very name of the genre raises philosophical problems. For instance, we shall soon recognise in the negative prefix a form of Freudian denial, which rejects meaning at the cost of evincing a strong fascination with it – nonsense texts *need* meaning, at least as much, and perhaps even more so, than meaningful texts (a law of compensation is operating here: the more tenuous the meaning offered by the author of the text, the greater the reader's need and desire for full meaning). And we must also be aware that the word raises questions about the scope of negation. Is it exactly the same thing to 'mean nothing' and 'not to mean anything'?

A famous passage in *Through the Looking-Glass* immediately comes to mind:

> 'Who did you pass on the road?' the King went on, holding out his hand to the Messenger for some more hay.
>
> 'Nobody,' said the Messenger.
>
> 'Quite right,' said the King: 'this young lady saw him too. So of course Nobody walks slower than you.'
>
> 'I do my best,' the Messenger said in a sullen tone. 'I'm sure nobody walks much faster than I do!'
>
> 'He can't do that,' said the king, 'or else he'd have been here first.'[1]

We seem to be getting dangerously close to a dubious ontology of negative beings, where the 'nothing' that nonsense means risks being hypostatised into a something, a quasi-meaning, like the *quasi-Sein* that Meinong attributed to impossible or inexistent objects.[2] But rejecting negative ontology involves another pitfall, the equally dubious paradox of reflexivity, an insidious scion of the great Liar: how can I mean not to mean?

This reflexive paradox dominates the implicit philosophy of nonsense. The question 'What is language?' is merely the consequence of the raising of the more fundamental question, 'What is meaning?' And, as we shall see, the question of meaning – of its nature and of its construction – takes the privileged form of, 'Does the speaker mean what she says?' It takes, as I said, talent to produce nonsense – a far cry from mere senseless noises or emotionally charged verbal signals. But what kind of control does the speaker exert over an utterance the coherence of which is no longer given by its intentional meaning? At one level it is undoubtedly deliberate, since the nonsense writer is an artist who sets out to entertain his reader, not an inspired mystic or a possessed lunatic. But since the product of his art somewhat resembles the unintentional productions of logophiliacs, the question of the exact amount of the speaker's intentional control over his utterance must be raised.

In her study of intention, Elizabeth Anscombe isolates the class of intentional actions as those that are liable to induce the question 'Why?',[3] which in turn elicits answers beginning with, 'In order to' or, 'Because'. Why did you pick up the ashtray? In order not to drop my ashes on the carpet, or because it needs emptying. Thus is an intentional gesture distinguished from mere fiddling. Anscombe gives a token list of intentional actions in two columns:

Intruding	Telephoning
Offending	Calling
Coming to possess	Groping
Kicking (and other descriptions	Crouching
connoting characteristically	Greeting
animal movement)	Signing, signalling
Abandoning, leaving alone	Paying, selling, buying
Dropping (transitive), holding,	Hiring, dismissing
picking up	Sending for
Switching (on, off)	Marrying, contracting[4]

'Intentional', she claims, refers to a form of description of events. The description of actions occurs, or does not occur, in the form of intention. Or rather some descriptions are dependent on the existence of this form for their sense, while some are not. Thus, the actions listed in the right-hand column are always deliberate or intentional, while the actions in the left-hand column may or may not be voluntary. I can offend my hearer without meaning to do so, I cannot unwittingly marry.

The class of intentional actions is very large. It is composed of most of the acts 'effected by the movements of human beings which go to make up the history of a human being's day or life'.[5] Some of these actions consist of, or involve, speech acts: telephoning, calling, greeting, signing, hiring or dismissing, marrying and contracting. But what if we wonder about the (un)intentional nature of the most general action of the kind, uttering? The answer is that it will tend to dwell in the right-hand column. Why did you say that you felt cold? Because I wanted you to understand that the window ought to be closed – in order for you to close the window. The intentional nature of the speech act is what the link between 'meaning' and 'saying' expresses. An act of saying is intentional if what is being said is meant by the speaker. The French language aptly captures this, as the standard equivalent for the verb 'mean' is '*vouloir dire*', an intentional turn of phrase if there is any.

However, it soon becomes apparent that the question is not as simple as it seems, as the relationship between meaning and saying is not clear. If we hypostatise the separation of the two nominalised verbs into two separate actions, we find ourselves burdened with a dubious ontology of mental acts. As a 'mental act' indeed, meaning cannot be said to be intentional in Anscombe's sense – there is no asking the question '*Why* did you mean this?', in the hope of eliciting an 'in order to ' or a 'because' answer. The only possible question is, 'What do you mean by this?', and the only answer a paraphrastic explanation – we now dwell within Searlian intentionality, a far cry from '*vouloir dire*'. Yet that there is something intentional, even in Anscombe's sense, about meaning is clear – what distinguishes intentional saying is that it is meant by the speaker. But then the spectre of unintentional saying, of saying without meaning, looms on the horizon. It will come as no surprise – is not 'saying without meaning' a definition of nonsense? – that nonsense texts explicitly raise the question of the relationship between meaning and saying, meaning and intention.

MEANING AND SAYING

There are three occasions in *Alice's Adventures in Wonderland* when the question of meaning and saying crops up. The first occurs when Alice is asked by the Caterpillar to repeat 'You are old, Father William', a poem that should be Southey's 'The Old Man's Comforts and How He Gained Them', but turns out to be vastly different. The Caterpillar is not taken in:

> 'That is not said right,' said the Caterpillar.
> 'Not *quite* right, I'm afraid,' said Alice timidly: 'some of the words have got altered.'
> 'It is wrong from beginning to end,' said the Caterpillar, decidedly; and there was silence for some minutes.[6]

What else is there to say indeed, since saying has been separated from meaning, and the question 'Who meant that, if Alice did not mean it?' looms large. And we note that the Caterpillar does not say 'you said that wrong', but 'that is not said right', a passive without an agent. Poor Alice is reduced to the state of a tape recorder, a possessed mystic or a raving lunatic. The words that come out of her mouth are not hers. In a way this is a natural state of affairs, since in any case she is reciting a poem. But it raises the awesome possibility that we are all, to some extent, mere mouthpieces, repeating words that are not ours. Even worse in this case, Alice's words are not hers not only because they have a previous author, but because she no longer has any control over them. Quotations, at least explicit ones, can be controlled. Here the words come out of her mouth without confessing an explicit origin, a meaning that would precede the saying. (An obvious defence would be to remind us that what she says, the parody, is meant by Carroll – but even this will not do: his meaning is in turn preceded by a saying, the original poem.) No wonder this state of affairs raises doubts about her identity in Alice. This is the scene where she utters the famous sentence: 'I am not myself, you see', to which the Caterpillar answers, with apparent common sense – but a common sense so excessively literal that it threatens to subvert the generally accepted view it is supposed to express – 'I don't see'.[7]

There are several episodes similar to this in the tales. Whenever Alice recites a poem, and whatever she means to say, the saying always goes wrong. My second occasion is more specific. It occurs during the Mad Tea-Party, when Alice is drawn into verbal battle, cornered and defeated by unscrupulous opponents. A riddle is proposed by the Hatter: 'Why is a raven like a writing-desk?' It is a strange sort of riddle. When asked for the solution, the Hatter will confess that he does not know the answer. And Carroll himself claimed that he did not know the answer either. This is an interesting case of saying without meaning. Of course, both Carroll and the Hatter know what the words mean, but in an important sense they do not know what the utterance means. Worse even, both speakers do not want to know what it means – they want it not to mean, what they mean is not to mean. Thus causing in generations of readers an inordinate desire to produce the absent meaning, as an expression without a meaning, of which the riddle without an answer is the emblem, is a scandalous object, which must be reduced by an ascription of meaning: a riddle *must* have a solution. In his *Annotated Alice*,[8] Martin Gardner mentions a few answers, from which I extract the most imaginative, or the crankiest: 'Because [Edgar Allan] Poe wrote on both.' And when I stated that the Hatter, too, meant not to mean, perhaps I was imagining things, or trying to reassure myself. For there is something comforting – we have already encountered such comfort – in Carroll's provocative trick. It is not cooperative, but at least it conforms to a strategy, albeit an agonistic one: as long as someone is in control, as long as there is something meant beneath this apparent piece of nonsense, all is safe. But the Hatter, being mad, may not be in control. He may not have meant anything at all,

119

not even 'not to mean', and this is a much more disquieting thought – a case of expression without meaning at *any* level, a *dire* without the least trace of *vouloir dire*. This is the ultimate non-sense of madness, which literary nonsense attempts to deny, as the rest of our text shows. Alice is eager to join in the fun:

> 'I'm glad they've begun asking riddles – I believe I can guess that', she added aloud.
> 'Do you mean that you think you can find out the answer to it?' said the March Hare.
> 'Exactly so,' said Alice.
> 'Then you should say what you mean,' the March Hare went on.
> 'I do,' Alice hastily replied . . .'[9]

She is right, of course, when she says 'I do.' The March Hare appears to be holding an extreme structuralist position, extending the Saussurean concept of value to sentences. In a Saussurean system, for instance the system of phonemes in a given natural language, there are no perfect 'synonyms', that is, no two elements which are substitutable or indiscernible. An element in the system is defined not through its intrinsic characteristics, but through its opposition to all the other elements in the system, which gives it its differential value. If the system in question is a semantic one, the implication is that there will be no synonyms in the strict sense, not even 'oculist' and 'eye doctor'. Extended to the level of sentences, this conception implies the impossibility of paraphrasis. If we follow the March Hare, we shall have to grant that,when Alice said 'I believe I can guess that', she meant that she believed that she could guess that. Had she meant that she thought she could find the answer to it, she should have said: 'I think I can find the answer to it.' All this is, of course, sheer sophistry. Our heart goes out to Alice, because we know that, in spite of certain appearances, such as the presence of the danger word 'believe', this is no intensional context and that in this case substitution preserves truth – we are even prepared to add that it also preserves meaning: the March Hare offers a straightforward paraphrasis, and Alice is right to recognise it as such, although the word she uses, 'exactly', is perhaps ill-chosen (there may be a nuance in presentation between the original sentence and its paraphrasis: this is where the Fregean distinction of *Sinn* and *Bedeutung* emerges), but this is only due to the slight exaggeration caused by her using a common form of a natural language, not the careful language of philosophers.

However, this is not a cooperative Gricean conversation, but another instance of verbal *agon*. The Hatter and the Hare mean to win the battle, by foul means or fair. By answering 'hastily', Alice shows that she is not sure of her ground, that the eristic sophistry of the Hare has undermined, if not her position, at least her confidence:

'I do,' Alice hastily replied; 'at least – at least I mean what I say – that's the same thing, you know.'

'Not the same thing a bit!' said the Hatter. 'Why, you might just as well say that "I see what I eat" is the same thing as "I eat what I see"!'[10]

Alice has become seriously muddled. She has made a gross mistake. Linguistic inversion does not preserve meaning, as the Hatter, soon followed by the March Hare and the Dormouse, tells her in no uncertain terms. This is the Dormouse: ' "You might just as well say," added the Dormouse, which seemed to be talking in its sleep, "that 'I breathe when I sleep' is the same thing as 'I sleep when I breathe'!" "It *is* the same thing with you," said the Hatter, and here the conversation dropped, and the party sat silent for a minute.'[11]

In spite of our natural antipathy for the Hatter, we must confess he is right. 'I say what I mean' is not the same thing as 'I mean what I say'. But on the other hand, we may also understand Alice. She is speaking a natural, not a logical, language, where the situation is not clear cut. Transformations that involve the inversion of elements of the sentence do not always, or at least do not always *significantly*, alter meaning. We remember that the analysis of the passive transformation, where a similar rule of inversion operates, induced Chomsky to formulate his principle: 'transformations preserve meaning'. But we also remember that taking this principle seriously has meant that in the latest versions of the model there is no longer a passive transformation, as the old passive transformation was discovered to alter meaning after all. But take topicalisation, which goes from 'I say what I mean' to 'what I mean, I say'. Can we not understand Alice's willingness to go one step further and say 'I mean what I say'?

In fact, in a natural language, rather than a straightforward logical opposition we will have a gradation of semantic differences. 'I eat what I see' is clearly different from 'I see what I eat.' What about 'I eat what I chew' and 'I chew what I eat'? The entailments are not the same – in the first sentence, I may eat without chewing and in the second, I may chew without eating. But the possibility of constant association between two events makes the logical distinction less easy to grasp, as clearly appears in ' I breathe when I am alive' and 'I am alive when I breathe.' But this explanation is still purely contingent: it does not affect the logical distinction. What about synonyms, though? My dictionary gives 'catch sight of' as a perfect synonym of 'espy'. What then, if Alice had said 'I espy what I catch sight of' and 'I catch sight of what I espy'? In this case, we must admit that inversion does preserve meaning, unless we deny the possibility of synonyms.

But Alice believes in synonyms. At least she is consistent in her beliefs. And her mistake turns out to imply a theory of the relationship between meaning and saying. For her, there is semantic synonymy, or reciprocal entailment, between the two verbs: 'if I mean, then I say', and 'if I say, then I meant'. 'Whenever I say something, I meant to say it'; and 'whatever I mean I say.' I am not claiming Alice's theory is right, at least in its strong version, but it could easily be made more palatable in a weaker version: 'Whenever I say something, there is some meaning behind it'; and, 'Whatever I mean, I always have the possibility to say it.' I may, of course, not actually say it for contingent reasons, such as fear of the Queen of Hearts's 'off with his head!', but I always can, if only *sotto voce*, or *more jesuitico*, in my mind at least – while my head is still on my shoulders. Thus expressed, Alice's position is no different from John Searle's.

Perhaps we should also note the exchange ends in stalemate – silence. This is strange, as the Hatter appeared to have defeated Alice. But at the end of the exchange he scores an own goal, by stating that, in the case of the Dormouse at least, inversion preserves meaning. He therefore concedes that consistently concomitant events can induce us to bridge the logical gap between the inverse propositions. The point he gained through a mixture of sophistry and straightforward logic, he loses because he wants to be witty. He ends by implicitly conceding that Alice may have a point after all. Not that it matters, in any case, since this is an agonistic exchange and what counts is not the overall coherence of his position but the efficiency of his argument at the moment it is used. Inconsistency and contradiction may be blessings if the game is ruled by the PS rather than by the CP.

The third episode I announced occurs in the course of an intimate conversation between Alice and the Duchess. Alice is irritated at the Duchess's advances, and is playing a game of perfidious reminder. This reminder takes us back to Chapter 6, where the Duchess is speaking to Alice: ' "If everybody minded their own business," the Duchess said, in a hoarse growl, "the world would go round a deal faster than it does." '[12] This is Alice:

> 'The game's going on rather better now,' she said, by way of keeping up the conversation a little.
> ' 'Tis so,' said the Duchess: 'and the moral of that is – "Oh, 'tis love, 'tis love, that makes the world go round!" '
> 'Somebody said,' Alice whispered, 'that it's done by everybody minding their own business!'
> 'Ah, well! It means much the same thing,' said the Duchess, digging her sharp little chin into Alice's shoulder as she added, 'and the moral of *that* is – "Take care of the sense, and the sounds will take care of themselves." '[13]

The Duchess appears to be holding a rather straightforward conception of the relation between meaning and saying. Not 'I mean what I say and say what I mean', but, 'Whenever I say, I have meant first.' Or rather, since this is a recommendation, as opposed to a statement of fact: 'Whenever I say something, I ought to have meant something first.' Meaning goes before saying. That goes without saying, or rather that is said in the very general and very obvious form of a proverb. However, the Duchess's position is undermined by the very context of what she says, in two ways. First, she appears to be claiming that ' 'tis love, 'tis love, that makes the world go round!' means 'much the same thing' as 'everybody ought to mind their own business', a paraphrase even more problematic than Alice's previous one, without even the extenuating circumstances we found for Alice. It would appear, therefore, that the Duchess does not practise what she preaches, and does not let herself be unduly troubled by the sense before producing the sounds. Second, and more dramatic, her statement is undermined by the very words she uses, to the point of self-destruction. As we know, her 'moral' is a parody of a proverb, 'Take care of the pence, and the pounds will take care of themselves.' But in this case at least, it is not possible to say, as she does, that meaning is the origin of saying, for the origin of her idiosyncratic, falsely proverbial meaning is to be found in the saying of the original, conventional, proverb. *In this case at least,* saying precedès meaning. She can only mean this because the speech community has been for ever and ever in the habit of saying that. This is a deconstructionist's dream – this is is a text so paradoxical that it destroys itself. (And the reason why it does so is of course, not difficult to conceive – this is, again, a form of *agon*, and the main purpose of the text is not to express the Duchess's meaning but to reveal her desire in what is undoubtedly a scene of seduction.)

The three episodes from *Alice's Adventures in Wonderland* that I have quoted have one point in common. They put forward, in various guises, a theory of the relationship between meaning and saying, the general moral of which, as the Duchess might say, is that meaning, logically and chronologically, precedes, or ought to precede, saying. And at the same time they deeply subvert this conception, impelling readers to work out another for themselves. This is not only another instance of the familiar dialectics of subversion and support, which characterises literary nonsense. This is the very core of nonsense. Is not, after all, a nonsense text non-sense, i.e. a text which is said, and certainly not meant, or only paradoxically so, as it means not to mean?

This shows the quality of Carroll's philosophical intuitions. His solutions are a century old, but the problematic within which they are naturally inserted is contemporary. In other words, Carroll's path is meandering, in anticipation, through a famous philosophical battlefield, the polemic between Searle and Derrida, which started with Derrida's critique of Austin in his essay 'Signature, event, context', went on with Searle's reply in *Glyph*, and eventually provoked Derrida's massive rejoinder, *Limited Inc.*[14] I am a little baffled by this transatlantic *scène de ménage*, and I do not intend to add my brick to the pandemonium. I can only advise anyone wishing to take a crash course in verbal *agon* to read the texts. Meanwhile, I shall try to follow my path, which is also Carroll's path, through the wreckage – my aim is to explore the philosophical intuitions of nonsense. More precisely, I shall explore the dialectics of subversion and support by looking for the emergence of radical non-sense within nonsense, of an expression so far in excess of any possible meaning that it cannot be ascribed any meaning whatsoever.

One of the weak positions I have attributed to Alice, 'We say what we mean', in the sense that for every meaning there is at least the possibility of its adequate expression, is well known under the name of 'the principle of expressibility',[15] 'Whatever can be meant can be said', in which the important word is the modal verb. What the principle denies is inexpressibility, or the ineffable. Meaning may well remain unexpressed or implicit, but only for contingent reasons – expression is always possible. There is nothing that I can mean and not express: there is no such thing as an epiphany. Or rather, the mystic's epiphany cannot be talked about in terms of meaning – which, however, it usually is. Searle provides examples of this contingent unexpressed. I mean but do not say because I am not proficient enough in the language (a few sessions at a Berlitz school will help), or because I am deaf and dumb (but I can learn sign language). In these cases, which are trivial enough, meaning is temporarily in excess of expression.

But the drift of nonsense takes me in the other direction – expression in excess of meaning. Is such a thing possible in the terms of Searle's theory? He provides one such example in his book on *Intentionality*.[16] Suppose I utter the words 'es regnet', not because I mean that it rains, or anything at all for that matter, but because I want to improve my spoken German. In this case I certainly say more than I mean, namely that it rains. Although I am not sure that this involuntary, perhaps even unfortunate, excess of saying over meaning can qualify as nonsense, if nonsense is defined as non-sense, something which is said but in no way meant. Here is another perverse example, also involving translation. It is borrowed from an uncharacteristic passage in Davidson.[17] Suppose, he says, that I utter the sounds 'Empedokles leaped'. What I have just said is, ambiguously, either, in English, that he jumped into the Etna, or, in German, that he is in love. I cannot have meant both at the same time, so that one meaning is in excess, arbitrarily induced by the shape of my saying. (On the other hand, it seems to me that what I have just done by writing the last few sentences is precisely to mean both meanings at the same time, as a kind of interlingual pun.) However, the Duchess's theory of the saying–meaning relationship, which nonsense both denies and protects, is not seriously affected by such limited and marginal counter-examples – superficially at least, for our analysis is not at an end.

In saying 'I say what I mean', Alice is an excessive, because over-enthusiastic, follower of Searle. I would now like to show that Searle is a secret follower of Alice, or at least of a weak version of the converse thesis, 'I mean what I say.' I shall call this converse thesis the *principle of expressivity*. It is not to be found as such, i.e. in its strong version, in Searle, who certainly does not mean to say, which would be absurd, that whatever I say I mean. It is only too obvious that I can lie (although here we could argue that I do say what I mean, since I wish to deceive – we need to distinguish between levels of meaning), that I can speak compulsively, in buttonholing garrulousness, that I can speak deliriously. Not everything that is said is actually meant. The strong version of the principle does not hold water.

But Searle is, to my mind, committed to a weaker version of the principle – for every utterance, there is some meaning, even if only an indirect one. I can now give a better account of the case of lying. I say something, intending you to believe that I mean it, whereas I mean something else (there remains an uncertainty about the exact value of 'mean' – in what way is it different from 'believe', 'hold true', etc.?). The important point is that there is always something that I mean, even if I do not seem to mean it. It is easy to understand why Searle is committed to this weaker form of the principle. It is the rationale behind his theory of indirect speech acts[18]– it is also the main content of Grice's cooperative principle, what allows the calculus of implicatures to apply. In Alice's terms, the general formula of indirect speech acts might be: he did not mean what he said and he said what he did not mean, or, using Searle's simple formalism in *Intentionality*:

$$\forall p \, \exists q \, S(p) \, . \sim M(p) \supset \, \sim S(q) \, . \, M(q)$$

(where S and M represent 'say' and 'mean'). True, he meant to say what he did, as this is a deliberate speech act, except that he did not mean *it*, but something else. Searle's *Expression and Meaning*[19] is largely devoted to such speech acts, which go under the name of irony, metaphor, and even fiction. I am now in possession of a vast class of utterances, where saying is separated from meaning. Although they are frequent in nonsense (except for metaphors), and especially, as we saw, in the Alice books, they are not strictly speaking non-sense and remain well within the scope of the Duchess's proverb. Behind every saying there is still a meaning, which is, perhaps, literally inadequate, but always pragmatically apt. This has nothing to do with nonsense proper: true nonsense would not be expression and meaning, but expression without meaning. It is time to remember that *Alice's Adventures in Wonderland* is a work of fiction, and to look for non-sense in the wonderland of fiction. Searle may be of help there, as he is the author of an essay on the logical status of fictional utterances.

Suppose we read the following sentences, each in its appropriate context. 'On an evening in the latter part of May, Lord Lucan was walking homeward along Pall Mall'; and 'On an evening in the latter part of May a middle aged man was walking homeward from Shaston to the village of Marlott.' The first is a fanciful attempt at torrid journalism, of which I am the proud author. The second is the opening sentence of *Tess of the d'Urbervilles*.

According to Searle these two sentences are (1) textually impossible to distinguish – there is no textual feature, syntactic or semantic, which identifies a text as fictional; and (2) pragmatically vastly different, and easily distinguished. The journalist is committed to the truth of his proposition, and to belief in its truth (this is a somewhat optimistic view of the profession); he must be capable of adducing proof, etc. Not so the novelist, who is committed to none of these requirements and can be as mendacious as he likes, with an easy conscience. A fictional utterance is not an assertion – at best it is a non-serious assertion, the idol of the iconic assertion of the journalist. By using these two specialised words, I am suggesting that Searle's conception is not as modern as it seems.

As a result, the illocutionary force of the act of fiction is closer to that of performatives than of assertion proper. With the performatives, fiction shares a world-to-word direction of fit, as opposed to the word-to-world direction of fit of assertions. And the only distinction between a fictional and an assertive text lies in the illocutionary intentions of the author. 'Pretend' is an intentional verb, and pretending to assert, i.e. writing fiction, has its source in, and must be judged from, the author's intention.

This is a solution to our problem, albeit a negative one. The saying can be as quaint as it comes, but on another level there is always a meaning-as-intention behind it. There is no *dire* without its *vouloir dire*. When he seems not to mean anything, the author of nonsense intends that it should be so: he has taken care of the sense, or rather of the non-sense, and the nonsense sounds take care of themselves. The trouble with this theory is that it is caught in what Derrida calls 'the metaphysics of presence'. I will not rehearse Derrida's argument.[20] I share with him the idea that when a text is treated as *écriture*, as writing in the technical sense, meaning as intention is at best of limited importance, as a result of the general laws of citationality and iterability that govern language (this is why the Duchess's proverb deconstructs itself). Instead, I shall take up a point or two. The first is the non-seriousness of fiction as pretence. This is rather similar to the non-seriousness of the performative act when uttered on stage by an actor – it is not even infelicitous, it is not serious. One recalls that Derrida's critique of Austin starts precisely from this. This 'interference' (*parasite*, as on a radio set), Derrida claims, is an integral part of the workings of language. Since it is always possible for a speech act to fail through infelicity, the necessity of this possibility, the fact that such potential failure is integral to the workings of language, must be taken into account, and not excluded as marginal or non-serious. So that instead of dismissing fiction as a devious form of assertion, perhaps we should start from its specific characteristic – not pretence but iterability. A text remains beyond the physical presence of its original speaker, like a riddle the solution to which has been lost. It can be quoted, reworked and reinterpreted. Each reader is like an actor: he or she re-enacts the original speech act, but such reproduction is a reproduction of the same text, and at the same time a different text, a different reading, in both senses of the term. So in fact a text not only does not need the presence of its original speaker, but it structurally excludes it, and only accepts the inscribed, and iterable, 'presence' of a system of places. That riddle never had a solution in the first place: in such a context, to quote Derrida, 'the category of intention will not disappear; it will have its place, but from that place it will no longer be able to govern the entire scene and system of utterance'.[21]

The first characteristic of fiction as writing, which Derrida calls its remainder capacity (*restance*), can be understood, at its most trivial, in chronological terms. I cannot ask Shakespeare whether in a given line he meant to make a pun or not. The perusal of his carefully preserved laundry lists will not always solve my hermeneutic dilemma. Here, meaning as intention finds a rather trivial, because contingent, limit. The fact that I no longer have access to Shakespeare's meaning makes the task of the critic more difficult – it does not preclude the possibility that meaning *is* intention-of-meaning. But the question of hermeneutics becomes less trivial if we consider the case of Borges's 'Pierre Ménard'.[22] Pierre Ménard, the eponymous hero of Borges's tale, is a twentieth-century French critic who has rewritten, word for word, several chapters of Cervantes's *Quixote*. It is not, of course, a simple case of copying. Nor is it a case of possession or even empathy. Pierre Ménard has firmly rejected the idea that he might become a seventeenth-century Spaniard in his mind, so that, by recovering the original intention of meaning, he might reproduce exactly the same saying. That, he claims, is too easy. He wants to produce the same saying, but from an entirely different meaning, from the point of view of a twentieth-century Frenchman. Hence the fact that although the saying is exactly the same, the meaning is so different: where Cervantes's style is robustly contemporary, Ménard's is precious and archaic (the passages from the *Quixote* that the narrator quotes to illustrate this striking difference are, of course, word for word the same passages).

We could account for this in the manner of Searle, or rather along the same lines as Davidson on metaphor.[23] The literal meaning of both versions of the *Quixote* is the same, but the use that is made of it is entirely different. Or even, perhaps, this is a case of textual ambiguity: one surface meaning corresponds to two deeper illocutionary intentions. But I think that in this case a Derridean account would be more elegant, perhaps even more faithful to Borges's perverse games. The alteration of the text is due to its iteration (Derrida stresses the etymology of the term: '*iter*', the same, is linked to '*alter*', the other: iteration, or the same *qua* other).[24] If we grant that the original *Quixote* may have been the result of a Gricean intention of meaning, we must grant, for Borges's tale as for the Duchess's proverb, that Ménard's intention of meaning is the effect of the text of the *Quixote*, which precedes and maximally constrains his intention – since his intention is to write the *same* text. This inversion of the relations between meaning and saying is contagious. In turn, it opens up the possibility that Cervantes's text is the product of an Ur-text, a saying that precedes the author's intention. Which, of course, it is, as the *Quixote* is a pastiche of older tales of chivalry. Ménard is only doing to Cervantes, in his exaggerated way, what Cervantes did to his own predecessors. They, in turn, etc. – the chain of inter-textuality is endless. The inversion is no longer temporary or contingent: saying and meaning are in the same relation as the chicken and the egg. This is why the fact that Pierre Ménard never existed, that his text is an impossible one, is of no importance. Apart from the fact that, with the Duchess's proverb, I have already produced a similar text, the situation can be generalised.

Borges's tale merely exaggerates what any literary text offers its readers.

This is where radical nonsense emerges. Instead of meaning as the origin of saying, as in the superficial reading of the Duchess's proverb, we now have saying as the source of a proliferation of potential meanings. We have the same reversal as in Marx's theoretical account of the emergence of capital, when he goes from the commodity chain, C–M–C, to the money chain, M–C–M', where the accumulation of capital becomes possible. In our case, we start from a Meaning–Saying–Meaning chain (an original intention of meaning is a source for a saying which in turn is interpreted), to a Saying–Meaning–Saying chain, where an Ur-text inspires a meaning that results in a text. (In the economy of signifiers, Pierre Ménard is the emblem of simple reproduction, as the end-text is the same as the Ur-text; the normal process is, of course, one of expanded reproduction, where the 'end-text' adds something to the Ur-text, and in turn becomes the Ur-text for a new text – this could be rephrased in terms of two other chains, Lyotard's *montage en parallèle*, where there is an origin of meaning, and his *montage en série*, with its potentially infinite sequence of texts.[25]) In this new chain the position of the author is secondary, as the saying is unmeant in an important sense (it is the temporary end-product of a potentially endless chain of saying and meaning). Unless of course I have recourse to a myth of origins, and imagine an arbitrary first Meaning, God's, which produces the truly original text, a text that turns all other texts into commentaries and all human authors into emulators of Pierre Ménard. This, as we saw in the Introduction, is how Ettelson treats Carroll's *Through the Looking-Glass*. And even if our chain is agonistic and rejects the possibility of an origin of meaning, this is how we treat texts when we interpret them. We are interested to know the local intentional meaning, the author's meaning, but we can do without it if we must. And even if it is available, we shall still appeal to an objective global meaning, that is to the effect which the endless saying–meaning–saying chain has on its latest link. Such a 'meaning' is largely unmeant. Suppose that I acquire the conviction that in one of Shakespeare's sonnets there is, undoubtedly, a pun – whether he meant it or it was merely a slip of the pen is irrelevant. Suppose, then, I read one of the 'will' sonnets,[26] and realise that something is afoot, namely that there is extensive punning on all the senses of 'will', including the author's Christian name and the sexual meanings of the term. Must I not then read into any of the sonnets the potentialities for punning that language allows? Must I not decide that, whenever a pun is possible, *there is* a pun? 'Meaning' has become objective, the product of an intertextual chain, in which each intentional act of *vouloir dire* is caught between two sayings, the one it imitates and the one it re-creates. Incidentally, this is the way the editors of the Arden Shakespeare go about their task – it is their duty to do so. The only limits to the proliferation of such puns are not intentional and biographic but philological – the state of the language in Shakespeare's day, that is the point reached by the intertextual chain, may preclude the possibility of a pun in a given context.

I have reached a paradoxical conclusion. The radical non-sense that emerges through the higher nonsense of Lewis Carroll has turned out to be at the same time a radical threat to meaning (as intention) and the foundation of our reading of (literary) texts. We must take care of the sounds, and the sense will take care of itself – it will appear retroactively, like Lacan's 'upholstery button' (*point de capiton*), as behind every meaning there is the previous saying that induced it, so that the originality of the meaning is at best an illusion. The door of the room is slowly, and it seems deliberately, opened, yet there is nobody behind it. There is no longer an implicit or explicit *vouloir dire*, to be computed through pragmatic calculus, but an ascription of meanings after the event – of meanings in the plural because there is no guarantee that the chain will be unique, as it is in the extreme case of 'Pierre Ménard'. From the belated point of view of the interpreter of the text, the saying which he analyses, even if it is the product of an explicit meaning, can also be the end of a multiplicity of intertextual chains of retroactive possible universes of intertextuality, on which interpretation must play. Figure 3.1 attempts to picture this:

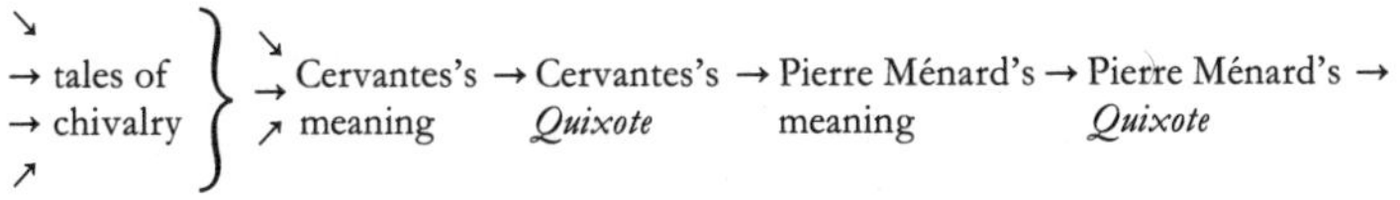

Figure 3.1 'Pierre Ménard'

An obvious objection can be made to Figure 3.1: there is someone missing in the diagram, whose presence would offer a solution to my false dilemma: the author, Borges. He, and only he, it is who means the saying. He invented Pierre Ménard and the whole story. My chain is not a chain, since it has an absolute origin in Borges's idea, which is the pretext for his text.

But things are not as simple as they seem, and a pretext is never more than a pre-text. In the case of Lewis Carroll's riddle without an answer, we saw that an author's text may well be in excess of his or her intention of meaning. (It is only too easy to produce a riddle without an answer: why is George Bush like a warming pan? – don't ask me, I am only the author.) Even if Borges invented it all, he will inevitably be captured by Pierre Ménard his character, so that a place in Figure 3.1 is always already ascribed to him. The strange thing is that by quoting extracts from the *Quixote* and interpreting them in an entirely different context, as he does in the story, he, *qua* author, does what he claims his character is doing in the fiction, even if we can reasonably decide that he did not reconstruct the extracts, but simply copied them. In other words, iteration is always as much alteration as repetition. Recourse to the intention of meaning of the actual author, therefore, is a dead end, the 'author' being as much a textual figure as his or her character. Lewis Carroll's riddle is the playful image of the tragedy of uttering as a kind of writing – our utterances inevitably escape our control and turn us into mere authors, that is temporary bearers of utterances, occupying a position in a chain of meaning, which is never the noble place of origin, or end. We could try to generalise this, and still preserve a place for the author's 'meaning', albeit a modest one, as shown in Figure 3.2.

→	Ur-text 2	→	meaning 2	↘		
→	Ur-text 1	→	author's meaning	→	text	→
→	Ur-text 3	→	meaning 3	↗		

Figure 3.2 General case

Even as in the theory of possible worlds, the real world is given pride of place, the author's meaning, where it is available, will be given first consideration – but it can never be the sole meaning of the saying that follows it, nor is it allowed to dominate the whole scene, since it follows another saying. And the arrows to the left and right indicate that the chain has neither origin (there is no word of God except in a myth of origins), nor end (the task of interpretation is never ended). The interpreter's myth is the mirror image of the myth of origins: it claims to provide an end for the chain by identifying the right meaning and producing the final text, so that the Good Chain (as one says the Good Book) will go from meaning to saying, according to the Duchess's proverb:

Meaning 1 (God's) → text 1 (word of God) → . . . . → text n − 1
→ meaning n (final) → text n (final interpretation)

Only the philosopher's paranoia can produce such a chain. The interpreter's task, therefore, is to take into account the plurality of intertextual chains as one global objective meaning, as opposed to the local subjective meaning of the author's intention. This can be captured by using Searle's formalism again, which is a means of rehearsing the steps of the argument, and introducing a Principle of nonsense:

1 Principle of expressibility:
$\forall a \ \forall p \ M(a,p) \supset S(a,p)$
2 Principle of expressivity (strong):
$\forall a \ \forall p \ S(a,p) \supset M(a,p)$
3 Principle of expressivity (weak):
$\forall a \ \forall p \ \exists q \ S(a,p) \supset M(a,p) \lor M(a,q)$
4 The case of Pierre Ménard:
$a, b, p, \exists q \ M(a,p) \ . \ S(a,p) \ . \ M(b,q) \supset S(b,p)$
5 Principle of nonsense:
$\forall a \ \forall p \ S(a,p) \supset M(a,p) \ . \ M(\emptyset,p) \supset S(L, p_1 \ldots p_n)$

The first three formulae are entirely straightforward: 'a' and 'b' are speakers, 'p' and 'q' propositions, and the predicates M and S, meaning and saying respectively. The fourth formula, which is restricted to Cervantes ('a'), Pierre Ménard ('b') and the *Quixote* ('p') has one considerable advantage: it makes the meaning–saying chain apparent. The fifth formula is entirely illicit, an impossible chain of consequences. It reads thus: if a says p then a means p *and* nobody (ϕ) means p, which implies that language (L) derives from this an indefinite number of utterances ($p_1 \ldots p_n$) which, in a strange sense, it 'says'. The interesting point about the formula is that it is symmetrical around the central 'and' dot, so that its illegitimacy may be interpreted as paradox. This paradox I have formulated elsewhere[27] as 'I speak language' (this is what the left half of the formula represents: there is a sense in which the principle of expressivity is correct) versus 'language speaks' (this is what the right hand of the formula represents: no one means the multiplicity of utterances that may be derived from the text, no one except the free play of language, as the receptacle of multiple intertextual chains).

We have come a long way from the pragmatic intuitions of Lewis Carroll, as embodied in the three passages from *Alice's Adventures in Wonderland* – a whole philosophy of meaning and of language can be derived from them. We understand why Carroll is the philosopher's favourite teller of tales, why he provides an inexhaustible fund of quotations and episodes for illustration and analysis, why his literature is so thought-provoking – there lies the modernity of Carroll.

It is time, therefore, to make up the balance sheet. What we have obtained is first a theory of the emergence of texts, and therefore of nonsense texts, as the output of intertextual chains. But a nonsense text is not any text, if the theory is correct. It is an *en abyme* text, the text that contains in its very structure the lineaments of such a theory – this is what Lewis Carroll spelt out more than a century in advance of the current formulation. And those lineaments account for the dialectics of subversion and support, which lies at the heart of nonsense as a genre. In their very being nonsense texts subvert the dominant conception of language as an instrument of expression and communication, i.e., in our terms, of saying as the result of a speech act governed by meaning-as-intention. The 'I speak language' pole of the contradiction is subverted by nonsense texts: there are too many linguistic traps for Alice to fall into, and the Duchess's proverb deconstructs itself. But it is also supported. The 'language speaks' pole of the contradiction is perceived as a danger, the danger of the speaker's linguistic slavery. Nonsense, therefore, is a constant effort towards mastery, towards blocking the emergence of the radically unmeant, the true or radical nonsense of possession or delirium. Alice's possession is a mild, even if disquieting, case – it is limited to recitation. The repetition of the failure to recite the right words is nothing other than the compulsive re-staging of the primitive scene of language, where mastery over language is mythically acquired – the compulsiveness of the re-staging being due to repeated, inevitable failure.

HUMPTY DUMPTY'S THEORIES OF LANGUAGE

Is he an egg or a person?

In a way, Humpty Dumpty is the embodiment of our discussion of the relationship between saying and meaning. The chapter devoted to him, Chapter 6 of *Through the Looking-Glass*, opens with the following paragraph:

> However, the egg only got larger and larger, and more and more human: when she had come within a few yards of it, she saw that it had eyes and a nose and mouth; and, when she had come close to it, she saw clearly that it was HUMPTY DUMPTY himself. 'It can't be anybody else!' she said to herself. 'I'm as certain of it, as if his name were written all over his face!'[28]

Alice has been trying to purchase an egg in the Sheep's shop. For some reason, the Sheep refuses to 'put things into people's hands', and has placed the egg on a shelf, where it appears to be getting larger and larger, while the shop itself turns into a forest – Humpty Dumpty is the result of this metamorphosis. What is interesting here is that Alice instinctively recognises him. The name appears to her consciousness through a sort of illumination. True, she has been looking at an egg, and there are very few human eggs around, but this cannot satisfactorily account for the certainty of her identification of him. After all, she has no expectation of meeting him, no previous knowledge of the person, or egg, she is about to meet. Nobody has said to her: 'Allow me to introduce Humpty Dumpty'; she has not seen any sign saying: 'To Humpty Dumpty's wall', as she saw a sign that read: 'To the house of Tweedledee'. So she ought to find herself in the same situation she was at the beginning of *Alice's Adventures in Wonderland*, when she was afraid, as she was falling down the rabbit hole, of ending up in the antipodes:

> 'I wonder if I shall fall right *through* the earth! How funny it'll seem to come out among the people that walk with their heads downwards! The Antipathies, I think – . . . but I shall have to ask them what the name of the country is, you know. Please, Ma'am, is this New Zealand or Australia?' . . . 'And what an ignorant little girl she'll think me for asking! No, it'll never do to ask: perhaps I shall see it written up somewhere.'[29]

In this case, she does not have to ask – she just knows the answer. The reason, of course, is clear: because of the intertextual origin of Humpty Dumpty; because she knows the nursery rhyme, which she 'softly repeats to herself' on the next page. Apart from the fact that it is an egg she is beholding, two hints would help her reach the right conclusion, were she to reach it through process of reasoning rather than, as she does, in an intuitive flash: this egg is actually sitting on a wall ('Humpty Dumpty was sitting, with his legs crossed like a Turk, on the top of a high wall – such a narrow one that Alice quite wondered how he could keep his balance'),[30] and the sentence just quoted promises the fulfilment of the narrative programme set by the text of the rhyme. So the name of the creature is not reached through a link in the chain of naming that originally stems from the primal act of baptism, in the approved Kripkean manner.[31] It is not 'written all over its face' in the literal, but in the metaphorical sense: it is derived from the 'meaning' of the creature, that is from a cluster of descriptions (he is an egg – he is also human – he is sitting on a wall), in descriptivist fashion. But the origin of this 'meaning' is a saying. The cluster of descriptions does not refer to properties of Humpty Dumpty that he would naturally possess or to characteristics conventionally or stipulatively ascribed to him (of the type: 'If it is an egg, then it will not keep its balance easily, unless placed in a cup'; or 'This egg shall be sitting on a narrow wall!'), it has an entirely intertextual origin, the words of the nursery rhyme, which exhaust the 'meaning' of Humpty Dumpty by determining its fate down to its minutest details. Hence the exchange, a few pages later, between Alice and Humpty Dumpty:

'Don't you think you'd be safer down on the ground?' Alice went on, not with any idea of making another riddle, but simply in her good-natured anxiety for the queer creature. 'That wall is so *very* narrow!'

'What tremendously easy riddles you ask!' Humpty Dumpty growled out. 'Of course I don't think so! Why, if ever I *did* fall off – which there's no chance of – but *if* I did —' Here he pursed up his lips, and looked so solemn and grand that Alice could hardly help laughing. '*If* I *did* fall,' he went on, '*the King has promised me* – ah, you may turn pale, if you like! You didn't think I was going to say that, did you? *The King has promised me – with his very own mouth* – to – to —'

'To send all his horses and all his men,' Alice interrupted, rather unwisely.

'Now I declare that's too bad!' Humpty Dumpty cried, breaking into a sudden passion. 'You've been listening at doors – and behind trees – and down chimneys – or you couldn't have known it!'

'I haven't, indeed!' Alice said very gently. 'It's in a book.'

'Ah, well! They may write such things in a *book*,' Humpty Dumpty said in a calmer tone. 'That's what you call a History of England, that is. Now, take a good look at me! I'm one that has spoken to a King, *I* am: mayhap you'll never see such another: and, to show you I'm not proud, you may shake hands with me!'[32]

The humour of the passage lies in the fact that Humpty Dumpty presents as new information what has always already been known to Alice – hence her 'unwise' interruption – and also that, like a hero of tragedy, he misinterprets the oracle, and fails to comprehend the fate assigned to him by the Gods – this arch-commentator is in fact a poor reader of texts, since he does not seem to realise that 'all the King's horses, and all the King's men couldn't put Humpty together again.' The passage is a study in comic hubris, where Humpty Dumpty's pride, which announces a fall, is stressed (note, again, the intertextual chain of meaning: the nursery rhyme illustrates another text, a proverb). Thus, not only does he look grand and solemn, but he can only interpret his intertextual origin, which deprives him of all freedom and also of any psychological depth – he is what the critic calls a 'flat', as opposed to a 'round' character – as a historical one. At first sight, his beliefs in this respect are naive. He seems to think that what is written in a *book* is always true (this is the fictional character's archetypal bid for existence). And he also seems to think that a book is even truer if it is a *history* book. Presumably, the difference is that fiction is fictitious and history real. In these our postmodern times, we are inclined to believe that the dividing line is not all that neat (on history as fiction, see the work of Paul Veyne).[33] All the more so as Humpty Dumpty's claim is self-defeating, since he, the most fictional of characters, states that he is historical because of verbal contact (*'with his very own mouth'*) with an unspecified King. Indeed, there is something postmodernist about Humpty Dumpty. By claiming to be a historical character, he suggests that historical characters too are caught in a web of words, in a narrative, and that in spite of their being anchored in the world of solid things by certain hard facts (such as Clive defeated the French at Plassey in 1757), they are also constructed through ever renewed and ever changing interpretations (as the latest biography of Clive

137

offers an entirely new picture of him, to be dispatched into oblivion by the next biography). Historical characters, in spite of their objective solidity – they after all did exist in the fullest sense of the term – have, like characters of fiction, a certain plasticity which allows the historian the same sort, if not the same amount of freedom as the novelist. They did exist, but they share one great quality with their inexistent colleagues: they are no longer with us to contradict and expostulate. In the immortal words of E.C. Bentley:

> What I like about Clive
> Is that he is no longer alive.
> There is a great deal to be said
> For being dead.[34]

Humpty Dumpty, however, is not dead – nor can he ever be. Which means that he too is endowed with a sort of ontological solidity – here the fixity involved in a narrative programme that plays the role of fate.

This is the fate common to all objects of representation, real or fictional. It is the joy and sorrow of the world of the Grecian urn;

> Fair youth, beneath the trees, thou canst not leave
> Thy song, nor ever can those trees be bare;
> Bold Lover, never, never canst thou kiss,
> Though winning near the goal – yet, do not grieve:
> She cannot fade, though thou hast not thy bliss,
> For ever wilt thou love, and she be fair![35]

There is more to this, and to Humpty Dumpty's fate, than an accession to immortality at the cost of immobility. What is involved is the eternal repetition of the same chain of events, which makes Humpty Dumpty a comic embodiment of the eternal return of the same. In the saying–meaning chain that determines his essence, each meaning, each new version of the adventures of Humpty Dumpty, is constrained by a previous saying, which in turn is constrained by a previous meaning. So that what has to be explained is not that Humpty Dumpty will fulfil his fate (the chapter ends on 'She never finished the sentence, for at this moment a heavy crash shook the forest from end to end'),[36] but the possibility of innovation, of a text deviating from its arche-texts, of Humpty Dumpty injecting new meaning into his story by predicting his survival from the fall. How can a meaning and a text deviate from the identity bequeathed to them by their predecessors? How can Humpty Dumpty be a person, for instance, rather than what he is in the nursery rhyme, an egg?

The easiest answer, of course, is to dismiss the framework I have constructed, and deny that a meaning is determined, or even constrained, by previous sayings. Such an answer, however, is not open to Humpty Dumpty – in his case at least, the intertextual chain is at work. So Carroll suggests another answer, which is based on the non-transparency of language. Every new saying, being a linguistic representation of a previous meaning, is open to misunderstanding, as natural languages are riddled with ambiguity, vagueness, and the possibility of mistake or equivocation. There is a game which involves two opposite rows of sitting children. A sentence is whispered at the same time to the two children sitting at one end of their respective rows. They must whisper it to their neighbour as fast as they can, and the process is repeated till the sentence reaches the last child in the row, who utters it aloud. The object of the game, as presented by the adult who organises it, is swiftness of transmission. The real object, which clearly appears when the sentences are uttered aloud, is the deformation that transmission involves: the end-product is usually misshapen to the point of being unintelligible. Our saying–meaning chains have the same effect on meanings and utterances: they are not preserved intact, they do not weather well, thus allowing considerable scope for innovative interpretation (this is in fact the most notable, and creative, characteristic, of what Lyotard calls *montage en série*).

This state of affairs is represented in the text by Alice's mistake as to the 'meaning', or identity, of Humpty Dumpty:

> 'And how exactly like an egg he is!' she said aloud, standing with her hands ready to catch him, for she was every moment expecting him to fall.
>
> 'It's *very* provoking,' Humpty Dumpty said after a long silence, looking away from Alice as he spoke, 'to be called an egg, – *very*!'
>
> 'I said you *looked* like an egg, Sir,' Alice gently explained. 'And some eggs are very pretty, you know,' she added, hoping to turn her remark into a sort of compliment.
>
> 'Some people,' said Humpty Dumpty, looking away from her as usual, 'have no more sense than a baby!'[37]

Alice is quibbling. She *has* said, or at least strongly suggested that he *is* an egg, she has not just innocuously stated, in spite of linguistic appearances, that he looks like one. But, having learnt the rules of *agon*, she is immediately able to exploit those linguistic appearances, for a worthy social purpose, i.e. to retrieve her blunder and placate the injured creature. But her mistake is understandable. She has merely followed the intertextual cue, according to which Humpty Dumpty is only an egg – although the very fact that this egg is given a name in the rhyme tends to personify him. In truth, equivocation is the order of the day in the Ur-text of the rhyme, since in a riddle the meaning must be concealed as carefully as it can be. The textual ambiguity is redoubled (and represented) by Alice's further hesitation as to the status of his cravat or belt:

> 'What a beautiful belt you've got on!' Alice suddenly remarked . . . . 'At least,' she corrected herself on second thoughts, 'a beautiful cravat, I should have said – no, a belt, I mean – I beg your pardon!' she added in dismay, for Humpty Dumpty looked thoroughly offended, and she began to wish she hadn't chosen that subject. 'If only I knew,' she thought to herself, 'which was neck and which was waist!'[38]

As Humpty Dumpty's reactions show, the ambiguity in the Ur-text, which produces hesitation in Alice, also causes a contradiction in the character. Subjectively he is – he does not say exactly what he is, since he contents himself with denying he is an egg, but we must naturally take him to consider himself as a person, certainly a centre of consciousness, well deserving the pronoun 'he'. But objectively, he is an egg, in shape and vulnerability. One might object that he is alive – well, so is an egg; that he talks – well, it is true that eggs do not talk, but some do *in potentia*, as the foetus is *potentially* (in an important philosophical sense of the adverb)[39] a fully developed human being. The interesting point is that both sides of the contradiction are tenable because of the manoeuvring that language allows. For language constructs interpretations and thus creates represented objects, but it ruins those interpretations by making them incompatible and contradictory, or else it makes them so coherent and logical that they end up betraying what they purport to represent. Humpty Dumpty is constructed, by the nursery rhyme, by Alice's interpretation, by Carroll's text (particularly the immediate context of the episode), as an egg. But the text threatens to destroy the interpretation by producing another, contained in Humpty Dumpty's vigorous protest, which is incoherent with the first and yet, as we have seen, not without textual backing. So that, inevitably, his conversation with Alice turns around questions of identity, as indeed it will again, at the very end of the chapter, when Humpty Dumpty criticises Alice's lack of distinctiveness:

> 'I shouldn't know you again if we *did* meet,' Humpty Dumpty replied in a discontented tone, giving her one of his fingers to shake: 'you're so exactly like other people'. . . . 'Your face is the same as everybody has – the two eyes, so –' (marking their places in the air with his thumb) 'nose in the middle, mouth under. It's always the same. Now if you had the two eyes on the same side of the nose, for instance – or the mouth at the top – that would be *some* help.'[40]

Identity, the identity of the speaker's self and of the other speakers, is what interpretations construct, a never-ending process, in language. Because language is not transparent, because representation is always also betrayal, all we have access to is images, that is conflicting interpretations, not persons 'as they really are', hence the need to defend one's interpretations against those of others, and the agonistic turn the exchange inevitably takes.

The plight of Alice and Humpty Dumpty can be generalised. They find themselves in the banal position of characters in novels, who by definition are nothing but strings of sentences, that is interpretations, a situation which, at the end of the nineteenth century, with the novels of, for instance, Henry James, became the very object of narratives. One could summarise the implicit chain of argument behind this conception of characters, of Humpty Dumpty as well as of James Strether in *The Ambassadors* or Milly Theale in *The Wings of the Dove* by the following propositions:

1 Every perception is also a projection.
2 Every projection involves an interpretation.
3 A subject (a character) is a centre of interpretation.
4 Intersubjective relationships consist of confrontation between interpretations.

If we interpret the 'also' in a weak sense (1) is innocuously Kantian. The perceiving eye has no access to the thing-in-itself but projects the forms of intuition on to the phenomena. If we give the 'also' its strong sense, we leave Kant or some form of idealism. This is exactly what we shall be doing in order to proceed to (2), where a form of constructivism is offered. But there is a Nietzschean twist to this constructivism.[41] Language is one of the forms of intuition: it constructs our *Lebenswelt*, which is a network of interpretations. Those are at best temporary, in need of constant revision, and of uncertain relevance. How do we know that the characters that our interpretations hallucinate will behave in the predicted way (characters in nonsense are particularly prone to behaving contrary to Alice's expectations, i.e. interpretations – this is part of their charm). Hence (3) and (4): a subject, or a character, is merely a centre of interpretations, about herself and others, which she puts forward in order to test them in the intersubjective exchange. In such (agonistic) exchanges, interpretations are imposed, vindicated, defeated. Their success or failure does not depend on their adequacy to an unknowable 'true' state of affairs, but on their acceptance by the community, be it local or global, of interpreters, and therefore largely on the skill with which they are defended.

Thus, in a late novel by Henry James, the baffled reader realises that the world of objects and events is never 'objectively' described, but, on the rare moments when it is evoked, only within the interpretation of a character. In turn, the interminable conversations which meander through most of the chapters are never about 'things', objects or events, but about interpretations of them – they are confrontations of interpretations, with all the vagueness, the implicitness and the possibilities for misunderstanding that this implies. Even the narrator is a centre of interpretation – the epitome of characters, a voice that does not utter truths from an omniscient outside position, but rather an umpire, arbitrating between different interpretations without really showing preference for any. Henry James's characteristic style can be seen as a consequence of this.

Humpty Dumpty is hardly a character out of Henry James, nor is Lewis Carroll's style, God forbid, in any way similar to that of the master – we have learnt to cherish the crystal clarity and the (apparent) simplicity with which the adventures of Alice are told. But the confrontation between Alice and Humpty Dumpty throughout the chapter is one between interpretations. There are at least two views of Humpty Dumpty, both of which are entirely rational, i.e. coherent and textually founded. Humpty Dumpty's *cogito*, 'I think, therefore I am not an egg', is opposed to Alice's conventional reasoning: the nursery rhyme says this is an egg, *ergo* it *is* an egg. No wonder conversation is difficult and mutual understanding impossible to attain. Let us see how the conversation proceeds.

A theory of naming

If conversation is a confrontation of interpretations, each speaker defending a view of his and other speakers' identities, and seeking to impose those views on others, it is natural that the subject of naming should be the first to be broached:

'Don't stand chattering to yourself like that,' Humpty Dumpty said, looking at her for the first time, 'but tell me your name and your business.'

'My *name* is Alice, but —'

'It's a stupid name enough!' Humpty Dumpty interrupted impatiently. 'What does it mean?'

'*Must* a name mean something?' Alice asked doubtfully.

'Of course it must,' Humpty Dumpty said with a short laugh: '*my* name means the shape I am – and a good handsome shape it is, too. With a name like yours, you might be any shape, almost.'[42]

Alice's puzzlement, 'Must a name mean something?', shows that although she defers to the authority of the expert, as a good little girl should, she has her doubts, and would intuitively prefer J.S. Mill's theory of names, in which they are meaningless counters in the communication game. Humpty Dumpty, however, is more advanced. His conception anticipates on the descriptivism which was to dominate the field until the advent of Kripke. For him, a name is not a mark, but a cluster of descriptions. Those 'descriptions', however, are hardly straightforward. They are not of the type, 'the main character in the sixth chapter of *Through the Looking-Glass*', 'the eponymous hero of the famous nursery rhyme', or 'the talking egg', but such as can be derived from (a) the onomatopoetic suggestions of a name that turns out to be motivated; (b) the elements of information to be derived from the Ur-text of the rhyme; and (c) the fate to which this intertextual origin sentences him, i.e. a set of (all too predictable) deeds. Only (b) could count as an unambiguous source of 'descriptions' for the meaning of a name ('he that sits on a wall'); one could derive genuine ones from (c) – one could not do it from (a). Of course, Humpty Dumpty chooses (a) as the source for the meaning of his name: '*my* name means the shape I am.'

That name should be meaningful, *pace* Mill and Kripke, is not so surprising, and it is based on a general property of language, known to rhetoricians as *conversion*. If your language is plastic enough – English is so to an amazing degree – words can easily change their parts of speech. You can always name your child Faith, Hope or Charity (the only limits are legal, therefore historical and contingent), thus turning a common noun into a proper name. And you can always say of your best friend that he is 'the Lenin of our time', thus doing the opposite. But there is a logic for these conversions, as the example I have just used shows. An arbitrary name is associated, by metonymy, with a number of remarkable deeds. Such deeds provide the meaning of the converted common noun. I am aware that Lenin was called Ulyanov, and that his *nom de guerre*, like Stalin's, was motivated, not arbitrary. Like Humpty Dumpty, they both felt the need to adopt a name that 'meant the (moral) shape they were'. My example, then, is not as good as if I had said 'Jeffrey Archer is the Dickens of our time.' But it is a good example nevertheless, as it illustrates the tactics of adopted nicknames, which is Humpty Dumpty's tactics. An Ur-text about deeds (and fate) produces a (nick)name, through a metonymy which is always already there, in the language, as a piece of common sense and a cliché ('steel' is associated with a number of qualities); from this a motivated name is derived – this, I take it, is what the sounds 'Humpty Dumpty' evoke: plumpness, roundness, etc.; lastly, actual deeds will fulfil the fate inscribed in the name. The irony, of course, is that it is all too easy, after the event, to establish an essential link (although one metaphorically reached) between the man of steel and the gulag. But the favoured locus of Humpty Dumpty's tactics is not history, but literature. It is the novelist who is fond of naming his characters through *adnominatio*, the deliberate choice of motivated names, which tell the reader what to expect. We do not expect anything good from Uriah Heep. If we wished to know exactly why, we would have to embark on a discussion of phonesthemes, the sub-morphematic 'units' that seem to be endowed with meaning,[43] of the association of phonemes with instinctual drives:[44] behind Saussure's 'arbitrary character of the sign' there may well lie a deeper motivation, which makes us sure, without being able to pinpoint the exact reason, that 'Heep' is not a nice name, and enables Humpty Dumpty to claim, to the reader's satisfaction, that his name means his shape. No rigid designator or primal baptism for Humpty Dumpty. Rather than the mastery of Adamic naming, he demonstrates the servitude of a subject towards the name he or she must bear as a fate. This accounts for the tone of the discussion between Alice and Humpty Dumpty in the pages that follow our passage. He answers her obvious anxiety about his fate, and her kind advice on how to avoid it ('Don't you think you'd be safer on the ground?') with hubristic confidence – which takes us back to the conflict of interpretations. If names are motivated, then one of man's deepest urges will be satisfied – everyone will be able to know the future, as far as it concerns them. All Humpty Dumpty has to do is to purchase a book and read a few lines – it is all written down there, not up there as in the heavens of determinists. But, alas, language as *nomothetes* is as oblique as the Apollo Loxias of Greek oracles. If a name is determined by sounds or by a text, we cannot be assured of a true or even a firm interpretation. All we can obtain is a multiplicity of interpretations, one or more per speaker – not *a* meaning in the Gricean sense, intended to be recognised as such by the audience, but a multiplicity of potential meanings. It is, as we have seen, entirely fitting that the Ur-text from which Humpty Dumpty's name derives its meaning should be a riddle.

A theory of conversation

If a subject, or speaker, is a centre of interpretation, and intersubjective relations a confrontation of interpretations, it is understandable that the subject of conversation should crop up next:

> 'However, this conversation is going on a little too fast: let's go back to the last remark but one.'
> 'I'm afraid I can't quite remember it,' Alice said, very politely.
> 'In that case we start afresh,' said Humpty Dumpty, 'and it's my turn to choose a subject —' ('He talks about it just as if it was a game!' thought Alice.) 'So here's a question for you. How old did you say you were?'[45]

On the face of it, Humpty Dumpty anticipates the work of Grice, or ethnomethodology. He is interested, for instance, in

145

turn-taking – albeit, as usual, in a caricatural way: if conversation is interrupted by a breach in the maxim of speed, which he introduces, no doubt, as a sub-maxim to the maxim of manner (which, we have seen, is a rag-bag of injunctions, and therefore open to indefinite enlargement), his demand that they should start again at the 'last remark but one', rather than at the last, can only introduce confusion. (Do we count remarks as we speak? And do we know what, if we did, would count as a 'remark'?) This, his usual tactics of excess, is given by the word 'game' which Alice feels authorised to apply to it. And we must take it literally – not in the general sense of 'language game'. Humpty Dumpty is not practising an established language game and drawing Alice's attention to it for pedagogic reasons. He is turning the common regulative language game of conversation (as described by Grice's maxims) into a game in the sporting sense, where rules are constitutive, and explicitly stipulated. This is taking the co-operative principle to excess. In order to function smoothly, like a game of chess, his conversation needs an explicit agreement between the participants before the game can start – as when two children open their Christmas presents and play a new game for the first time.

This has two consequences. Since 'conversation', far from being a new game, is not even a game in that sense, at least in Alice's opinion and in ours, the game has already started when Humpty Dumpty invokes a rule. Alice is in the situation of someone who plays without having been given all the rules, and who therefore is entirely dependent on her opponent's decision as to the legality of the next move. How can we be sure Humpty Dumpty has not just invented the 'start again' rule as the King of Hearts so obviously invented Rule Forty-two? Such games are usually played by a cat and a mouse. But this is not as bad as it sounds – this is the norm in Wonderland, and Alice is no longer surprised. The second consequence, although apparently more innocuous, in fact goes further. By turning conversation into a game of chess, Humpty Dumpty introduces competition, and therefore confrontation – he moves from a non-zero sum to a zero-sum game. The main question becomes: who is going to win? This, of course, is a far cry from Grice: excessive (because excessively formal) *irene* produces *agon*, the mild *agon* of a game (this is only a game!), but strong enough to induce passion and cause some form of violence – the frightening ghost of the conversation hooligan, or word-mugger, looms on the horizon. The French sociologist Roger Caillois distinguishes between two kinds of playing: *paidia*, the childish activity of free play, usually based on imitation and acting (for instance dressing up for the Christmas party) and *ludus*, the playing at games, usually competitive, governed by constitutive rules.[46] What Humpty Dumpty is doing is turning the *paidia* of cooperative conversation into *ludus*, and an agonistic form of it at that, as will soon appear.

But we must also note that there are advantages to this, and we must remember that the creator of Humpty Dumpty was a logician. Conversation is a messy affair. It is sometimes too fast, and sometimes too slow. It loses its thread in infinite digression, or abruptly ends as the mood changes – or sometimes, as we saw with Patrick Hamilton, it fails to end and is painfully protracted. The orderly type of conversation advocated by Humpty Dumpty is not at all like this. Constitutive rules enjoy a considerable advantage over all others: they are neat, i.e. explicit, definite, complete and consistent. Were Humpty Dumpty to spell out his rules in full, no doubt we would have an opening move and an end move as well as the intermediate moves he stipulates, and the conversation would proceed in an orderly fashion. We might even draw an end move from his rule: if you fail to remember where you are in the conversation, the game is at an end, and you start afresh. What Carroll is suggesting, of course, is *a contrario* a picture of real conversations, of which the conversation between Alice and Humpty Dumpty is a perfect example.

Real conversations are not cases of *ludus*. They develop in a haphazard fashion, meandering their way through association of ideas, inconsequential sallies and anacolutha. What Humpty Dumpty is trying to do is not only to regulate this disorderly flow (in which, however, conversation analysis will discover an underlying thread: ordinary conversations are not strings of *non sequiturs*), but to make it mechanical. This is the source of the comic effect the exchange produces, if we believe in Bergson's definition of the comic, '*du mécanique plaqué sur du vivant*', mechanism forced upon life.[47] The humour in the passage, of course, does not simply lie in Humpty Dumpty's attempted imposition of a mechanical rule – it lies in the contradiction between his mechanical theory and absent-minded practice. This, Bergson's theory of laughter and comedy enables us to understand. According to him, laughter has a deep-seated link with forgetfulness. Gestures and utterances

147

become mechanical when life becomes absent-minded, when the spontaneous in 'life', the purposefulness of meaningful action for instance, turns into absent-minded repetition. The mechanical is not so much a deformation imposed on the naturalness of life by our technological culture as life forgetting itself into empty repetition or predictable movements. Thus, there is a sense in which nonsense is a comic genre because it stages *the absent-mindedness of language*.

This, for Bergson, is the main source of linguistic comedy. It takes three forms, all richly represented in nonsense. The first is *cliché* – a set phrase, mechanically repeated, becomes comic if something hampers the smooth workings of the machine, at the same time making its mechanical aspect manifest. The instance Bergson gives is the well-known comic cliché, 'I never work between meals' a ludicrous variation on hackneyed, if sound, dietetic advice. The numerous false proverbs of nonsense, one of which was analysed in the previous section, belong to this category. The second is *literalism*: interpreting a phrase or dead metaphor according to its lost, but easily recoverable, literal meaning. This can be a rich source of jokes. The instance Bergson gives is the following dialogue, the object of which is a notorious bore: A: 'He is striving after wit' – B: 'I'll take a bet on wit.' Literalism in this sense is a notorious characteristic of nonsense. Alice's 'I beg your pardon' is usually greeted with, 'It is not nice to beg.' In *Sylvie and Bruno*, a pompous character declares: 'This movement has assumed the dimensions of a revolution.' The immediate rejoinder is a demand for the exact width, length and breadth of this revolution. The third is *transposition*: inversion, pun or sudden change of tone or register. Language absent-mindedly sings the tune an octave higher or lower than it should be sung. A solemn proclamation is delivered in vulgar style, or ruined by the presence of a few puns. Nonsense, as we have had the opportunity to realise, is fond of puns, in the form of a mechanical series of them. And, being a parodic genre, it is fond of playing with tone and register.

This detour through the comic aspects of nonsense has not taken us as far from the theory of conversation as it seems. The absent-mindedness of language disrupts the *irene* of cooperative conversation in two ways. Because it is a sign of life, it prevents the smooth flowing of the exchange of information and argument by introducing an element of unpredictability and irrationality that baffles the maxims and threatens the CP. Because it is a mechanism forced upon life, it provides ready-made weapons for a strategy of *agon*. Because of its nature, the PS is much more capable of adapting to inconsequentiality and syntactic anacoluthon. Irrationality is a mark of total breakdown for the CP; for the PS, it is merely another tactic. The very next passage in our chapter provides a striking illustration of this.

An agonistic use of literal interpretation

Humpty Dumpty's 'rule' is not in fact a means for him to regulate the game in order to make it more cooperative. It is a pretext for verbal aggression:

> 'In that case we start afresh,' said Humpty Dumpty, 'and it's my turn to choose a subject — ' ('He talks about it just as if it was a game!' thought Alice.) 'So here's a question for you. How old did you say you were?'
>
> Alice made a short calculation, and said 'Seven years and six months.'
>
> 'Wrong!' Humpty Dumpty exclaimed triumphantly. 'You never said a word like it!'
>
> 'I thought you meant "How old *are* you?" ' Alice explained.
>
> 'If I'd meant that, I'd have said it,' said Humpty Dumpty.
>
> Alice didn't want to begin another argument, so she said nothing.[48]

This sounds familiar. Alice has been caught again. Only this time she knows better, that is she has learnt to accept defeat, well knowing as she does that argument with Humpty Dumpty would only lead to further defeat. And again we must sympathise with her. The conventional sense of Humpty Dumpty's question is an indirect meaning. The question does not necessarily presuppose that Alice has already mentioned her age. It *pretends* that she has, in order not to ask the question directly, out of tact perhaps, or in order to demonstrate the speaker's right to elicit information from his hearer, whom he thus places in a position of conversational subservience. Alice understands, and responds to the utterer's meaning, well knowing that it does not correspond to the utterance meaning. Humpty Dumpty unfairly uses the discrepancy for his own ends, in order to triumph, and backs his move with a general theory of the relationship between meaning and saying which denies the possibility of indirect speech acts, thus adopting the (untenable) position of a supporter of the strong version of our principle of expressivity.

But Humpty Dumpty's move is not only tactical. Behind it, there lies an implicit theory of interpretation: the best interpretation of an utterance is always the most literal. The next paragraph illustrates this:

> 'Seven years and six months!' Humpty Dumpty repeated thoughtfully. 'An uncomfortable sort of age. Now if you'd asked *my* advice, I'd have said "Leave off at seven" – but it's too late now.'
>
> 'I never ask advice about growing,' Alice said indignantly.
>
> 'Too proud?' the other enquired.
>
> Alice felt even more indignant at this suggestion. 'I mean,' she said, 'that one ca'n't help growing older.'
>
> '*One* ca'n't, perhaps,' said Humpty Dumpty, 'but *two* can. With proper assistance, you might have left off at seven.'
>
> 'What a beautiful belt you've got on!' Alice suddenly remarked.[49]

There is more to this than *agon*. This is Humpty Dumpty's interpreting machine, which automatically (hence comically) produces the preferred interpretation for any utterance, by reducing it to its narrowest literal meaning. We understand Alice's indignation: the machine works without a hitch, and there is no stopping it. In the first instance, Alice relies on linguistic common sense: 'grow' is not a verb denoting an intentional action, at least not in this sense (the verb also has a transitive use, on which Humpty Dumpty is implicitly punning). Therefore, there is no point in asking advice or help about this kind of growing, since there is no possibility of not growing – the mark of agency lies in the possibility *not* to act. But Alice's phrasing is ambiguous, and susceptible of a more literal emotive interpretation, which is absent from her more correct paraphrase, 'one ca'n't help growing older.' But, of course, she can never win, for if the second version is semantically safe, it does contain syntactic or lexical ambiguities, which are unavoidable, if her utterance is to be expressed in natural language. If Humpty Dumpty had not chosen to exploit the ambiguity of 'one' he probably would have distorted the sense of 'help' to suit his purpose. He does so, in fact, using a characteristic of language which I have called the 'remainder work': the ambiguity he forces on the word 'one' (it can hardly be said that, on any definition of a 'normal' or 'standard' reading, the sentence is ambiguous) is strengthened by the fact that a concomitant play on the two main senses of 'help' becomes possible. The metaphorical drift clearly appears if we go from 'one ca'n't help doing this' to 'two can help doing it'. What is so surprising about this – but language is full of such 'coincidences': this is what the remainder is about – is that the pun on 'one' should occur in a sentence in which another, related, pun also occurs. Lastly, we must note that although Humpty Dumpty's exploiting of ordinary language is outrageous, there is a rationale to it, which he shares with the more theory-inclined linguists. Many linguists conceive their task as showing that a form (like 'one' or 'may') has, at a deeper level, only one semantic value, whatever the superficial multiplicity of its meanings. You will accordingly find treatments of 'one' which insist on the fundamental value of the word,[50] which accounts for both its ordinal meaning (one, two) and its generic and prop-word meanings ('one is never sure of choosing the right one').

There is no escaping Humpty Dumpty's interpretation machine. Alice, who does not want to start an argument, attempts to avoid one by abruptly changing the subject. But, as in a situation of double bind, she fails. Indeed, she unwittingly imitates Humpty Dumpty by offering an interpretation of an ambiguous object: she decides that it is a belt, and of course it is a cravat. Why should she not be allowed to do this, since, like Humpty Dumpty, she is only exploiting a perceptual ambiguity – in his case at least, it is impossible to tell the waist from the neck. But this is not allowed to pass, as the following lines show: ' "It is a – *most – provoking –* thing," he said at last, "when a person doesn't know a cravat from a belt!" "I know it's very ignorant of me," Alice said, in so humble a tone that Humpty Dumpty relented. "It's a cravat, child, and a beautiful one, as you say. It's a present from the White King and Queen. There now!" '[51] In fact, Alice has made two mistakes. First, she tries to use a perceptual paradox (in the sense of *Gestalt* psychology) rather than a linguistic ambiguity. Humpty Dumpty's commonsense view is that language is treacherous (hence the need to exert power over it, as we shall see), but sense impressions not so. Some people, he might say, have no more sense impressions than a baby. The difference, then, is that perception is only marginally ambiguous and can generally be trusted, whereas language is essentially ambiguous and lacking in transparency. The second mistake derives from the first. It is all a question not so much of an object, or a perception (what Alice unambiguously perceives is a piece of cloth round Humpty Dumpty's person), as of naming – and Humpty Dumpty, as we know, has a stipulative conception of definition. Which means that Alice can never know, but only guess, for in this case at least, because eggs, even when human, have no waists or necks, the ascription of a name to the object can only be arbitrary. Humpty Dumpty chooses to call the object in question a cravat; but he might easily have called it a belt, and there is no way for Alice to know. What we are witnessing is, in fact, the equivalent of an act of primal baptism in Kripke's anti-descriptivist theory of naming. That is why Alice eats humble pie (as long as the baptism has not taken place, she can only be ignorant) and why Humpty Dumpty relents (he is occupying the exalted position of the *nomothetes*). There is no point in saying that Humpty Dumpty contradicts himself – he does so all the time. It is more interesting to note that he is passing from a descriptivist view (as far as proper names are concerned) to an anti-descriptivist conception of common nouns – an inverted Kripke. It is therefore natural that the next paragraphs should deal with naming again, in the form of a theory of definition.

A theory of definition

'. . . There's glory for you!'

'I don't know what you mean by "glory",' Alice said.

Humpty Dumpty smiled contemptuously. 'Of course you don't – till I tell you. I meant "there's a nice knock-down argument for you!" '

'But "glory" doesn't mean "a nice knock-down argument",' Alice objected.

'When *I* use a word,' Humpty Dumpty said, in rather a scornful tone, 'it means just what I choose it to mean – neither more nor less.'

'The question is,' said Alice, 'whether you *can* make words mean so many different things.'

'The question is,' said Humpty Dumpty, 'which is to be master – that's all.'

Alice was too much puzzled to say anything; so after a minute Humpty Dumpty began again. 'They've a temper, some of them − particularly verbs: they're the proudest − adjectives you can do anything with, but not verbs − however, *I* can manage the whole lot of them! Impenetrability! That's what *I* say!'

'Would you tell me, please,' said Alice, 'what that means?'

'Now you talk like a reasonable child,' said Humpty Dumpty, looking very much pleased. 'I meant by "impenetrability" that we've had enough of that subject, and it would be just as well if you'd mention what you mean to do next, as I suppose you don't mean to stop here all the rest of your life.'

'That's a great deal to make one word mean,' Alice said in a thoughtful tone.

'When I make a word do a lot of work like that,' said Humpty Dumpty, 'I always pay it extra.'

'Oh!' said Alice. She was too much puzzled to make any other remark.

'Ah, you should see 'em come round me of a Saturday night,' Humpty Dumpty went on, wagging his head gravely from side to side, 'for to get their wages, you know.'[52]

This is when Humpty Dumpty appears to be contradicting himself. The interpretation machine relied on exploiting ambiguity through motivation and re-motivation. This text states that common nouns receive their meaning through stipulative definition. In the preceding paragraphs, he relied on an excessive awareness of what Saussure calls the 'relative motivation' of signs; in this text he draws on an absolutist view of their arbitrary character. And arbitrary they are with a vengeance: not only are definitions stipulative, but they depend on the decision of the individual speaker (a move that Saussure certainly would not have condoned).

There are two possible explanations for this apparent contradiction. If we treat the whole exchange as agonistic, a verbal struggle the object of which is to defeat Alice and make her leave the field (there is a clear hint of that in his definition of 'impenetrability', which could be vulgarly glossed as 'buzz off!' − Alice must be either a little dim or skilled in the game, since she fails to take the hint), then the contradiction, as part of a rational strategy, is welcome. Alice is in fact reduced to a state of abject subservience, confessing ignorance, 'talking like a reasonable child', and so on. But I would like to think there is more to it than

153

this – that Humpty Dumpty is a true theoretician, not an opportunist. So I shall embark upon a defence and illustration of Humpty Dumpty linguistics.

Like all speakers, Humpty Dumpty is caught up in a dialectics of mastery and servitude in language – except that, unlike most, he is aware of it. This dialectics is captured in the two metaphors which Nietzsche applies to language: the bee and the spider.[53] Articulated language, like a bee, constructs a liveable world for the speaker, giving her an impression of control over the world of phenomena through her control over language. It also, like a spider, captures and imprisons her in a network of constraints, thus enslaving her, dictating her vision of the world to her. Humpty Dumpty's theory of arbitrary definition corresponds to the moment of Adamic mastery when the speaker entirely controls the language she speaks. While his reliance on the ambiguity and relative motivation of words and phrases demonstrates that, in the words of two other of Nietzsche's pronouncements about language, (a) language is a disease of thought, and (b) thought is a disease of language – both formulas representing the moment of servitude. In other words, Humpty Dumpty is aware that language is both a bee and a spider. The (a) formula is illustrated by the exploitation of the ambiguity in 'one'. If language allows us to do this, then it is sick, and threatens to corrupt logical thought. This is the well-known position of logicians and logical positivists, which Carroll shared. But (b) is also valid; thought *is* a disease of language. This appears in Humpty Dumpty's interpretation that immediately precedes our present text, the explanation of the word 'unbirthday'. The explanation has a logical ring about it. If my birthday is the day that commemorates my birth ('birthday' is an eminently motivated word, being one of those words that 'mean the shape they are'), then my unbirthday is either the day(s) when I was not born and the day(s) commemorating my unbirth (two classes with different intensions but the same extension). In this case, where Humpty Dumpty's reasoning has nothing arbitrary about it, it is (logical) thought that waylays and trips language, not the reverse. Through a work of analogy and deduction, Humpty Dumpty is forcing the English language to mean what it does not, since 'unbirthday' does not exist outside *Through the Looking-Glass*. Except of course, that the word has become famous, and will crop up here and there, in allusions or jokes: to that extent does thought corrupt language.

Let us go back to the moment of mastery – to Humpty Dumpty's Adamic theory of naming. When I said that Humpty Dumpty is an inverted Kripke, this statement was not entirely correct, and must be qualified. We have witnessed a Kripkean moment of original baptism, when the name is given a meaning by ostension (i.e. by pointing at the referent) or description – in our case, by description only, since the baptism applies not to proper names, as in Kripke (you can name a person by pointing at him, or a natural kind by saying, with the appropriate gesture, 'this is silver'), but to common nouns – and it would be difficult to define 'glory' or 'impenetrability' by ostension. But there is an important difference. In Kripke, the result of an act of baptism is a rigid designator; according to Humpty Dumpty it cannot be that, as the baptism is temporary, dependent as it is on the decision, perhaps we ought to say the whim, of the individual speaker. The anticipatory inversion of Kripke consists in this: on the global level, Humpty Dumpty rejects Kripke's theories where they apply (names) and adopts them where they do not apply (nouns) – a fascinating negative image.

I seem to be suggesting that Humpty Dumpty's theory is so topsy-turvy as to be untenable. And on the face of it, this picture of language is an impossible one. No language thus constituted could work: it would not provide the elementary stability of meaning on which intersubjective communication must rely. At worst, it would be an instance of that notorious impossibility, a private language. At best, it would be a linguistic variant of the practices indulged in by the inhabitants of Swift's Laputa, who, for sheer laziness, carried the referents of their utterances on their backs, and pointed at them, which saved them uttering their names. But is such a practice, as a part or an aspect of language, so impossible? Of course it is not – it is the common practice, or should I say the privilege, of scientists and philosophers. A scientist is entitled to her technical language, which she will obtain either by outright coinage, or by waylaying common words into new areas of meaning. Lewis Carroll not only was aware of this practice, but approved of it, as a famous passage in his *Symbolic Logic* shows: 'I maintain that any writer of a book is fully authorised in attaching any meaning he likes to any word or phrase he intends to use. If I find an author saying, at the beginning of his book, "Let it be understood that by the word '*black*' I shall always mean '*white*', and that by the word '*white*' I shall always mean '*black*', I meekly accept his ruling, however injudicious I may think it.'[54] The extremism of this position lies in the 'any', which allows the practice to be extended from the scientists, who need to talk a different language from the rest of the tribe, to everybody – and this includes Humpty Dumpty – who will do it out of sheer perversity. For it is obvious that if I decide that from now on 'white' means 'black', I am relying on our shared awareness of the meaning of the word 'black', and am only confusing matters and putting communication at risk.

Humpty Dumpty's extreme practice, however, does find its source in a socially recognised custom. But perhaps we might make a distinction between the scientist and the philosopher, which will show that Humpty Dumpty sides with the latter – we shall not be unduly surprised by this. A simplified account of the creation of scientific jargons might go like the following. The scientists' need of a technical language without any link to normal language is so great that they will tend to prefer coinages to other sources of new meanings. Once adopted in the scientific field, the coinage may expand out of it and appear in common language through a metaphorical use that extends or dilutes the original limited and precise sense. Our everyday vocabulary is full of corpses, dead metaphorical remnants of forgotten scientific theories. Many of what Lakoff and Johnson call 'ontological metaphors' are traces of antiquated science. Thus, 'temperature' goes back to the physics of Aristotle, and there is a long history for the word 'revolution', which goes from science to politics. Philosophers or social scientists, on the other hand, have other constraints. They may choose the scientific path of coinage, but they may also wish to remain as close as possible to common forms of speech, since their concern is also the concern of the average person in everyday life. In the field of ethics, for instance, there is no avoiding the use of words like 'good' and 'right'. But the sense the philosopher gives those words may be entirely new, and may have to be distinguished from all previous senses. This is, if the philosopher is lucid enough to be explicit and to proceed *more geometrico*, where stipulative definition comes in. Often, there is good reason for this – it is to be presumed that in a new ethical theory the definition of the word 'good' (for instance 'I approve of this. Do the same!') would claim to cover the previous or 'common' meanings of the word. But sometimes the link is not so clear. A famous linguist wanted a name for his brand new concept of language as system, as opposed to the individual speaker's use of the system. Nobody will claim that the words '*langue*' and '*parole*' which he chose for his concepts have kept their common meanings – the proof of this is that they are hardly ever translated into English.

Humpty Dumpty is an extreme case of philosophical linguistic creativity – a paranoid coiner, who is merely aping equally paranoid philosophers, with their outlandish jargon. This is only another instance of the dialectics of subversion and support. There is a solid British no-nonsense attitude in this comic exaggeration: only foreigners or talking eggs would behave in that extravagant manner, not our very own Locke and Hume. But this apparently conservative support for a commonsensical view of language and philosophy is subverted by Humpty Dumpty's partly justified practice; the no-nonsense attitude must accept the inevitability of nonsense. Indeed, as Humpty Dumpty's further explanations to Alice show, his exaggeratedly stipulative theory of definition evokes older, and deeper myths about language, namely language as a living organism, and the linguistic exchange as, metaphorically, an economic one.

Humpty Dumpty is the 'master' of potentially unruly words. If the question is 'which is to be master', the implication is that words have a will of their own, and therefore a force of their own, and must be kept down. The speaker is king over a rebellious population of words. And since Humpty Dumpty claims to be that sort of king himself, we may well imagine that such sovereignty over words places the speaker in a position as precarious as that of Humpty Dumpty on his wall – a revolution by words, toppling the speaker who utters them, is always to be feared. It is, after all, language that speaks. The irony is that the masterly speaker is entirely subjected to a number of words, the words of the rhyme that spell out his fate – the so-called master is a slave after all.

The whole picture is again obtained by playing on ambiguity in language. Humpty Dumpty exploits Alice's rejoinder: 'The question is . . . whether you *can* make words mean so many different things.' Taken in its 'normal' contextual meaning, the sequence of words 'you can make words mean . . .' raises the question of the speaker's control over the meaning of his utterance, involving the familiar principles of expressibility and expressivity. Taken in its 'looking-glass world', nonsensical context, the words personify the objects of the causative 'make': can we make words do this (i.e. mean) against their will? The consequence of this semantic drift is a show of force, implicitly playing on an intuition that utterances or words have force, as will become apparent in speech act theory. The personification is made explicit when the words come round to ask for their wages.

The second myth is as venerable as the first. The word 'exchange' in 'the communicative exchange' is a metaphor for the economic type of exchange. From this, a whole metaphorical system of words as coins and conversations as money transactions has developed (on this, see the seminal work of J.J. Goux).[55]

Humpty Dumpty, because of the breadth of his vision and the depth of his intuitions is the archetypal philosopher of language. No wonder that he should be appealed to by Alice as the authoritative interpreter of texts: the rest of Carroll's chapter is devoted to his explanation of 'Jabberwocky', which we evoked in the introduction.

Interpretation revisited

Humpty Dumpty's interpretation technique does not apply only to texts that come to him from other people – it also applies to the texts he himself recites, and in which it appears he is personally involved. Here, his literalism will not concern individual words, but fiction in general. Thus, he makes a rather unwilling Alice ('so she sat down, and said "Thank you" rather sadly') listen to a poem, which, he claims, 'was written entirely for your amusement':

'In winter, when the fields are white,
I sing this song for your delight – only I don't sing it,' he added, as an explanation.
'I see you don't,' said Alice.
'If you can *see* whether I'm singing or not, you've sharper eyes than most,' Humpty Dumpty remarked severely.'[56]

Not only does he take words like 'see' literally, again rejecting the possibility of indirect speech acts or metonymic transfer, but this time the literal interpretation applies to the immediate situation of utterances, so that the shifter, 'I', acquires a fixed referent, and ceases to shift. It is not merely the case that whenever he says 'I' he refers to himself – this is, after all, the definition of 'I' as a shifter – but he does it also when he quotes a text containing 'I'. He is so egocentric that he cannot conceive the possibility of reporting the speech of another ego. This has consequences for his attitude

158

towards language. It is no longer possible to separate various levels of utterance, various ways of uttering, as the difference between direct, indirect and free indirect speech vanishes. Were he consistent in his approach, communication would, of course, become complicated. Indirect speech would not be affected, but it would no longer be translatable from or into direct speech. Thus, the indirectly reported promise of rescue made by the King to Humpty Dumpty would still be valid, but a directly reported one (the King has said to me: 'I shall send all my soldiers, and all my horses') would only appear to be a promise granted to the recipient by himself, but above all an incoherent text, with conflicting indexicals. And metalinguistic commentary, of which Humpty Dumpty is so fond, would become impossible, as the inverted commas would lose their function, and there would be no way of telling utterance from 'utterance'.

These are, however, idle imaginings, as these potentialities of disruption are not developed by Humpty Dumpty or Carroll. The point of the exercise seems to be elsewhere. Humpty Dumpty's collapsing various levels of utterance into a single stratum concerns the theory and practice of fiction. In a sense, fiction is reported speech writ large. Someone may say 'I' in a novel, but this creature will often turn out to be rather different from the author of the text – there is no need to go as far as Nabokov's *Pale Fire* to realise this. So that blurring the distinction between author, narrator and character turns all fiction into autobiography, and implicitly makes rather large claims on the relationship between fiction and reality. We may note here that such blurring is contagious, as Alice seems to accept that the referent of the 'I' in the quoted text can only be Humpty Dumpty.

It is not difficult to understand why this is. There is something of the puritan in Humpty Dumpty. If fiction were allowed, the difference between truthful and lying assertions would become fainter. *Ergo*, fiction must not be allowed. Whatever is uttered must be true or false. Or, if we leave the high moral tone and go back to philosophy, we will see a referentialist in Humpty Dumpty, who has no quarrel with assertions, but finds questions, orders and opaque contexts somewhat of a problem. If the word 'I', or indeed any indexical, is allowed to refer to persons or objects other than those present in the immediate context of utterance, in other words if the text is allowed to become separated from its spoken origin, confusion becomes rife – we shall inevitably find ourselves in the situation of the King of Hearts, the White Rabbit and Alice quarrelling about the poem that the Knave has or has not written. '*Je*' must, therefore, never be '*un autre*', not even in the innocuous form of reported speech.

There is, of course, irony in this. Creatures of fiction, as we have seen with Tweedledum and Tweedledee, have a natural tendency to deny the existence of fiction and lay claim to full existence – that the shadowy existence of Meinong's *quasi-Sein* should be insufficiently attractive, we understand. In this text, as in others, the distinction between reality and fiction will insist, or even obtrude, in a textual form. This is how the recitation ends:

> 'I took a corkscrew from the shelf:
> I went to wake them up myself.
>
> And when I found the door was locked,
> I pulled and pushed and kicked and knocked.
>
> And when I found the door was shut,
> I tried to turn the handle, but —'

There was a long pause.
  'Is that all?' Alice timidly asked.
  'That's all,' said Humpty Dumpty. 'Good-bye.'[57]

The abruptness of the ending reminds us of the difference between fiction and reality. For if this is fiction, the situation is frustrating, but also reassuring. There is a lacuna in the text, the end has been lost, and we shall never know what terrible deed ensues, as we shall never be certain of the solution to the mystery of Edwin Drood. Or, if the absence of an ending is a deliberate gesture on the part of the author, we shall be in an even better position: once we have understood that this is a metafictional joke, we know everything there is to know. In other words, the whole affair is deeply reassuring: communication is maintained, or only accidentally broken, and we are aware of the author's strategy. But if this is reality, as it is to Alice, the situation is rather disquieting. There are no lacunae in the text of life, and there is no possibility of an abrupt interruption, as long as the speaker is available for comment. This is why Alice asks 'Is that all?' – something unforeseen and unfamiliar has happened, the teller of tales has wilfully refused us the climax of his tale, that towards which all his narrative tended. We can only interpret this as an act of aggression, hence Alice's 'timid' question. Our worst fears are confirmed in the next line, when Alice is summarily dismissed from the presence.

This, of course, makes an important difference between fiction and reality manifest. The text of reality never ends – it can only end with the death of the subject that experiences it. In this case, the 'but — ' is not an ending at all, as the text continues in the exchange between Alice and Humpty Dumpty, which is entirely coherent, since there is no difference between reported text and reporting context. Whereas the text of fiction *can* end abruptly, and illegally, in the middle of a sentence. However, as is usual in nonsense, this sharp distinction, which the passage denies in order to reveal, soon becomes blurred again, as in *this* case a least, the abrupt ending of the text becomes the harbinger of the only end reality knows, the death of the speaker. This is the last paragraph of the chapter:

> Alice waited a minute to see if he would speak again, but, as he never opened his eyes or took any further notice of her, she said 'Good-bye!' once more, and, getting no answer to this, she quietly walked away: but she couldn't help saying to herself, as she went, 'Of all the unsatisfactory —' (she repeated this aloud, as it was a great comfort to have such a long word to say) 'of all the unsatisfactory people I *ever* met — ' She never finished the sentence, for at this moment a heavy crash shook the forest from end to end.[58]

In *this* context, the context of nonsense, reality and fiction are joined again. The ending of the text accompanies the brutal end of the extralinguistic situation. Humpty Dumpty's fall is announced twice: in the abrupt ending of his poem, in the interruption of Alice's exclamation which, like the poem, will never be finished (even if, in this case, we feel we could supply the missing words). And it was always already announced in the text of the rhyme that determines his fate. There is, of course, no 'reality' in all this, only the multiple layers of representation in a playful text. The chain of quoting has no origin and no end – like the chain of meaning: it is indeed the same chain. But because it is also the chain of dreaming (who dreams whom), perhaps reality will be invoked after all. We may then discover that, even as there is only a blurred separation between dream and reality, there is no telling where the text ends and where reality begins.

CONCLUSION

I would like to be able to say that this chapter has demonstrated the quality of the philosophical intuitions of the writers of nonsense, particularly Carroll, but if I can define a linguistic or pragmatic intuition more or less clearly, a 'philosophical' intuition is harder to define. In what sense can one 'anticipate' in philosophy, which presupposes that philosophy evolves and develops like a science? My usual argument seems to have lost its edge.

Yet there is little doubt that contemporary philosophers use the texts of Victorian nonsense as a source of situations and propositions to be quoted, commented upon, and variously exploited. In this sense the attitude of philosophers towards nonsense does not differ from that of linguists. With the added interest that philosophers, both analytic and continental, seem to find reading nonsense texts rewarding. So that, retrospectively, we can ascribe a lot of local intuitions to nonsense texts. In the fields of philosophy of meaning, philosophy of language and of logic (the theory of naming, the concept of definition), philosophy of action (what is intentional action?), nonsense texts raise questions that still fascinate philosophers. And, as usual, there is a sense in which nonsense is in advance of the current state of the art – the brand new discipline of philosophy of fiction or of literature has something to learn from a consideration of the workings of nonsense texts, not least *Alice's Adventures in Wonderland*. If I had to add one more field to prove my point, I would add that part of the philosophy of mind that is concerned with the question of personal identity over time – the Locke–Reid–Hume tradition. Perhaps we could add Carroll to the list, by reading the chapter where Alice loses her name and meets a fawn, who, no longer knowing who and what he is, is temporarily not afraid of a human child.[59] The theme is also present in nursery rhymes, where an old woman who has forgotten her name has lost her identity, and despairingly exclaims 'this is none of I'. In order to reassure herself, she seeks recognition from her dog, who of course fails to recognise her, leaving her with the conviction that 'she is not herself', a plight that also befalls Alice. We would have to note, were we to pursue the matter, that Carroll's solution – the solution of nonsense – is not, like Locke's, based on the persistence of memory, but on the continuity of a name. If the chain of baptism is interrupted, as it is in the wood without a name, the chain of person-states is also interrupted. The situation is, of course, complicated by the fact

162

that Alice is dreaming, so that we cannot claim a continuity of consciousness for her – Tweedledum and Tweedledee's paradox of the reality of dream and the dream of reality is again looming large.

The general conclusion must be, again, that the texts are plastic enough to be inserted in the philosophical tradition – particularly of Anglo-Saxon philosophy – and intuitive enough to enable us to raise questions about the present state of the art – even perhaps to go over to the other side ('There is another shore, you know, upon the other side./ The further off from England the nearer is to France – / Then turn not pale, beloved snail, but come and join the dance.')[60] The *dire/vouloir dire* dichotomy, as exemplified in the *Alice* books, lends itself only too readily to deconstructive manoeuvring and a Derridean reading. This, I suppose, is another consequence of the negative prefix in the name of the genre, as embodying the dialectics of subversion and support, which culminates in transversion. Nonsense transverts, in advance, the analytic philosophy that stems from the same intellectual tradition.

Perhaps there is more to it than this. The general aim of the dialectics of subversion and support is pedagogic. As she moves from perversion (of language) to inversion, conversion and transversion, Alice undergoes a learning process – she becomes a philosophical figure, the embodiment of the figure of the philosopher. Nelson Goodman once jokingly defined the philosopher as someone who does not know anything himself, but asks questions from others, and elicits from them a knowledge they possess but do not necessarily know they possess.[61] This, of course, is a classic description of the philosopher – this is Socrates questioning the young slave in *Meno*. Characters in nonsense often find themselves in similar pragmatic situations. Alice, an apprentice philosopher, falsely naive like all the members of the tribe, asks awkward questions (is it a tie or a belt?). Humpty Dumpty, a plump Socrates, overbearing like all the philosophers in their dealings with laymen, behaves towards her as if she were the young slave. Were I to air a little prejudice, I would even describe the scene as an encounter between a humble analytic philosopher and a continental prophet. Except, perhaps, that I am not entirely sure that humility is an intrinsic characteristic of analytic philosophers.

We can even take one step further. Nonsense texts represent, in the theatrical sense, the pragmatic position of the philosopher as professional asker of the wrong questions, and also, in the

163

intercourse between Alice and Humpty Dumpty, its transversion. They also make manifest the importance of a fundamental intellectual instrument of contemporary philosophy, the thought experiment (this is where, perhaps, nonsense is closer to the analytic side of the debate, which makes systematic use of thought experiments). Because nonsense lies outside the realm of common sense, *idées reçues* and the illusions of appearances, it can ask stupid questions, and represent idiotic or impossible states of affairs. This is the rationale behind a phrase I have often used to account for a nonsense situation: 'but in *this* case at least . . .'. The proverb, 'a cat may look at a king' is subverted in *Through the Looking-Glass*,[62] because it is uttered in a situation where the two opponents in the verbal struggle are, precisely, a cat and a king. In *this* case at least, the proverb does not function normally, as this is both the best and the worst context for it. The best because the two nouns have literal, not metaphorical, reference. The worst because this literalism precludes the generalisation from which the proverb draws its force. The phrase is in fact the indication that a thought experiment is going on – the objects of these experiments in the *Alice* books are the nature of language, of meaning, of personal identity, of communicative exchange. To prove my point, I could easily indulge in the inverse test: read the thought experiments of philosophers as nonsense tales. And truly, the thought experiments relating to personal identity, the Tweedledum and Tweedledee transplants of half-brains, Reid's brave officer who remembers storming the bastion but not being flogged for stealing a pear, the ship of Theseus in Hobbes's *De Corpore*, which gives birth to a double of itself, are all excellent material for nonsense tales. A ship is a ship is a ship, but in the case of the ship of Theseus at least, it is both itself and another ship. Here is perhaps the best definition of nonsense: *la philosophie en riant*.

4

THE POLYPHONY OF
NONSENSE

INTRODUCTION

So far, my approach to nonsense has been *synchronic*. I have
analysed the formal characteristics of a genre. The corpus of texts
was Victorian, but the object of the analysis was a timeless
language game, to be found anywhere and anywhen. What I have
conducted is the literary equivalent of a philological study of texts
from the point of view of *langue*, concentrating on the internal
coherence of the texts, on the rules and maxims that could be
derived from the corpus. The result is a structure, expressed
through a number of conceptual dichotomies: 'I speak language' v.
'language speaks', *agon* v. *irene*, subversion and support. We may
even go further, as nonsense is doubly concerned with synchrony.
Like all genres, it is the object of a synchronic formal analysis; but
being a genre that thematises the workings of language, a
metalinguistic genre, it welcomes synchronic analysis as particularly adapted to it. There appears to be a reflexive relation
between the constitution of the genre and the mode of its analysis.

Because of this, we can extend synchrony a little further, and talk
of the *achrony* of nonsense. Nonsense is not only a language game,
not only a mere name for a literary practice, but a concept. The
movement which goes from the word 'nonsense' to the concept,
the movement of all abstraction, is described by Lakoff and
Johnson under the category of 'ontological metaphor'.[1] The result
of this linguistic construction is an ideal object, viewed *sub specie
aeternitatis*, endowed with stability in time and extension. Various
objects will fall under it, sometimes unexpectedly, but the
substance will persist in spite of these variations. The cultural and

165

historical differences that affect various types of nonsense are contingent. But are they? It is true that widely different objects may be captured under the concept 'nonsense': Rabelais's verve, Shakespeare's taste for unlimited punning, or certain pages in Dickens, when the reader has the impression that the sheer pleasure of comic verbal excess takes over. Or again, the word 'nonsense' may be used to describe certain aspects of the work of the French Surrealists or the Russian futurists. But it is clear that such captures are always mythical, not an assessment of fact, but an intervention in a historical and cultural conjuncture. And there always will be an implicit restriction to 'our Western culture'. I may conceive of Russian, or Renaissance, nonsense, but is there any sense in talking of Japanese nonsense? Or would Grice's maxims of conversation hold among the Quechua Indians? The most determined achrony always finds its historical or cultural limits. Even if the achronic abstractions in question are established as conventional idioms or dead metaphors. Lakoff and Johnson's central metaphor, ARGUMENT is WAR,[2] although present in the languages we all speak, has little that is 'natural' about it. It does not reflect a property of the human mind, it is a cultural construct. As they themselves observe, one could construct an equivalent irenic metaphor, ARGUMENT is a COLLECTIVE WORK OF ART. The choice of *irene* over *argon*, or vice versa, is a historical choice, which tells us something about the culture that makes it.

Time and history are creeping back. The main symptom is the *anachrony* of nonsense. After all, the declared object of this book is the intuitions of Victorian nonsense writers – how literary practice anticipates theory. The possibility of such anticipation lies in a fundamental characteristic of language, best described in Kojève's reading of Hegel.[3] Language possesses the striking capacity to make error persist. A simple thought experiment will illustrate this. I look at my watch, see that it is 11.30, and write this down on paper. By the time I have done this, and look again at my watch, it is 11.31, so that my sentence, which purported to express a true proposition, is (always) already false. And the thing works both ways as, since I have not mentioned the date, the sentence will forever be true twice a day, including the day on which you read this. The situation inspired Lewis Carroll to state that, if he had a choice between a watch that was always a minute fast and another

THE POLYPHONY OF NONSENSE

that did not work at all, he would plump for the latter, since it gave the right time twice a day, whereas the former never did. There is more to this than a trivial account of the elusive nature of the present instant, the moment of consciousness. A theory of fiction emerges from this, where a fictional proposition can be not only an entirely fictitious, because imaginary, one, but a delayed truth turned into an error, or an anticipatory error waiting to turn into a truth. Language has the strange capacity to make its monsters survive. That is the difference from Nature, where, Hegel says, monsters soon disappear – calves with five legs have a short life expectancy, and no issue. Whereas linguistic monsters, under the polite name of fiction, increase and multiply.

This is of interest to us because of the notorious teratology of nonsense. Not only does the genre provide a breeding ground for monsters like the Jabberwock and the Snark, but it is also rife with coinages, fallacies, paradoxes and absurdities of all kinds, that is with all the varieties of error that the human brain can devise and language allows. The interesting point is that these monsters are the main source of the intuitions of the genre, of its power of anticipation. Like history, linguistic consciousness progresses the wrong side up. So the function of this type of literature is not only to read philosophy (which was the implicit claim made in the last chapter), thus reversing the usual relationship of exploitation, but to read it *in advance*. Nonsense is anachronic because it blurs the question of the origin of the philosophical theses it anticipates: it is the anoriginal illustration of theoretical theses, the 'truth' of which was still dormant at the time. There lies the profound 'originality' of such texts.

There is an easy way out of this quandary, out of the contradiction between on the one hand the achrony and synchrony of nonsense and, on the other hand, its anachrony. I shall call it, if you will pardon the coinage, *syntopy*. Nonsense is seen to have cultural and historical limits because it has geographical ones. This is the old theme of the Englishness of English nonsense. Only mad dogs and Englishmen can enjoy and understand nonsense (here you may sense a slight resentment on the part of a foreign author, who feels excluded from the game). The problem, of course, is that this 'national psychology' of the English, if it is not an illusion, can only be accounted for by reference to the historical conjuncture. So history is back: the appearance of Lear and Carroll there and then cannot be a sheer piece of luck, the blooming of one aspect of the English genius. For the question immediately arises of why this talent has waned since, or at least not persisted in the same glorious fashion. An attempt at grounding this 'sense of nonsense' in the characteristics of the English language, in its analyticity (an analytical, as opposed to a synthetic language, is one in which most morphemes are also words that can be used in isolation, ready tokens for a game with language), or its plasticity (English is well known for its massive use of conversion, the device whereby a word can change its part of speech), is also bound to fail. Behind those characteristics of language, historical processes are concealed: I have attempted to account for this type of linguistic history under the concept of 'corruption'.[4] The English language, like all others, is a locus for the remainder work and the process of historical corruption. In this it reflects, or refracts, historical conjunctures.

Nonsense, therefore, is more than a language game: it is a *chronotope*. The term comes from Bakhtin, where its meaning is so wide as to defy precise definition:[5] it denotes the intrinsic connectedness of temporal and spatial relationships that are expressed in literature, something like literary forms of intuition. This, for Bakhtin, is the locus for the relationship between the work of art and reality, which goes beyond simple mimesis. I would like to explore the anti-realist, but also anti-formalist intuition that the concept expresses: there is no simple reflection of reality in the work of art, but there is no linguistic closure either. We can understand this by again using a comparison with the characteristics of language. Bakhtin has a distinction between propositions, which exist in *langue* as potentialities of meaning, and utterances, which actualise those potentialities in a given situation or conjuncture. The failure of structural linguistics, and of formalism, is due to their choice of propositions as objects of study. This makes them miss the polyphony of texts. Only the utterance has full meaning, and its structure, its relationship with the context of utterance, with reality, is given by the chronotope. Envisaged in this way, the chronotope is not a reflection (of a historical period, of the *Zeitgeist*), but rather the locus for the plurality of voices and points of view to develop. Language,

168

Bakhtin says, is not only a system of abstract grammatical categories, but also an 'ideologically saturated' worldview.[6] In the phenomenological terms of Bakhtin's early work, we could say that reality is the *horizon* of the utterance, a horizon that is not a source of reflection, but a receptacle for the polyphony of conflicting voices that will find their way into the text. The chronotope is the name for this relationship.

It is possible to claim, therefore, that there is a chronotope of nonsense, as there is for Bakhtin a chronotope for the Roman family. The contradiction between achrony and anachrony in nonsense is the expression of this chronotope: it can be viewed as a manifestation of the *chrony* of nonsense, i.e. of the anchoring, which is not a reflection, of Victorian nonsense in a cultural and historical conjuncture. If nonsense, because of its intuitions and anticipations, is able to look towards the future, it is because it has a present and a past.

There is, therefore, a *diachrony* of nonsense, which is the object of this chapter. Since it is not the diachrony of reflection (where nonsense would reflect society, and Victorian nonsense Victorian Britain), we shall attempt to develop three aspects: (a) Nonsense has an *intertext* – it is a characteristic of nonsense texts that they are always secondary, always after-the-event rewritings of other texts, hence the importance of parody in the genre. The chronotope emerges in this distance between the nonsense text and the text it parodies. (b) Nonsense also has a *tradition* – a mythical, fictitious tradition, created *a posteriori* (like all traditions) to justify the texts, to organise their polyphony into a mythical chronology. (c) Lastly, nonsense texts are the locus for a *polyphony of discourses*: this multiplicity of voices refracts (to us Bakhtin's term, which he carefully distinguishes from 'reflects') the historical conjuncture, by anchoring nonsense in ideology and its apparatuses. The result of this diachronic study is that nonsense will appear in the light of a *narrative*, in the sense of Lyotard.

PARODY

The nonsense chronotope does not reflect, it refracts. This is not merely distortion, but also inscription. A nonsense text literally inscribes other texts through ironic quotation – this is the distance of parody. Metaphorically, it inscribes elements of the extra-linguistic world within itself, but of course elements already translated into words and discourse. The literal is the medium of the metaphorical: it is because nonsense inscribes texts that it inscribes reality – in the guise of discourses. Because this is a little abstract, I shall give an example of this inscription of the extralinguistic. 'Wonderland', that archetypal garden for nonsense characters to frolic in, is not a place, not even in the sense in which, in other chronotopes, geography is metaphor. I am thinking, of course, of the novels of Thomas Hardy, or of Graham Swift's *Waterland*. Bakhtin has a page on such 'local cults', which manifest the emergence, within literature, of a new feeling for time and place – he analyses such a chronotope in Goethe.[7] But Wonderland is no such place as Wessex or Goethe's mountains. It has a more abstract quality. It is instead a *textual locus*, the scion of a literary tradition of Gardens of Eden that goes from *Paradise Lost* (Adam and Eve's bower) to Frances Hodgson Burnett's *Secret Garden* (which has been adopted as a cliché by the English language). It is also a *linguistic universe*, which deploys the abstract space of games, a chessboard for instance, and the immaterial, or linear, space of embodied words. Such a space is aptly represented by the flatness of the playing cards in *Alice's Adventures in Wonderland*. There lies the difference between Lewis Carroll and the mawkishness of Kingsley's *Water Babies*, or conventional Tolkieneries (as I seem to remember Peter Conrad once wrote, the world of Tolkien is 'the West Midlands blown up into a universe'). Parody is the name for this type of inscription, for this internal distance, for this abstract chronotope. That it is all-important in the genre of nonsense is obvious: parodies are very frequent in nonsense texts, which they sometimes punctuate (as is the case with *Alice's Adventures in Wonderland*), and they are the privileged locus for the dialogue between the author and his child readers. I shall distinguish between two types of parodic intertext in nonsense. The first is parody proper: if I may say so, a *textual* intertext, ascribed by an erudite footnote to a specific author. The second is pastiche, where the ascription of authorship is blurred or impossible, where the parodic distance is even greater – pastiche is the parody of a parody, where the style, the clichés, the slips of the pen are recognised as somehow 'other', but no name can be given to this other. Pastiche is the result of what we might call blurred Morellism, from the name of the nineteenth-century Italian art critic who revolutionised the techniques of attribution by deciding that one was not to look for the obvious, i.e. shape, colour or composition, but for the details, which escaped the conscious intentions of the painter, and betrayed his touch the more surely. In pastiche, the details are there to tell us that the text has a model, except that the ascription fails, as they do not all point in the same direction (the usual definition of pastiche is 'a patchwork', of words or sentences from other authors).

As an example of nonsensical parody, I shall consider Carroll's 'I never loved a dear Gazelle', a parody from a well-known passage in Thomas Moore's 'The Fire-Worshippers'. Here is the original:

> Oh! ever thus from childhood's hour,
> I've seen my fondest hopes decay;
> I never loved a tree or flower,
> But 'twas the first to fade away.
> I never nursed a dear gazelle,
> To glad me with its soft black eye,
> But when it came to know me well,
> And love me, it was sure to die!

That this amply deserves burlesque is obvious (there is another well-known parody of it by C.S. Calverley). Carroll is not particularly lenient. Here are the first two stanzas:

> *I never loved a dear Gazelle* –
> Nor anything that cost me much:
> High prices profit those who sell,
> But why should *I* be fond of such?

> *To glad me with his soft black eye.*
> My son comes trotting home from school,
> He's had a fight but can't tell why –
> He always *was* a little fool![8]

The 'theme and variation' aspect of this text enables us to distinguish parody from pastiche. The italicised initial lines are straightforward quotations (except for the substitution of 'loved' for 'nursed' – the parodied text is etymologically vulgarised, it undergoes distortion by going through the collective memory of its vast readership), which are the objects of a process of inversion through punning (the farcical 'black eye' is a good instance), that is through recontextualisation of their original meaning. Thus, the 'never' of the first line, having lost the 'but' that modifies it in

Moore's text, becomes the bearer of absolute negation: not 'all the gazelles I loved died', but 'there is no gazelle that I loved'. This becomes cheekily explicit at the beginning of Carroll's fourth stanza, which goes: 'And love me, it was sure to dye/ A muddy green, or staring blue.' A similar process occurs in Calverley's version, which combines inventory (a list of unlikely animals is provided: I never nursed a gazelle, but I had a parrot, etc.) with ironic inversion, the catastrophe being not that the animal dies, but that it lives to a state of advanced dotage. The advantage of parody is that we know where we are. In this it is like irony, at least according to the trivial definition (irony is inversion of meaning). Once we have grasped the language game we are in, meaning becomes easy to compute, through a maxim of parody or irony, which gives rise to implicatures. The text works according to recognisable dichotomies: parodying/parodied; comic/serious; in it a voice can be heard, which controls the meaning, the voice of the author.

But Carroll's text goes further than this, into what I call pastiche. In Moore's poem, a voice is speaking. As a result, the text is unified in diction and feeling, and we understand Bakhtin's criticism of poetic texts as monological. Not so in Carroll's text, where the displacement of the theme introduces different variations in each stanza, with the consequence that we no longer have a single voice, but a polyphonic babble (in the first stanza a miser is speaking, in the second a parent). The only unity of the text is textual rather than pragmatic: in the regular form of the stanza, but also in the recurrent querulousness of the tone, which seems to indulge in a form of hysteria (witness the stressed word in the last line of both stanzas). This excess of feeling is what characterises Moore's gushing sentimentality. The process is, of course, helped by the semantic disruption which is due to the grossly materialist, matter-of-fact contents of Carroll's text. Sentiment is destroyed by reference to money and bodily accidents, so that the reader is reminded that a dead gazelle is not only an occasion for mawkish tears, but also a stinking carcass. The sheer excess of Carroll's verve (in which he shows himself to be an admirer of Dickens) is what subverts the unifying control of the authorial voice, what liberates the multiplicity of discourses. This is the *pasta* of pastiche: an ungodly and excessive mixture, the source of a textual *fuite en avant* whereby the text escapes the control of the speaker and the words take over.

My opposition between parody and pastiche has its origin in Barthes. In his *S/Z* we find a theory of parody, but with paradoxical consequences for my dichotomy.[9] According to Barthes, there is a non-trivial link between parody and irony: parody is irony at work. It operates through a simple rule of inversion, it is easily recognisable, even blatant (*la parodie s'affiche*), and substitutes another controlling voice, the parodist, for the voice of the original author. What it does is '*mettre les codes ventre en l'air.*' Such topsy-turvydom does not change the nature of the text: 'codes', even when 'belly up', retain their usual functions − only this time these are made manifest. The parodying text, therefore, is strictly monological: the redoubling of the authorial voice reproduces the relation of property the author has over her meaning, and the propriety of the text. Parody, he concludes, is '*une parole classique*'. This classicism he opposes to the multiplicity, to the polyphony, the undecidability of *écriture*, the kind of writing that escapes the control of the author, and can no longer be ascribed to a voice. The texts produced by such writing he calls 'multivalent'. They blur the dichotomies of the original and the derived, the comic and the serious, the true and the false, which parody supports (the falsity in parody lies in a Gricean exploitation of authorial meaning). The multivalent text breaks down the unifying control of the author, rejects recognition, refuses to label itself or the texts it works with or on. In so doing it liberates the polyphony of writing.

Barthes's hostility to parody is misguided, at least as far as nonsense is concerned. What I have called pastiche has two contradictory characteristics. On the one hand it belongs to the genre of parody − pastiche, as the parody of a parody, needs parody as the mistletoe needs the oak. But on the other hand, it corresponds to Barthes's *écriture*, and what I have tried to show is that 'I never loved a dear Gazelle' is a 'multivalent' text. My contention is that Carroll's text is merely a clearer version of nonsense parodies, in that it separates parody (the theme) from pastiche (the variations). But nonsense parodies, even if they mix the two aspects, are always caught up in the hysteria, or the verve, of pastiche; they always are the locus of a multiplication of words, discourses or points of view. In fact, all nonsense texts − this is a defining characteristic of the genre − are parodies in this sense. I shall come back to this later in the chapter, in 'The Institution of Nonsense'.

In Chapter 8 of *Through the Looking-Glass* the White Knight sings a song, in order to comfort Alice. It is long, he says, but very very beautiful, and it either brings tears into the hearer's eyes or else, he adds, it doesn't. The title, or name, of the song is rather complicated, but the important point is that the tune is his own invention. None of this is true, as Alice soon recognises the tune as one she knows already, and the reader recognises the poem as a parody of Wordsworth's 'Resolution and Independence'. Here are the first three stanzas:

> I'll tell thee everything I can:
> There's little to relate.
> I saw an aged aged man,
> A-sitting on a gate.
> 'Who are you, aged man?' I said.
> 'And how is it you live?'
> And his answer trickled through my head,
> Like water through a sieve.
>
> He said 'I look for butterflies
> That sleep among the wheat:
> I make them into mutton-pies,
> And sell them in the street.
> I sell them unto men,' he said,
> 'Who sail on stormy seas;
> And that's the way I get my bread –
> A trifle, if you please.'
>
> But I was thinking of a plan
> To dye one's whiskers green,
> And always use so large a fan
> That they could not be seen.
> So, having no reply to give
> To what the old man said,
> I cried 'Come, tell me how you live!'
> And thumped him on the head.[10]

In 'Resolution and Independence', the old man is a leech-gatherer reduced to poverty by the scarcity of leeches, and the only survivor of a family which once comprised a wife and ten children. The poet meets him in a mood of deep dejection, and the meeting has a cathartic effect, as he confides in a letter to Sara Hutchinson, where he gives a running commentary on the poem:

I describe myself as having been exalted to the highest pitch of delight by the joyousness and beauty of Nature and then as depressed, even in the midst of those beautiful objects, to the lowest dejection and despair. A young Poet in the midst of the happiness of Nature is described as overwhelmed by the thought of the miserable reverses which have befallen the happiest of men, viz Poets . . . . I can *confidently* affirm, that, though I believe God has given me a strong imagination, I cannot conceive a figure more impressive than that of an old Man like this, the survivor of a Wife and ten children, travelling alone among the mountains and all lonely places, carrying with him his own fortitude, and the necessities which an unjust state of society has entailed upon him.[11]

And this is the crucial meeting with the leech-gatherer, which occurs in the middle of the poem. To the poet's question, 'What occupation do you pursue?' the old man answers this:

He told, that to these waters he had come
To gather leeches, being old and poor:
Employment hazardous and wearisome!
And he had many hardships to endure:
From pond to pond he roamed, from moor to moor;
Housing, with God's good help, by choice or chance;
And in this way he gained an honest maintenance.

The old Man still stood talking by my side;
But now his voice to me was like a stream
Scarce heard; nor word from word could I divide;
And the whole body of the Man did seem
Like one whom I had met with in a dream;
Or like a man from some far region sent,
To give me human strength, by apt admonishment.

My former thoughts returned: the fear that kills;
And hope that is unwilling to be fed;
Cold, pain, and labour, and all fleshly ills;
And mighty Poets in their misery dead.
– Perplexed, and longing to be comforted,
My question eagerly did I renew,
'How is it that you live, and what is it you do?'[12]

In the wake of Carroll's take-off of Wordsworth's mannerisms, it would be only too easy to note the comic potential of the poet's failure to listen to the answer to the question he himself has asked, and to remember that part of the poem was included in D.B. Wyndham Lewis's anthology of bad verse, *The Stuffed Owl*. This would be unjust to a poem that rather successfully fulfils a complex task. The old man is an objective correlative for the poet's mood, the real subject of the text, which enables us to interpret the poet's absent-mindedness in less unfavourable terms. More important, the old man is seen as a moral emblem, whose status has textual grounding in a paronomasia indirectly but vividly suggested by the text: the leech-gatherer's moral resolution and independence, in spite of the plight 'an unjust state of society' has reduced him to, evoke a political revolution and independence, the model for which is not far. In this light the choice by Wordsworth of this deliberately simple and down-to-earth poetic diction becomes a reflection of his revolutionary views about language and poetry, whose task is 'to speak a plainer and more emphatic language', in order to 'retrace the revolutions not of literature alone, but likewise of society itself'. No wonder such a language, 'though naturally arranged and according to the strict laws of metre [should] not differ from that of prose' (all quotations are from the Preface to *Lyrical Ballads*).

This is not a commentary on Wordsworth's poem, only an attempt to take it seriously. And, in a way, this is what Carroll does too. For a start, his is a double parody. The tune that Alice recognises is 'I give thee all, I can no more', a love lyric by Thomas Moore, the metrical pattern and rhyme scheme of which Carroll follows – his poem, therefore, is a portmanteau parody, in which the authorial voice is blurred, not only because there are now two parodied authors instead of one, but because the parodying voice itself becomes uncertain. This is a love poem offered to Alice by Carroll as both the White Knight and the aged aged man (who, in Tenniel's illustration, is a carbon copy of the White Knight), the bearer of an affect strong enough to emerge into print, but so unsayable as to remain repressed in the indirection of the text. And this is also a parody of Wordsworth's stylistic idiosyncrasies, in which the usual inversion of parody can be felt, as the incongruity and matter-of-factness of Carroll's poem ruin the Romantic poet's revolutionary pretensions and make them appear in the light of narcissistic pretentiousness. The result of all this, of course, is pastiche – a polyphony not of voices, but of discourses, or rather of

seemingly individual voices that actually embody social discourses. Thus, Carroll's poem intermingles his own voice with the
voices of Wordsworth, Moore, and 'the people', of Alice as the
addressee of the love poem, of the Knight, the aged aged man and
the leech-gatherer. Not persons of course, hardly individuals, but
personae whose points of view are never completely fused. This,
again, is the hodge-podge, the *pasta* of pastiche. And the discourses
of which those personae are the bearers are all social: the discourse
of the Romantic poet is part of the historical development of
subjectivity, the discourse of 'the people' part of the history of the
constitution of this ontological metaphor into a political force; the
take-off of the revolutionary language of the people is part of the
history of political and literary reaction to the revolution in
language and politics (as exemplified in Canning's savage attack on
Southey in *The Anti-Jacobin*). Not a babble of inane voices, but a
polyphony of historically relevant, because historically constituted, discourses.

We can derive a theory of texts from this account of nonsense
parody. A text is conceived as a *singularity* that *expresses* other texts.
I draw here on an intuition of Bakhtin's, who compares a text to a
monad,[13] in so far as an utterance is separate, and yet refracts, in
actual or potential dialogue, all the other utterances in the same
sphere. The metaphor has its limits, of course, since a monad has
neither door nor window, and only pre-established harmony
allows it to express (that is to realise its potentialities in unfolding)
or represent other monads – this goes far beyond Bakhtin's
concept of a text that is eminently open to intercourse and
dialogue. But the concept of expression allows us to go beyond the
mere reflection of the extralinguistic, and makes us take Bakhtin's
term, 'refraction', more seriously. Refraction implies not representation as mimesis and reproduction, but both linkage and
distortion – it produces some kind of image, but not a straightforward mimetic image. Consequently, expression (by a text, of
other texts) has three main characteristics: (a) the text *qua*
singularity expresses all the other singularities (monads) in its field
(in its dialogic catchment area); (b) it also expresses, that is refracts
and works on, the relations between those singularities – a text,
especially a parody, is not dialogic only because it sets up a
dialogue between itself and the parodied text, but because it

registers, and inscribes in its own space, the dialogues between other texts (in the case of 'The Aged Aged Man' the dialogue between Wordsworth and his poetic predecessors, as well as the dialogue between the progressive Romantic poet and his reactionary parodists); (c) it also expresses the background, historical and institutional, to those relations, i.e. it refracts not only elements in the field, but the structure of the field itself – nonsense parodies are interested in problems of genre, because genres are like concretions of the structuring of the discursive field. There is a programmatic aspect in this, as (a) corresponds to a *citational* intertext, which is the object of the next section, (b) to a *discursive* intertext, analysed later, in 'The Discourses of Nonsense', and (c) to the institutional background of the *genre* of nonsense, the object of 'The Institution of Nonsense'. Before I go further, however, I would like to illustrate this theory of the text as simply as I can, with a phrase, a metaphor and a figure. The basic idea is indeed simple. There is nothing new under the sun, and a new text is constructed with odds and ends from other texts. The French language has an apt phrase for this: *'faire du neuf avec du vieux'*. Hence the metaphor of the text as radio set, which catches several programmes at the same time, so that the discourse we pick up and interpret is heard over a background of interference. The commentary of our football match is interspersed with fragments of Mozart and of a political speech in Albanian. This is illustrated in Figure 4.1.

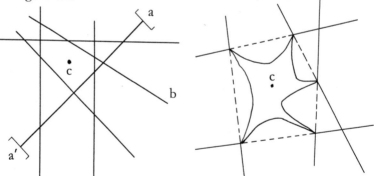

Figure 4.1 The field

Figure 4.2 The singularity (an enlarged version of point c in Figure 4.1)

The text as singularity is a point in the field of discourse in which it emerges (this field is defined by a historical conjuncture): point c in

Figure 4.1. Around it there are social discourses, represented by lines (b in Figure 4.1): not individual texts, but discourses, carried by language in the shape of clichés and *idées reçues* for instance. Such discourses can be defined in the same way as Lévi-Strauss's myths, as imaginary solutions to contradictions in reality. That they do not float freely in the ideological atmosphere but are anchored in reality is shown by the anchoring points a and a' in Figure 4.1 (that there should be two such anchoring points for each discourse is understandable: the discourses are contradictory or, in Bakhtin's terms, dialogic). The anchoring points are institutional, institutions being defined here as sites for the production of social discourses (the interesting consequence of the figure is that an institution does not produce its own singular discourse – that a discourse is always the product of a dialogue, or a clash, between institutions). Lastly, and this is Figure 4.2, the text as singularity is a *point of attraction*, which attracts and refracts (hence the substitution of curves for dotted lines) the neighbouring discourses. The text so conceived is the locus of a work of inscription it turns a multiplicity of discourses into a unity, it distorts in order to shape. The rest of this chapter will be a detailed commentary on this figure.

THE INTERTEXT OF NONSENSE

I am moving from the local intertext of parody (already made rather complex by the passage to pastiche) to the global intertext of a genre. The question raised here is that of the historical constitution of nonsense as a genre through the invention of a tradition. For the monologism/dialogism dichotomy must not be the object of a value judgement, but the occasion for a dialectical process. As Bakhtin notes,[14] consciousness is not only a place for dialogue but also the site of a monologising process, as the polyphony of dialogue is gradually 'forgotten' into monological unity, a unity which in turn will take part in a new dialogue and become dialogic. Individual texts are caught in this process, which is the condition for their survival in what Bakhtin calls 'long term temporality'. Genres, on the other hand, are not the subjects but the results of such a process – they are constituted by it. Thus, nonsense as a genre is the weaving together, into a tradition, of two different, even opposed, threads, one literary, the other folkloric, one poetic, the other childish, one 'high', the other 'low'.

The opposed threads produce naturally dialogic, or contradictory, texts – texts that capture this contradiction in some sort of unstable and provisional unity. In nonsense, this dialectic of monologism and dialogism is inscribed in the very name of the genre. I take the negative prefix as both a symptom of the dialogism of the genre, of its two divergent orientations, and of the inscription of the historical conjuncture in which the genre was formed. On the one hand, non-sense is to be taken not so much as the trace of a cognitive judgement ('I assert that there is no sense in this text'), but rather as an elliptic exclamative, calling for dialogic response. Not so much the recognition of an absence as the defiant and provisional formulation of a value judgement, calling for contradictory response, as when Alice, irritated beyond what she can possibly bear by the Wonderland characters' quirks and absurdities, exclaims: 'Stuff and nonsense!' This is no absence of sense but a calling for the sense that the answer will provide – in this, literary nonsense is only the manifest staging of the language game of sense, at least as defined by Bakhtin: 'sense can be assimilated to response. It is always the answer to a question.'[15] On the other hand, nonsense bears the mark of a conjuncture, of the moment when two generic threads, one low or 'folkloric', the other high or 'literary', pass from the external dialogue of rejection (of the low by the high) to the internal dialogue of mingling into a new genre. This is why nonsense can be treated as a discourse, that is a line in my figure, a myth in the sense of Lévi-Strauss: the imaginary solution to a discursive contradiction, itself dependent on anchoring points in the reality of society, in other words an already mediated contradiction between what Bakhtin calls 'discursive genres', i.e. groups of relatively stable utterances. The modernity of nonsense lies in the fact that the blending of those contradictory genres is not effected through an inversion of value (where the low comes to oust the high from its position of dominance), but through a transversion. We shall now analyse this transversion of values, of the natural hierarchy of genres.

We shall start with the initial situation, with the historical conjuncture out of which nonsense emerged. Incipient nonsense – the name of course precedes the object – definitely belongs to the low aspect of the contradiction, and as such is subject to rejection.

This is how Addison, in *The Spectator* of Tuesday, 10 April 1771, describes the genealogy of true and of false humour:

FALSEHOOD	TRUTH
NONSENSE	GOOD SENSE
FRENZY – LAUGHTER	WIT – MIRTH
FALSE HUMOUR	HUMOUR[16]

What is striking in this is that the main characteristics of Victorian nonsense – its sense of excess, or frenzy, its rejection of the cognitive element of truth for the falsehoods of exaggerated, because over-imaginative, fiction, its difference from mere wit, are all present, only under a moral cloud. Here, there is no question of substituting the amiable playfulness of the imagination for truth and good sense: from top to bottom, nonsense falls under the moral condemnation of falsity as a sin. One is reminded of the Puritan father who allowed his daughter to sing 'Hey diddle diddle, the cat and the fiddle', as there was nothing false in it, but not 'the cow jumped over the moon', an impossibility and therefore a lie. There is a trace of this moral condemnation in the rejection of metaphor by Victorian nonsense – as we have seen, metaphors are false, blatantly so. From such condemnation was nonsense born, not by inversion (falsity is better than truth) but by transversion, by leaving the semantics of truth value for the pragmatics of dialogue, where falsity is only a provisional step, like truth, in a chain of statement and response.

But transversion must go through a stage of historical subversion, where the dominance of the dominant discourse is questioned. If the first sense of the negative prefix was rejection, exclusion and domination, the second is subversion and defiance, where the low becomes of equal importance to the high, the comic to the serious, the nonsense of triviality to the sense of the literary canon. The historical moment of this subversion occurs in nineteenth-century Britain, through the rediscovery of the national past. In the wake of the Romantic revaluation of popular culture and language it was realised that such childish trivia as nursery rhymes and nonsense tales were monuments of the English national past. In his short text on the *Bildungsroman*,[17] Bakhtin evokes this discovery of national folklore whereby a whole range of genres, folk tales, songs, sagas and legends became respectable – with them the time

181

of local folklore (the *Ur*-time of archaism) invaded the chronological time of literary history. Victorian nonsense is very much part of this process, as witnessed by the career of J.O. Halliwell, who edited the first collection of nursery rhymes and tales, *The Nursery Rhymes of England*, in 1842. The constitution of nursery rhymes as a literary corpus, which his collection achieves, anticipates the emergence of nonsense – it has also contributed to it. Halliwell, not unlike the brothers Grimm in Germany, brought to the task all the seriousness and authority of the scholar – he began his career as a Shakespeare scholar – and aimed to produce a scientific edition of the nursery rhyme corpus, even if he sometimes confused the antiquary with the scholar and it has since been proved that he made up a few of his rhymes. The interest of Halliwell lies in his explicitly ethnographic tendency, much influenced by the contemporary development of philology in Germany. Even as words bear the traces of the history of the language, nursery rhymes and folk tales, whose ancient origin he sets out to demonstrate, bear the marks of the cultural history of the English nation, a national history open to nationalistic manoeuvres, as those texts, being treated as negligible, have escaped the cultural domination by the French invaders and their courtly culture, and bear witness to the culture of our Saxon ancestors. Their very lack of literary sophistication or elegance becomes an asset, as it turns them into 'the natural literature of Great Britain', faithful to its humble origins. That such history is entirely mythical is obvious – it is closer to the novels of Walter Scott than to actual historical events. But the process of subversion has begun – high literature is no more valuable than the folk productions of the people. Of course, nonsense is not yet a positive term – Halliwell's strategy is to ascribe the present superficial nonsense of nursery rhymes to the work of historical corruption: who could have thought, he says, that those rhymes were ever anything but unmeaning nonsense? Nevertheless, by devoting his time to such nonsense, Halliwell takes part in the creation of the genre, that is in the invention of a tradition by the promotion of dominated texts.

The lineaments of the genre emerge in the discursive genres that helped to form it. To cut the story short, Victorian nonsense can be said to have a number of folk origins: the nursery rhymes of children and the counting rhymes of shepherds (there is a long and well-established tradition for the likes of 'eena meena mina mo'); animal tales and fairy tales, the British equivalent of the tales collected by Perrault and the brothers Grimm; limericks, envisaged here as an example of the comic poetry of the pub, the brothel and the racecourse – the tradition of bawdy songs is infinitely rich, even if the origin of limericks, a clean, not a bawdy, origin, is obscure, and has nothing to do with the town of Limerick; lastly, school rhymes, like those collected by the Opies,[18] which can be said to be the link closest to literary nonsense, because of the ironic distortion they impose on the rather tame rhymes of the nursery.

To grasp the complexity of the historical process, I shall concentrate on the nursery rhymes. Halliwell is only a turning point in an age-old tradition of oral transmission (the first nursery rhymes were written down in the early eighteenth-century; they started being 'collected' with Halliwell; and the definitive edition of the corpus was the Opies' *Oxford Dictionary of Nursery Rhymes*, published in 1951).[19] Let us consider the history of one of the best-known rhymes, 'London Bridge is broken down', as reconstructed by the Opies. Its first appearance in writing is in 1726, in Henry Carey's *Namby Pamby or A Panegyric of the New Versification*, a satire on the mawkishness of nursery rhymes, which has made a gift of the first word in its title to the English language. An allusion to it can be found in a comedy published in 1659. The rhyme was sung in the course of a game, mentioned by Urquhart, the translator of Rabelais, in 1653. The game itself is evoked by Rabelais and was extant in France as far back as 1328; lastly, it seems that the rhyme alludes to ancient pagan rites, whereby a newly built bridge had to be protected from the anger of the gods by the sacrifice of a child, walled up in one of the piles. The line 'Set a man to watch all night' thereby acquires sinister overtones.

The Opies' detective work of reconstruction is admirable. It produces a *nachträglich* (retrospective) history of the corpus that overcomes the philological obstacles of the diversity of periods (few, if any, rhymes can be traced as far back as 'London Bridge'; quite a number are contemporary), the uncertainty of origins (some rhymes refer to specific historical events, like 'Little Jack Horner', which alludes to the dissolution of the monasteries; some refer to the archaic time of myth and magic), the complexity of the sources and the difficulty of their identification. The corpus appears

183

as a melting-pot, an easy prey for Halliwell's ideological manipulations, by which he seeks to turn the aggregate of singular texts into a monument to the national past, by finding Nordic origins for the rhymes and treating them as linguistic documents – the Opies' detective work is the literary equivalent of the detective work of the German grammarians who reconstructed Indo-European.

But if we consider the corpus of rhymes from the point of view of production, as a text, we find a formidable machinery for textualising the oral past, for turning sense into nonsense (which is only the mirror image of the interpretative process of making sense out of nonsense which I analysed in the case of Ettelson). Nursery rhymes are formed through *distortion*, as the history of 'London Bridge' shows, a process of corruption whereby historical events, practices or texts disappear, but not without leaving a trace. Sometimes this distortion takes the form of *extraction*: the nonsense of the rhyme is due to the fact that it is a quotation separated from the context that gave it its meaning. Or it takes the form of *censorship*. The Opies tell us that 'Elsie Marley is grown so fine' alludes to an eighteenth-century prostitute, which gives quite another sense to the lines 'She lies in bed till eight or nine/ Lazy Elsie Marley.' Lastly, it is formed by *absorption* whereby myriad texts, written for other purposes, are reappropriated by the nursery after being suitably doctored. What we have here is a rewriting machine, the textual equivalent of the work of corruption in language, which captures a wide range of meaningful texts, separates them from their historical and textual context, and de-semantises or re-semantises them for the purposes of the nursery. Victorian nonsense is the same textual machine that has turned literature, i.e. that has passed through one further stage, where the work of corruption becomes reflexive, in the two senses that it becomes deliberate, and that it it brought to bear on the corpus itself, to produce 'clever' out of 'primitive' nonsense. This is the stage reached with school rhymes – the last stage before the nonsense of Carroll and Lear and their direct, almost explicit, inspiration. For in the corpus of school rhymes collected by the Opies, the voice of literary nonsense is already clearly heard. Here is how the archetypal speech at the end of the school year by one of the school governors is parodied:

> Ladles and Jellyspoons,
> I stand upon this speech to make a platform,

184

The train I arrived in has not yet come
So I took a bus and walked.
I come before you
To stand behind you
And tell you something
I know nothing about.[20]

But Victorian nonsense results from the fusion of two main threads: it also has a literary source. However, there is a difference. Even if reinterpreted after the event, the folk origins of nonsense may be said to follow the usual chronological order. The filiation which goes from nursery rhymes to school rhymes to literary nonsense is fairly straightforward. First there were nursery rhymes, then there was *Alice's Adventures in Wonderland*. First, there were proto-limericks, like those collected in *The History of Sixteen Wonderful Old Women*, published in 1820, then there was Edward Lear. Not so in the case of the literary origins of nonsense: the tradition is blatantly an *a posteriori* creation of the contemporaries of Lear and Carroll. The best instance of this is an essay published in 1888 (the year of Lear's death) by Sir Edward Strachey, an old friend of Lear's. The essay is tellingly entitled 'Nonsense as a fine art'. The objective of the text is clear – it is a kind of literary obituary, a celebration of a dead friend, whose work must be rescued from the all too easy accusation of triviality and childishness. Strachey reaches this self-imposed goal by showing that nonsense, far from being the childish or popular practice that its name seems to indicate, has a long and venerable tradition in the canon of English literature. The negative prefix in 'nonsense' acquires a new twist – it refers not to a negation but to a change in direction. The philosopher Gilles Deleuze widely puns on the directional meaning of the French '*sens*': here, nonsense means following the literary canon the wrong way, not by retracing the literary history of the genre, but by working one's way against the historical current, from Lear back to Chaucer, so as to allow a 'natural' reading of the newly established tradition, from Chaucer up to Lear. Thus, Edward Lear is given a host of glorious predecessors: Chaucer's 'Nonnes Preestes Tale', Shakespeare's Falstaff, Milton, Swift, Sterne, Lamb and Tennyson. The inventory even includes, *horresco referens*, Bunyan, who is not known for frisky mischievousness. This historical tradition is supported by the extension of nonsense to all fields of writing and art, as

185

Strachey discovers nonsense in theology (in uneasy jokes about the devil) and in the visual arts (for instance in the British art of caricature). It is easy to dismiss this as mythical in a trivial sense, a genealogy as doubtful as that of Addison. Strachey's essay, however, does show that literary nonsense cannot be entirely separated from its literary past – the thread of high literature does contribute to its variegated texture.

My interest is not in the tradition of nonsense that Strachey outlines – being all inclusive, it is difficult to assess; yet it manages to be idiosyncratic, even quirky sometimes (with the inclusion of Bunyan and Milton – I am not impressed by the nonsensicality of the character of Satan). My interest lies in the process of transversion, whereby high and low are fused into a single genre. Rather than looking at the history of authors of proto-nonsense, from Skelton to Sterne, I shall consider two examples, the first of which shows nonsense at work in a mimetic text, Dickens's *Little Dorrit*, whereas the second illustrates the inscription of high literature, in this case Tennyson, within a nonsense poem.

The reason for my choice of *Little Dorrit* is, at first sight, incidental. One of the characters in the novel, Sparkler, has, in characteristic Dickensian fashion, a phrase that he incessantly repeats, like a signature. The phrase is 'a fine girl, with no nonsense about her'. The first half of the phrase may vary, the second never. This is a typical satirical trait, with hardly anything to do with my concern, nonsense as a genre. However, the novel also contains two other characters, the contents of whose discourses are rather high in nonsense. The first, Flora, on whom the hero was sweet when a child, and who constantly reminds him that she is now available and willing, is afflicted with a kind of logorrhoea in which we easily recognise the best of Victorian nonsense:

> Though indeed, she hurried on, nothing else is to be expected and why should it be expected, and if it's not to be expected why should it be, and I am far from blaming you or anyone. When your mamma and papa worried us to death and severed the golden bowl – I mean bond but I dare say you know what I mean and if you don't you don't lose much and care just as little I will venture to add – when they severed the golden bond that bound us and threw us into fits of crying on the sofa nearly choked at least myself everything was

changed and in giving my hand to Mr. F. I know I did so with
my eyes open but he was so very unsettled and in such low
spirits that he had distractedly alluded to the river if not oil of
something from the chemist's and I did it for the best.[21]

In this we recognise the linguistic excess that takes Dickens's verve
beyond the intelligibility of the merely comic into the incoherence
of nonsense. The character herself comments that 'she is running
into nonsense'. This character is often seen in the company of a
chaperon, an aunt of her late husband, who usually sits silent, but
sometimes breaks into incoherent aggressiveness, addressed to no
one in particular, but uttered in a tone of mingled earnestness and
malevolence:

> She now underwent a violent twitch, calculated to produce a
> startling effect on the nerves of the uninitiated, and with the
> deadliest animosity observed: 'You can't make a head and
> brains out of a brass knob with nothing in it. You couldn't do
> it when your Uncle George was living; much less when he is
> dead.'[22]

This goes beyond an acute psychological observation of the
eccentricity of madness, beyond even the exaggeration of caricature, for which Dickens is justly famous – this is the world of
Edward Lear's limericks, of the senseless animosity of the 'they',
or the world of the characters in Wonderland, with their gruff
aggressiveness. And the role of nonsense in the novel (other
instances could easily be mentioned) shows that the triviality of
meaninglessness has been adopted by and adapted to the seriousness of the mimetic novel, both as a theme (nonsense is the
symptom of eccentricity or madness) and as a literary device –
nonsense is one of the forms in which aesthetic pleasure, the
pleasure of writing, is experienced. In the passage from the one to
the other, the transversion of the low into the high, of the high by
the low, is achieved.

My second example is Lear's sonnet, 'Cold are the crabs',
originally published in *Teapots and Quails*, a posthumous
collection:

> Cold are the crabs that crawl on yonder hills,
> Cold are the cucumbers that grow beneath,
> And colder still the brazen chops that wreathe
> The tedious gloom of philosophic pills!

For when the tardy film of nectar fills
The ample bowls of demons and of men,
There lurks the feeble mouse, the homely hen,
And there the porcupine with all her quills.
Yet much remains – to weave a solemn strain
That lingering sadly – slowly dies away,
Daily departing with departing day.
A pea green gamut on a distant plain
When wily walruses in congress meet –
Such such is life —[23]

What interests me here is not the obvious nonsense of the text – the explicit allusion to Tennyson ('Calm is the morn without a sound,/ Calm as to suit a calmer grief,/ And only through the faded leaf/ The chestnut pattering to the ground': *In Memoriam*, section 11), the ironic reference in 'the tedious gloom of philosophic pills' to the philosophical and moral pretensions of Tennyson's poetry, or the ruining of the high moral theme of the parodied text by the grossly material reference to food (I would like to interpret 'chops' not only as part of the human head, but as edible flesh). What interests me here is the blank in the last line, a blank both easily recoverable and unbearable since some later editions of the poem have treated it as an accident in the manuscript and spelt it out:

'Such such is life – the bitter and the sweet.'

This, I think, is a mistake. We have a blank, not a conventional (even if ironic) moral ending. The blank is the 'upholstery button', to speak like Lacan, whose absence of meaning gives meaning to, and at the same time, if you allow the coinage, 'unmeans', the whole sonnet. This blank is the ultimate nonsense, the point where meaninglessness has contaminated and dissolved even the material texture of language. Yet, because the phrase that fills it is entirely predictable, even imposed by the structure of the text's rhyme scheme and prosody, it is also the ultimate, the most determinate sense. This absence is a fulfilment, this blank is full of words. As such it is the emblem not only of the dialectics of sense and nonsense which constitutes the genre, but also of the relationship between nonsense and its intertext – a denial which turns out to be a Freudian negation, as the sense denied on the surface of the text comes back in the multiplication of intertextual traces.

One might expect the intertext of nonsense texts, becaus
lack of sense, or because of their humble origins, to be p
least local, when the texts are explicitly parodic. In
superficial glance at the corpus gives the impression
emergence *ex nihilo*. Suddenly, in the middle of the nineteenth-
century, in Victorian Britain, nonsense was there, and predecessors can only be found *a posteriori*, through a *nachträglich*
construction. I have tried to show that such is not the case. The
intertext of nonsense is not only parodic, but global: the threads,
and the names they carry with them, soon multiply, and nonsense
is seen to have its source in a variety of texts, whether they be the
products of folk culture or of high literature. It is also seen to spill
over into other contemporary texts, like Dickens, and to take on a
new role in a new context. I can suggest two theoretical accounts
of this situation. First, the nonsense writer can be seen in the light
of an ephebe in the sense of Harold Bloom,[24] who ironically reads
his predecessors. But this would keep the relationship too
individual, too subjective: Lear would be Tennyson's ephebe,
whose parodying stance hardly conceals the deepest reverence (his
biographers tell us that this was actually the case – not only did he
illustrate Tennyson, but he would recite his poems in public, with
tears streaming from his eyes – 'Cold are the crabs' is only a
compensatory inversion of this sentimental relationship). Sec-
ondly, the emergence of a new genre can be seen, in the light of
Bakhtin's writings, as the monologisation of old dialogues (the
various threads of the global intertext) into a unified text, the unity
of which is constitutively unstable, and which is re-dialogised
through insertion into new dialogues (with contemporary texts).
Thus, Lear's sonnet inscribes the older dialogue between high
literature – it is a regular sonnet – and folk texts – it childishly deals
with victuals and belongs to the genre, popular in both senses of
the term, of the comic poem, a scion of the comic song. The
constraints of the sonnet genre and the pastiche, with the unity of
tone it implies, unify the text. But this unity is unstable, as is
materially indicated by the blank at the end of the poem. And the
parodic aspect of the sonnet introduces an explicit Bloomian
dialogue with the contemporary text of Tennyson, showing not
only that nonsense is receptive to its literary context but that, by
playing the critical role its very name evokes – this is the fourth
meaning of the negative prefix in 'nonsense' – it is prepared to
contaminate serious poetry and change it. There is little doubt that

the evolution of mainstream poetry from Tennyson to Eliot would not have been the same without the influence of nonsense. This Bakhtinian account, however, impels me to go further in my analysis of the intertext of nonsense. So far, the intertext was either explicit (parody as a relation between two authors, two names) or explicitly literary (even the folk sources of Victorian nonsense are literary texts in the sense that they are fiction). But the dialogue is much wider than this – it includes the anonymous, not always literary intertext of discourses.

THE DISCOURSES OF NONSENSE

Patchwork

In his essay on the genres of discourse,[25] Bakhtin produces an account of the 'complete utterance' as determined by the simultaneous occurrence of three factors. The first is the exhaustiveness of meaning (the utterance has a theme, and the contents of the utterance, from the point of view of meaning, must form a whole – I stop when 'I have had my say'). The second is the author's intention of meaning – we must be aware of the discursive purpose, the will-to-say of the author; this is the subjective element of the utterance, which combines with the objective element of the contents. The third is the constraints and form of the genre: the speaker is not entirely free in her utterance, she adapts it to the social context by selecting a genre that constrains what she is saying. It can be argued that in nonsense, because of the specific constraints of the genre, the first two elements are present, but deconstructed. There is indeed a dialogue between author and reader: the reader recognises the will-to-say of the author, the fact that he means to say what he says. She also recognises the paradoxical contents of this intention of meaning, as we saw in Chapter 2: he means to say nothing, or he means not to mean. This paradox, however, deconstructs the first two factors of the complete utterance. From 'the theme is the absence of a theme', one easily drifts towards 'nobody is speaking', 'nobody is making sense'. Even if the text has an author, he seems to have relinquished his responsibility and privileges – in other words his authority. And the two factors are deconstructed in yet another sense. Since nonsense texts are usually parodic, two other dialogues interfere with the author–reader, authorial and authoritative, dialogue: the dialogue between the two texts, the parodying and the parodied, and the dialogue between the nonsense text and the codes, in the sense of Barthes, around which the text is woven. This deconstruction means that both the theme of the utterance and the intention of the speaker are at best secondary and at worst non-existent (one should rather say they have dissolved). The result is that the third factor, the generic constraints, comes to the forefront: they are thematised and become the true theme of the text, and the voice, or voices, that are heard in it. This is the specific polyphony of nonsense. Because the text says nothing, the empty shells of discourse multiply, and the text says everything, becomes the bearer of a potential infinity of meaning – the blank in Lear's sonnet could in fact be filled by any sequence of words that would respect the metrical constraints (or perhaps even exploit them). This is why the metaphor of the radio set is apt: there is a specific receptiveness of nonsense texts, which is the mirror image of their semantic emptiness. Lack of sense is only the reverse side of excess of sense.

We understand now the importance that the opposition between *irene* and *agon* holds for the genre. Conversation, dialogue and verbal struggle are the explicit or surface manifestation of the constitutive dialogism of the text. They indicate that the text, like any utterance in a dialogue, aims at obtaining a response. Only the utterance, as opposed to the proposition, has full meaning, because it expects a response. This is the basis of Bakhtin's theory of dialogism and polyphony. Language is unified only in so far as it is an abstract grammatical system; from within this abstract grammatical language there emerges a concrete historical language, harbouring a multitude of worlds, of literary, ideological and social perspectives. Nonsense as a genre is like language in this: from within the abstract formal characterisation of the genre, a multitude of discourses, of literary and ideological perspectives, develops. Bakhtin, as we have seen, opposes the monologism of poetry to the dialogism of the novel. In poetry, only one voice is speaking, so that even the duality of meaning in a metaphor must be ascribed to a single voice, not to the dialogue between two voices (this is not far from the classic Aristotelian definition of genres, where the lyrical is characterised by the dominance of one voice, the lyrical I, and the epic by a mixture of voices, the narrating and the narrated). Nonsense as a genre cuts across this divide, since nonsense texts are both poetic and novelistic (from this point of view the tale is a short novel). This is understandable in Bakhtin's terms, since among the sources of the novel's dialogism, he ascribes a particular role to parody (the parodied text opposes an internal dialogic resistance to the interventions of the parodist) and to laughter. Nonsense poetry is never straightforwardly lyrical. This is another reason why nonsense texts should, as we have seen they do, shun metaphor: metaphor is too monological for them.

I shall give an example of the dialogism of poetic nonsense: Carroll's *The Hunting of the Snark*. This 'agony in eight fits' has always had a marginal position in the nonsense corpus, as influential critics, like Elizabeth Sewell,[26] have claimed that it takes itself too seriously in its evocation of death and ontological meaninglessness to be successful nonsense. Take, for instance, this Homeric simile, much disapproved of by Sewell:

> And my heart is like nothing so much as a bowl
> Brimming over with quivering curds![27]

The usual way of ruining the seriousness of poetic metaphor – a reference to the gross materiality of food – is used here in an ambiguous fashion. This is both something like Housman's parody of a Greek tragedy in translation and something distinctly close to a genuine simile. Nonsense, argues Sewell, should not play such games; it should be more clearly parodic. But I have tried to argue that pastiche, because it is dialogic, because it multiplies the voices and discourses, is not that explicit – it can accommodate a straightforward discourse and its parodic inversion. The word 'Homeric' was not used at random: the tone of *The Hunting of the Snark* is ambiguous because the poem is a nonsensical rewriting of a classical epic. There are numerous reasons why I am able to assert this. The eight fits are so many cantos, and the leitmotiv stanza ('They sought it with thimbles, they sought it with care;/ They pursued it with forks and hope;/ They threatened its life with a railway-share;/ They charmed it with smiles and soap') fulfils the same role as the notorious Homeric tags. The theme of the quest is an acceptable, even a usual one for an epic, and all the commonplace situations are there, in their usual order. The first fit gives us the traditional epic list of weapons and *impedimenta*, not unlike the celebrated description of Achilles' shield in the *Iliad*, although in this case what is lovingly described is the Baker's luggage. The second fit has the great speech before the battle, where the Bellman, in a parody of Nelson, describes the five unmistakable marks by which one can tell a Snark. The third fit has a prophecy – the tragic fate of the Baker is announced. The fifth has a scene of friendship between the Butcher and the Beaver, which reminds us of Achilles and Patrocles, and the sixth has the premonitory dream in which the Snark appears to the Barrister. Lastly, but most tellingly, the seventh fit has the Banker descend into Hell and back, in the best tradition of Ulysses and Aeneas. The result is a Victorian epic in a condensed form – it takes a few hundred lines, not many thousand.

There is, of course, a catch. A *Reader's Digest* version of an epic is hardly an epic, rather a burlesque of an epic. And the style mixes the serious and the comic to such an extent that the unity of the epic language is ruined. Worse even, the epic is a national poem where the nation is embodied in the person of its mythical founder, who is the hero of the poem. But there is no Aeneas in this *Aeneid*: each fit, and each *locus classicus*, has a different hero, as my summary shows. The only common points between them is that they are all members of the expedition, and that their names all begin with a B (the second criterion is more important than the first, as it is the reason why they were included in the crew). The would-be eponymous hero, the Snark, is remarkable only for its absence: it is present in the Bellman's description, in the Barrister's dream, and in the very last lines of the poem, when the Baker shouts, as he vanishes into thin air, that he has espied one. So there is both a multiplicity, an excess of heroes, and an absence, a lack of hero (this contradiction is embodied in the two names of the Snark, who is both excluded from membership of the crew, *qua* Snark, and potentially included in it, *qua* Boojum – note that the lethal form of the Snark, the Boojum, is the one whose name begins with B). The result of this is that we have not so much a burlesque of an epic as an explicit, or rather a reflexive, epic, one which brings its structure, the conventional techniques of composition that characterise the genre, to the fore. This is evident when we leave the text and find out the order in which the poem was composed by Carroll. A 'natural' way of going about it would be to follow the King of Hearts's advice and 'begin at the beginning', each situation following its predecessor because it is its logical or narrative consequence. But this is not what happened with *The Hunting of the Snark*. For the first line that came into Carroll's mind, out of the blue, before he knew what the creatures were or what the poem was about – perhaps even that there would be a poem – was the last line: 'For the Snark *was* a Boojum, you see.' We now know that this was inspired by the reading of some conventional children's verse written by one of his relatives.[28] But the important point here is that the composition of the text began with the last line, followed by the last stanza, followed by the rest of the poem. One would like to think that the poem is a looking-glass text and that the first fit to be completed was the eighth. This, we do not know. But what we do know is enough to show that *The Hunting of the Snark* is an epic in reverse, which takes the trivial definition of irony as inversion literally. As such, the poem is the locus of a complex dialogic activity: between the parodying text and a multitude of parodied texts (it is a parody not of a specific epic, but of a genre), between the language of High Romantic poetry (it is possible to construct a bona fide interpretation of the text as the lyrical expression of existential *angst*)[29] and the language of nonsensical debunking. The multiplicity is embodied in the character of the Snark, a free-floating signifier if ever there was one.

What I have suggested in this section is a Bakhtinian account of nonsense, according to the cardinal concepts of polyphony and dialogism. That this is a construction is obvious – but every tradition, as we saw in the case of Strachey, is a construction in this sense. What I have been suggesting is just another myth, a more apt one I hope. Indeed, Bakhtin's work, apart from his main concepts, provides elements for a theory of nonsense in his book on Dostoevsky,[30] in two places – in the pages devoted to carnival, and in his account of Menippean satire as a central genre in the constitution of the dialogic novel. Carnival is the embodiment of the negative prefix in 'nonsense' – it says no, locally and temporarily, to order and hierarchy, not least the hierarchy of the comic and the serious. And a complex network of similarities of detail emerges from a comparison between the texts of carnival literature and nonsense texts – to see an ancestor of nonsense in Rabelais, in spite of obvious and crucial differences, is not so difficult, mostly in his attitude to language. More generally, the four unmistakable marks of carnival, as given in the Dostoevsky book, topsy-turvyness, eccentricity, mismatching and profanation (one example of which is the parody of sacred texts) make full sense in the universe of nonsense. And since Menippean satire is the main carnivalesque genre, its formal characteristics will remind us – but also, interestingly, fail to remind us – of nonsense. The Dostoevsky book lists fourteen characteristics, some of which are nonsensical (the dominance of the comic over the serious, the phantasmagoria of the imagination, the themes of madness and eccentricity, the multiplicity of styles), and some not (the realism of the underworld, which recalls *The Beggar's Opera* rather than *Alice's Adventures in Wonderland*; the fantastic and the representation of Hell; the interest in contemporary political problems). The paradoxical conclusion is that there must be, and there cannot be, a filiation between Menippean satire and nonsense. There must be, because the universe described, the universe of carnival, is the same, and nonsense is the forgetful heir of a certain type of medieval literature (the texts that are closest to Victorian nonsense, true nonsense *avant la lettre*, are the French *fatrasies*). And there cannot be, not only because no concrete historical filiation can be traced, but because the contextual meaning of the same elements has radically changed – there is, for instance, nothing revolutionary about the topsy-turvy world of Victorian nonsense, and no attempt at sacrilege. Nonsense is not even a de-semanticised, non-political version of Menippean satire – it is rather the mythical repetition of the literature of carnival. Bakhtin reaches the same conclusion for the dialogic novel: the field of contemporary literature is strewn with the rubble of what he calls medieval or Renaissance 'grotesque realism'. Like the dialogic novel, but more insistently, nonsense has used this for its building materials.

Discourses

The text of nonsense is a patchwork – the pieces are of various origin, different materials, variegated colour. They are not only literary pieces, odds and ends of forgotten genres, borrowed bits extorted through parody – they are also echoes of the various discourses that made up Victorian culture. Nonsense texts are resonant with clichés, *idées reçues*, preconstructed thoughts. This is where nonsense fulfils, in classic Marxist terms, an ideological function. It has no ideology itself (there is no specific ideological position defended in nonsense texts) but it is one of the vectors of Victorian ideology, one of the forms through which, within certain ideological apparatuses, the Victorians experienced an imaginary relationship with the real conditions of their lives. Using the theory of the text adumbrated above, I shall try to illustrate the inscription within nonsense of Victorian discourses on language, fiction and logic, the natural sciences and madness. The list is not exhaustive – I have restricted myself to the types of discourse whose presence in nonsense is most 'natural', even if not entirely direct – it is natural, for instance, that medical ideas about madness should work their way into a genre which disclaims sense, even if they have to pay the price of distortion.

Language

In this book so far, I have insisted on the linguistic and metalinguistic intuitions of nonsense, on Carroll's capacity to anticipate the discoveries of later grammarians. But Lewis Carroll also read, or knew, the main linguists of his time, so that the state of grammatical knowledge is inscribed in the texts of nonsense – the influential work of John Horne Tooke, Richard Chenevix Trench and Max Müller can be said to have found its way into nonsense. To put it briefly, Victorian discourses on philology and language revolve round three *topoi*: the instrumental nature of language – the main use of language is communication; the imperfection of language, as natural languages fail in their attempt at smooth communication; and, contradictorily, the powers of language over the human mind and over culture. The first two are linked, and can be traced back to Locke, the third is a more recent contribution of the Romantics. All three pervade the texts of Victorian linguists, all three have left traces in nonsense. Here is Trench, whom Carroll had read, and who was perhaps the most popular linguist of the time, his *On the Study of Words* a classic worthy to be included in the Everyman Library:

> The imperfection which cleaves to our forms of utterance, to men's words and to their works, will make itself felt either in the misapprehensions of those to whom language is addressed (as in John III, iii), or by the language itself.[31]

Since Trench was dean of Westminster and later archbishop of Dublin, the tone is understandable. But the moral reprobation of the imperfection of language, as allowing lies and fiction, as a symptom of the Fall, is widespread, so that the mainstream view of language is deeply contradictory. On the one hand language must be preserved as a means of communication, but on the other hand it is made unfit for this task by its own imperfections and by allowing speakers to abuse as well as use it ('this falseness of words, whereof man accuses them, this cheating power of words, is not of their proper use, but only of their abuse').[32] A similar point is made by Max Müller, who taught at Oxford and whom Carroll knew, in his theory of metaphor as a disease of language. For Müller, metaphor is the source of myths and superstition. This is how he defines myth: 'Every case in which language assumes an independent power, and reacts on the mind, instead of being, as it was intended to be, the mere realization of the mind'.[33] The metaphorical power of language is the main source of such excess. Müller, having discovered a concrete etymology for the Latin word *nihil*, *ne-filum*, 'not a thread', proceeds to describe how metaphor has turned this inexistence into an existence (this is what one, nowadays, calls an 'ontological metaphor'), that is a metaphysical reality, nothingness, *le néant*, which comes to play a crucial part in philosophy and religion (under the form of 'Nirvana' for instance). 'What speculations [he exclaims], what fears, what ravings, have sprung from this word Nihil, a mere word, and nothing else.'[34] Metaphor, therefore, is the symbol of the imperfections that obfuscate language and make it of limited use as an instrument of rational communication. We understand once more why nonsense texts are shy of metaphor, why their consistent exploitation of other, less deadly, imperfections of language, like ambiguity, is, like a joke according to Freud, both local and temporary – why the very possibility of the dissolution of language is made to bear witness to the necessity of upholding its instrumental function. However, we have seen that in this dialectics of subversion and support, transversion follows conversion. This can also be seen in Victorian theories of language: Müller's denunciation of the evils of metaphor soon turns into a celebration of its poetic power; Trench's disapproval of the imperfection of our forms of utterance is only too easily changed into the expression of wonder about the force of language and the power of words. So that Trench's conception of language is not only post- but also pre-lapsarian: language after Babel has not lost all its pristine, Adamic, glory:

197

Words exercising so great an influence as they do, resuming the past, moulding the future, how very important it needs must be, that, in naming any significant fact or tendency in the world's history, we should give it its right name; since it is a corrupting of the very springs and sources of knowledge, when we bind up not a truth, but an error, in the very designations which we employ.[35]

Thus, says Trench, the name 'love child' applied to illegitimate offspring is one such error – the name may have prevented some unfortunate woman from resisting the appeal of sin. Male chauvinist prejudice is only the outer garment of a modernised form of Cratylism (the theory of the natural, or motivated, link between word and referent), the best, and most critical, version of which we have encountered in the conceptions of language held by Humpty Dumpty. Again, this shows the extent to which the linguistic anticipations of nonsense are rooted in the contemporary discourse on language – the dialectic of innovation and tradition is merely another version of the dialectic of subversion and support. I shall end this section by pointing at the presence, in the works of Lewis Carroll, of three vital threads of the Victorian discourse on language. The first is *etymology*, which was still of paramount importance to nineteenth-century linguists (it has now retreated into undeserved obscurity). Horne Tooke, for instance, built a whole system of language on dubious etymology. But the interpretative mania which characterises the thorough etymologist is also a striking characteristic of the creatures evoked in nonsense texts – Humpty Dumpty is again the obvious example. And the whole genre provokes the same mania in the reader – we are made to look for meaning with the same wily indirection that inspired speculative etymologists. The second is *Anglo-Saxon*. We know that the famous introductory stanza to 'Jabberwocky', perhaps the best known of nonsense texts, was first published by Carroll under the title 'A Stanza of Anglo-Saxon Poetry'. Anglo-Saxon philology at the time of Carroll was not only an essential subject, but also a field of scientific controversy (in the 1830s Oxford was the scene of the great Anglo-Saxon debate, in which Oxford professors, characteristically enough, defended out-of-date positions against the great German philologists). Carroll's nonsense is a more literary version of the work of the brothers Grimm, who collected fairy tales but also produced original work in philology ('Grimm's law') – if the grammarian is also a teller of tales, no wonder the teller of tales should become a folk linguist. The third is the *dictionary*. The interest that authors of nonsense have always shown for coinages (like the two words in 'Jabberwocky', 'galumph' and 'chortle', that have found their way into the OED), and for lists of words (like Lear's nonsensical alphabets) is another echo of a Victorian preoccupation with the making of dictionaries. Victorian England is, as is well known, the great era of dictionaries – not only Gilbert Murray and the *New English Dictionary*, but also the Greek lexicon of Liddell and Scott (the real model for Alice, Alice Liddell, was the daughter of the great lexicographer – there is perhaps more to this than coincidence). All three threads are inscribed in the first stanza of 'Jabberwocky' – this it is that turns these lines into an emblem of the genre: the Anglo-Saxon origin, the etymological bend of Humpty Dumpty's explanations, and the coinage of new words for which a dictionary definition will have to be provided. The most innovative of texts is also the one most steeped in contemporary culture.

Fiction and logic

There is a sense in which nonsense is a metanarrative genre, an intuitive, proto-reflexive view of fiction. In turn, this capacity for intuition is due to the genre's intimate relation to logic. The relation is not only subjective (in the case of Lewis Carroll), but also objective. The negative prefix indicates a relation of Freudian negation to the rules of sensible discourse, that which provides the bounds of linguistic sense, logic. And the wild imagination of nonsense is bound to exploit, and thereby make manifest, the constraints imposed on propositions by categories and logical form. Here is an excellent instance of this: an influential essay by the logician P. Alexander[36] shows that the impossible events in *Alice's Adventures in Wonderland* can be said to be the logical consequences of the first narrative proposition expressed in the tale, that there is a white rabbit who pulls out a watch from his waistcoat pocket and exclaims: 'Oh dear! Oh dear! I shall be too late!', if we reflect on the workings of the basic operation of material implication. The truth table for '$p \supset q$' tells us that the compound proposition is true in all cases, except when 'p' is true and 'q' is false. The consequence of this is that if 'p' is false, then '$p \supset q$' is true whatever the truth value of 'q'. If the first proposition in the tale is false (from the point of view of our world, we can consider it blatantly so), and if the relation of consecution with the other propositions that make up the tale is interpreted as one of material implication, then the tale can accommodate the wildest false propositions, i.e. the wildest nonsense, and remain 'true'. Of course, we have gone far beyond the boundaries of ordinary logic, and I have been playing on the words 'proposition', 'implication' and 'true'. But this shows that there is a natural link between logic (as a discourse on truth and falsity) and fiction. Take, for instance, the conception of false ideas, of chimeras, in, say, Locke and Leibniz. For Locke a chimera is obtained by the undue composition of simple ideas, the model for which is the centaur, or the nonsense coinage, like the Bread-and-butter-fly. The falsity of the compound idea does not reside in the idea itself (since the constituent simple ideas are straightforward) but in the undue attribution of existence to it. Centaurs do not exist – in other words, there is a distinction between fiction (where centaurs are welcome) and lying (where they illegally claim access to reality). Leibniz draws the boundaries elsewhere: for him, everything that is possible is real, and the false is self-contradictory. The status of fiction has changed: it is not a coiner of semi-lies, of second-order tall tales that can be forgiven only because they confess their ineptitude, but a creator of possible worlds, which, with the best possible world, reality, form a pyramid with a clear apex and a base lost in infinite distance. Nonsense hesitates between Locke and Leibniz. Wonderland is a blueprint for an imaginative possible world, one of those fictional worlds that are called 'salient' because they are sufficiently distant from our world for us to enjoy the exoticism. At the same time it is peopled with Lockean chimeras, eager to destroy the coherence of this salient world, to denounce its flimsiness, to show its linguistic origin, so as to prevent it from acquiring depth (the playing cards in *Alice's Adventures in Wonderland* are an emblem of this), to reduce the rich imaginative life of Wonderland to the incoherence of madness as described by Locke, that is to the temporary abandonment of common sense. Nonsense is both the name for the wildest imagination and the mirror image of common sense.

But in spite of this hesitation, nonsense, a true product of the venerable tradition of British empiricism, even if it is in a 'contrariwise' manner, as Tweedledee might say, is closer to Locke than to Leibniz, closer to the reduction and exclusion of the wildly imaginative as an aberration of the senses. This clearly appears in the inscription of Carroll's own discourse about logic into his nonsense texts. As a logician, Carroll was a reactionary. He was a contemporary of Boole, whose work he ignored, but his own conception of logic was strictly Aristotelian – he devoted his energy to a refinement of the theory of syllogism. Nowhere is this more apparent than in his theory, in which he is faithful to Aristotle, of the existential import of universal affirmative propositions.[37] The idea is that the truth of a universal affirmative (all men are mortal) entails the truth of the corresponding particular affirmative (there is at least one man who is mortal) – universal affirmatives are not merely concealed hypotheticals, they make an ontological claim as to their subjects. Modern logic has developed in the other direction, by severing the logical proposition from the ontological statement. This logically reactionary position, however, causes problems for the nonsense writer Carroll also was. He is best known, as a logician, for the inventiveness of his examples. His syllogisms are peopled with sharks dancing the minuet, green-eyed kittens and wise young pigs that fly in balloons. But such figures only appear in universal negatives ('no wise young pigs go up in a balloon'), which do not make any ontological claims – they never appear in their affirmative counterparts. This is where Locke wins – the negative prefix, here interpreted literally, makes sure that nonsense remains in the margins of sense, in etymological ex-centricity, and does not threaten to develop into an infinity of possible worlds all somehow connected to ours. The world of nonsense is closer to us – it is part of our world, which is the only world – and much further, being separated from us by the impassable barrier of negation, whose concrete embodiment is madness.

Nonsense, therefore, inscribes within its text the philosophical discourse on fiction and reality, as well as the technical discourse of logic. In the work of Lewis Carroll, because of his Janus-like identity as both logician and teller of tales, the inscription is reciprocal. *Alice's Adventures in Wonderland* fictionalises the discourse of logic (we could take Alexander's argument one step further, and say that the tale is the logical consequence of an Ur-proposition which turns out to be a universal negative: 'No white rabbit takes a watch out of its waistcoat pocket and exclaims: "Oh dear! Oh dear! I shall be too late!" '), and the sorites, those protracted syllogisms that were one of the main objects of Carroll's interest (he suggested new methods for solving them) logicise the literary discourse of nonsense – each sorite is an incipient Wonderland.

Natural history

The Victorian period is the great era of natural history, both because of the scientific progress that was made in the course of it (the name of Darwin is the symbol of this) and because of the popular success it enjoyed: railway trips to the countryside to observe the life and habits of insects; collections of butterflies which were so important to their owners that they sometimes painted the markings of the rarer specimens on to the wings of their more common brethren; the tourist attraction of fossil-hunting in the cliffs of Dorset; and the universal interest in the feats of explorers. That such a socially pervasive discourse should have found its way into the unlikely texts of nonsense is not so difficult to understand. In the case of Edward Lear, there is a subjective reason for this. He began his career as an animal painter in the tradition of Audubon, and his first published book was entitled *Illustrations of the Family of Psittacidae* (1832). Consequently, natural history is a direct source for his nonsense – the characters in his longer poems often go on explorations, and he is the author of a nonsense flora, in which the Latin names that Linnaeus provided for plants become the sources of inexhaustible nonsense. I would like, however, to make a more ambitious claim, and show that the discourse of natural history is present in the genre as a whole, even in Lewis Carroll, who had no special interest in the subject. There are two themes which nonsense borrows from natural history: exploration and taxonomy. The reader of *Alice's Adventures in Wonderland* is in the position of an explorer: the landscape is strikingly new, new planets swim into his ken, and a new species is encountered at every turn, each more exotic than the one before. Nonsense is full of fabulous beasts, mock turtles and garrulous eggs. As we read the text, we experience the same sense of wonder that Charles Darwin felt when exploring the Patagonian wonderland. There are indeed pages in *The Voyage of the 'Beagle'* that read like Carroll. Here is Darwin on the guanacos:

> That they are curious is certain; for if a person lies on the ground, and plays strange antics, such as throwing up his feet in the air, they will almost always approach by degrees to reconnoitre him.[38]

We can understand the guanaco's wonder – this is its first encounter with British nonsense in act. And it is a comfort to us that the famous scientist should behave like Lear's 'old man of Port Grigor', who 'stood on his head, till his waistcoat turned red'. The inscription of nonsense works both ways – the inchoate discourse of nonsense is already inscribed in the naturalist's behaviour, and in his description of the fauna he meets; witness his encounter with an irascible lizard, whose tail he has just been pulling, like an overgrown schoolboy:

> At this he was greatly astonished, and soon shuffled up to see what was the matter; and then stared me in the face, as much as to say, 'What made you pull my tail?'[39]

If the reader of nonsense tales is an exploring naturalist, the heroine, Alice, is the fictional equivalent of Mungo Park in the interior of Africa. Mungo Park is one of the last Europeans who saw Africa as it was before colonisation. This is because he used to travel without the accompaniment of a regiment of colonial troops, unlike the 'pilgrims' in Conrad's African tales. As a result of this, he was treated by the natives with a mixture of astonishment and contempt – not least because of the paleness of his skin. Alice is in the same position as Mungo Park – she is in the power of those strange creatures, and must obey their orders, even if she is secretly convinced of the superiority of her own world; they, in turn, treat her as a 'fabulous monster', even as the Africans sometimes mistook Mungo Park for a ghost. Alice, therefore, is the nonsensical reincarnation of the traditional figure of the British explorer *qua* traveller, a figure that disappeared with imperialist colonisation – *Alice's Travels in the Interior of Wonderland*.

The second form which the inscription of natural history within nonsense takes is taxonomy. The Victorian age is the great age of taxonomy. The intellectual instruments for it (the Linnaean classification) are fully mastered, and the task is to make an exhaustive inventory of the fauna and flora of the world. This is the age when the eager entomologist will be immortalised by giving his name to a number of species or subspecies. But the Victorian age is also the great age of collections. No longer the bric-à-brac of curios that antiquaries used to gather haphazardly, but the systematic organisation of a field of knowledge within a closed space, either private or public – the Victorian age is also the age of museums. Nonsense texts inscribe the discourse of taxonomy in their own terms. We have already noted the taste they evince for lists of carefully numbered items (according to Elizabeth Sewell the motto for the genre is 'one and one and one'), and a German critic has noted the contemporaneity of the emergence of the genre and of the development of museums.[40] The museum is the equivalent of the dictionary in the field of natural history: it turns living beings into separate items, each bearing a number, which can be manipulated as one handles tokens in a game of draughts, or words in a dictionary. Nonsense manifests a taste for naming in the classificatory sense of the term – the heroes of Lear's limericks are so many specimens. And it is part of a craze for discovering and classifying new species. Its advantage over natural history is that it can invent those species (like the Snap-dragon-fly) in the imaginative sense, whereas natural history can invent them only in the archaeological sense, that is discover what already exists. Nonsense is the entomologist's dream come true, or the Linnaean classification gone mad, because gone creative – it is the literary equivalent of Piltdown Man, that celebrated scientific fraud. The only difference, as Lyotard might say, lies in the 'regimen of phrases' – the phrases of nonsense are not cognitive, but at best narrative, and at worst delirious. From the rationality of natural history there is only a short step, in the inscription of nonsense, to madness.

Madness

The French language has no adjective for 'nonsensical'. The closest is *insensé*. The trouble is that it means not nonsensical but demented – 'out of his senses'. This points to a deep-seated relationship between nonsense and madness, which the Cheshire Cat acknowledges when he says to Alice: 'we're all mad here'. The characters of nonsense indeed tend to be delirious – they go from eccentricity to raving madness. It is natural, therefore, that the game should inscribe the discourse *of* madness. But the game itself, in spite of its name, is not mad. Its constitutive strategy is one of last-ditch defence against the contagion of madness. As such, it also inscribes the Victorian discourse *on* madness, in so far as it is the locus for an incipient, or inchoate, reflection on the language and behaviour of mad people. We have just seen that Lear's book of limericks was the literary equivalent of a museum: a collection of labelled items, each in the glass case of its limerick. But the species thus collected and classified are not biological, they are species of dementia or eccentricity (Foucault, in his *Madness and Civilization: A History of Insanity in the Age of Reason* reminds us that in the seventeenth-century the nosography of mental illness was conceived on the model of botanic taxonomy).[41] So the limerick is not only a glass case, but a cell, where the madman is kept under lock and key, and regularly exhibited for the enjoyment of audiences (as late as 1815, visitors could still go and see the inmates of Bedlam for a penny – the mental hospital was on a par with the menagerie). And if the position of the reader of the limerick is no longer that of the gaping audience, taunting the insane with their jibes, as 'they' persecute the characters for their eccentricities, it is nevertheless the position of the doctor, who examines, prods and experiments. The initial 'There was' in the limerick is the analogon of the pointing gesture of the doctor, as he introduces the next patient to an audience of medical students, as a new example in the nosography he is constructing. The patient will duly be labelled as paranoid, hysterical, or 'Old Person of Ischia/ Whose conduct grew friskier and friskier'. The reading of nineteenth-century psychiatry textbooks introduces us to a gallery of nonsense characters. And when they are not clinically mad, they at least deserve, like the White Knight for instance, to belong to the gallery of eccentrics whose portraits Edith Sitwell has drawn. Here is, for instance, Lord Rokeby. He lived in Kent in the eighteenth century, and 'became famous for his amphibious habits, and for possessing benevolence and a beard'.[42] He never shaved, lived in the company of pet animals, and spent his days in his bath:

> He erected a little hut on the sands at Hythe . . . and from his hut would dive, with commendable firmness, into the sea, remaining in this with the utmost persistence, until he fainted and had to be withdrawn forcibly from the water.[43]

No wonder he became a tourist attraction: people came to see him as he sat in his bath, with the secret hope that he might stand up, so they could catch sight of his beard, which went down to his knees. Lord Rokeby, of course – and this is entirely deliberate in Edith Sitwell's description: she calls him an 'amphibious old person' – is a character out of Lear's book of limericks. Fifty years before the emergence of nonsense, he was already a living parody of Lear and Carroll, a character in search of his author, who came too early on to the historical stage to find one. I would like to compensate for this injustice and give him the limerick he deserves:

There was an Old Person of Kent,
Whose beard was as long as it went.
For the whole of the day, in his bath he would stay,
That amphibious Old Person of Kent.

And if I were asked for the meaning of the second line, I would give Lewis Carroll's answer when questioned about the meaning of *The Hunting of the Snark*: 'Don't ask me, I am only the author.' Only adding, like the White Knight announcing his song, that 'it's very, *very* beautiful'.

The discourses of eccentricity and of insanity are discourses of exclusion. The nonsense character is isolated and pointed at, subjected to the wondering gaze of an audience of readers who laugh and gape at his eccentricities, as if he were a freak in a fair (the world of Tod Browning's film is only a sinister version of Wonderland), or who prod and interpret, before sending him back to his padded cell, like psychiatrists. But even as textbooks of psychiatry, before the fashion of *art brut*, were the only places where a distant echo of the speech of madmen (as opposed to the discourse about them) could be heard, those eccentrics manage to speak, albeit rarely and brokenly. Besides, the conception of Victorian psychiatry as merely repressive and unfeeling is a caricature. Not only because psychiatry had already become more humane (witness the 'moral management' school of psychiatry in early nineteenth-century England), but because the very resistance to an unbearable authority can be voiced only when that authority has already begun to waver, when it becomes subjectively unbearable (the general form of this is Marxian – mankind raises only the (political) problems that it can solve).

This is, for instance, what occurred in the case of Perceval,[44] who escaped from the institution where he was confined, to write an autobiography where he denounced the stupidity of the treatment meted out to him, and analysed his own disorder with impressive acumen. Nonsense also bears traces of this process. In fact, the genre's relationship to madness is pleasingly contradictory: it pictures the exclusion of madness in comic form, but at the same time constructs itself on the model of the speech of madmen. And this goes further than the mere reflection of the incoherence of delirium. The very rules of the genre appear to be the underlying laws of demented speech, as analysed by Perceval in passages which, according to Bateson, anticipate Freud's *Psychopathology of Everyday Life*. Perceval's analysis, based on introspection, enables him to understand what the psychiatrist and the pedagogue can only interpret as 'nonsense': the maxims that govern demented speech, which also underly nonsense texts (this is another instance of the intuitive power of nonsense). The first maxim is the maxim of *possession*. The madman does not speak in his own voice, he is spoken, often against his will, by spirits. Sentences often fail Perceval, or rather his control over them abruptly ends in the middle, and the end of the sentence escapes him. Sometimes the words are on the paper before he writes them down. This is a familiar situation in nonsense: whenever Alice tries to recite a poem, the words come out all wrong, and sentences have a tendency to let her down and utter contradictions, which she regrets but cannot help saying ('I'm not myself, you see', she says to the Caterpillar). On a more pleasant note, which takes us closer to Freud's psychopathology of everyday life, even her blunders, as when she cannot help praising her cat Dinah to the mouse and the other animals she meets at the pool of tears, are instances of words 'overtaking', and taking over, her thoughts. This, of course, is the old religious tradition of possession and speaking in tongues, which goes back to Paul's *Epistle to the Corinthians*. But in Perceval, things have already taken a comic turn – glossolalia is no longer possession by the Holy Spirit but by mischievous spirits bent on verbal or behavioural pranks at the expense of the speaker. Perceval's behaviour is often worthy of a character in Lear's limericks. At one point in his confinement, whenever his hands were freed he immediately took advantage of this to punch the warder in the face, as the spirits assured him that the man expected, nay welcomed, the blow with enthusiasm. The gesture, of course, is a successful *acte manqué* – it expresses, even if unwittingly, Perceval's revolt at the harshness of his treatment. But what is striking is the mixture of pathos (we should not laugh at such acute suffering) and high comedy, even farce (we cannot help laughing at a scene worthy of an early Charlie Chaplin film). The frontier between nonsense and madness is thin indeed. The second maxim is the maxim of *literalness*. The madman's speech is perceived as demented, Perceval explains, because he interprets the spirit's instructions literally. For the spirits speak poetically, he says, but man can only grasp the letter of the text. (We can interpret this as a translation, into the language of Victorian madness, of the four levels of meaning in biblical texts, the literal, allegorical, ana-gogical and tropological senses, in the Christian hermeneutical

207

tradition.) Again, this is close to nonsense. One of the constant comic devices of the genre is the literalisation of abstractions, set phrases or metaphors. Thus, to Alice's 'I'm not myself, you see', the Caterpillar answers 'I don't see', which is literally true, albeit irrelevant. And here we have perhaps reached the origin of the genre's wariness towards metaphor: the spirits speak metaphorically in order to deceive, and the only safe language is the literal. This is the world of the schizophrenic – this is also the world of nonsense, and they often overlap. Bateson mentions a schizophrenic patient who whenever he passed by the door of the doctor's office, on which there was a sign that read 'please knock', knocked (without entering, of course). Again, there is revolt, or retaliation, in the gesture – there is also comedy. The third maxim Perceval mentions is the maxim of *negation* – a predecessor of Freudian denial or negation. It is a rule of inversion, the very rule that governs *Through the Looking-Glass*: whenever we say we do not care about something, this means that the subject is infinitely important to us. The spirits speak through the speaker's slips of the tongue and the whole universe of nonsense is the universe of the mental patient. Not that the genre revels in madness – it inscribes it the better to contain it, again in a relationship of inversion striving towards conversion. The text of nonsense is a verbal asylum, in which madmen speak, but within the limits and constraints of the text, which phrases both the discourse of madness and the discourse on madness. The result of this complex inscription is what I have called, in the context of the dialectics of subversion and support, transversion.

The four discourses I have evoked are not the only ones to have found their way into nonsense. A case could be made,[45] for the discourses of the human body (of its health and cultivation through sport, of its sexual needs) of the family and the child (it is only natural that a genre addressed to children and whose main characters are children should echo, or rather inscribe, contemporary ideas about education and the place of children in society – more of this in the next section), poetry (nonsense poetry exploits the contemporary poetic code as laid down by Romantic or Victorian writers like Leigh Hunt or John Stuart Mill), and religion – the works of Lewis Carroll have been called 'inverted sermons', and we have seen that Perceval's nonsensical madness took a religious turn (he had his first attack in Scotland, when under the influence of the Pentecostal sect of Irvingites, who encouraged glossolalia). In the end, the rich texture of the Victorian frame of mind appears to have found its way into nonsense, but in an unexpected, because deeply distorted, form.

Inscription

In the last section I commented on certain aspects of Figure 4.2. I have shown that the singularity that a nonsense text is does not appear in a vacuum, but is constituted by a process of *inscription* of surrounding discourses. This process can be described in the terms of what Mark Johnson calls an image schema[46] – in this case the 'schema of attraction'. The universe of discourse in Victorian Britain is conceived as a field of forces, which act upon one another. An event occurs in this field, the appearance of a new point, or a new planet, which modifies the equilibrium of the system. This is done by attracting neighbouring texts and strings of texts (discourses, genres – the lines in Figure 4.1), or rather through a mixture of *deflection* (the lines curve – the discourses will be modified by the emergence of nonsense), *attraction* (the singularity of the nonsense text works upon the discourses it attracts – there lie the dialogism and polyphony of nonsense), and *extraction* (the process of attraction does not import words and sentences from neighbouring discourses, it extracts them, which implies a break and a contextual reworking – this creation of meaning through decontextualisation, and the dissemination of traces, is familiar to us since the work of Derrida). The function of my adopting this particular schema is tactical: it aims to show that the discursive intertext of nonsense cannot be accounted for under the metaphor (or schema) of reflection, the classic metaphor in Marxist discourse. In this I am following the course taken by Bakhtin, who, as we have seen, consistently distinguishes between reflection and *refraction* – dialogic texts do not reflect their discursive environment, but refract it. In reflection, an image of the extratextual and the extralinguistic is transferred to the reflecting text, as in the simple return of a light wave by the surface of a mirror. In refraction, on the other hand, an image is obtained, but only after deflection – a distorted, even if regular, image. There is a textual work of refraction as there is a psychic work of joke- or dream-making in Freud.

This, however, leaves out an important question. So far, I have concentrated on the singularity in Figure 4.2, and I have taken the rest of the figure, lines and anchoring points, for granted. I must explore my schema to the end. I shall do it by raising a second question, which has remained implicit – the figure deals with the individual nonsense text as a singularity, not with the genre. What is it, therefore, that drills singular nonsense texts into a line, with its anchoring points? The answer to this question is the object of the next section. It is easy to see why the answer to the second question will also provide an answer to the first – if I can account for a particular line, complete with anchoring points, the line of nonsense, I shall have at least the elements of a theory of lines and anchoring points, that is of genres.

THE INSTITUTION OF NONSENSE

So far, I have shown that nonsense texts inscribe/refract other texts (pastiche) and constituted discourses (the texts of ideology). I must broaden my field of research and wonder whether nonsense also inscribes or refracts the extralinguistic, that is the social. Here is Bakhtin, under the pen name of Vološinov, on the subject: 'The role of implied evaluations in literature is particularly important. We might say that the poetic work is a powerful condenser of unspoken social evaluations. Every word is saturated with them. These social evaluations indeed organise artistic form as their direct expression.'[47] The important words are 'unspoken' and 'evaluation'. We are no longer in discourse (so far my discourses were 'spoken' – there were monuments to them in the guise of texts, set phrases and clichés), and yet we are not directly in the realm of the social, outside language (in the realm of productive forces and relations of production, for instance), as another mediation has appeared, 'evaluation'. This blocks all interpretation of nonsense texts as superstructural reflections of the base, or of the political struggle – interpretations of the *Alice* books in terms of the class struggle there have been (mostly in the 1930s), but they are better forgotten, like Freudian interpretations that provide the answers before the questions are asked. Nevertheless, the social, *qua* 'social evaluation', is present in literature, and therefore in nonsense. I shall evoke this question by offering an example: the inscription of railways in Victorian literature.

It is difficult to exaggerate the importance of the changes brought about by the railways to the daily life of the British people in the course of the nineteenth century, so it is only natural that this should have been 'reflected' in the literature of the times. A 'reflection' theory of literature would look at Dickens, for instance, to sustain this hypothesis. Indeed, the railways play a vital role in *Dombey and Son*. Not only do we catch a glimpse of the social and geographical changes undergone by London suburbs as tunnels and cuttings plough through the landscape; not only do we catch a glimpse of the new proletariat in the person of Mr Toodle, employed by the railway company as a stoker; not only do we have delightful vignettes of social history, as we watch the London to Birmingham line cutting its way through Camden Hill; but Carker is the first (but not the last) villain in literature to be disposed of by a railway engine, that modern version of the juggernaut. This enumeration shows that, even in Dickens, we are moving away from simple reflection to 'social evaluation', as the railways acquire mythical power and play a vital part in the fabric of the novel, as the objective correlative of the forces of change that cause Mr Dombey's downfall. But at least, in Dickens, a case could be made for a process of reflection (this is, up to a point, what actually happened – there is, at times, a documentary side to Dickens, even if it is always tinged with nostalgia). But what about nonsense, where such reflection is out of the question? The answer is that trains are mentioned in *Through the Looking-Glass* (Carroll was extremely fond of them, and in his childhood had created a family railway system in his father's garden, for the pleasure of his innumerable brothers and sisters). In Chapter 3 Alice finds herself in a train, in the company of a gentleman dressed in white paper, a gruff goat, a beetle, and an unhappy gnat, who sighs at its own jokes. She has no ticket, of course, which attracts attention, and the train leaps over a brook – Alice, having moved one square on the chessboard, is suddenly somewhere entirely different, with no train in sight (the vanishing of this phantom train is not even commented upon by the narrator). This is a nonsensical train, whose only function is to fulfil the prediction in the game of chess in the Preface: '2. ALICE THROUGH Q's 3D (*by railway*) TO Q's 4TH (*Tweedledum and Tweedledee*)'.[48] Its intrusion into the tale gives the impression of being arbitrary and forced. There is a certain naturalness in Dickens's use of trains, the naturalness of allegory and symbol, which is ultimately based on image schemata, in this case the path schema: life is metaphorically conceived of as a journey from birth to death, and trains are literally used for journeys from London to Leamington Spa. It is therefore quite fitting that the railway engine should be the modern version of the Parcae. But there is nothing of this in *Through the Looking-Glass*. True, the occasion for the appearance of the train is Alice's journey on the chessboard. But none of the other characteristics of the schema are present: there is no starting point, since Alice, out of the blue, finds herself in the train, in the middle of a journey that never started. This train does not seem to come from anywhere. Nor does it go anywhere. It simply vanishes, after its task, jumping over a brook in a highly unorthodox manner, has been completed. In fact, it vanishes like an image on a screen, or a scene in a dream: Alice wakes up in the next square – she has switched channels. The train, however, has been present *qua* train, and with it some of the 'social evaluations' associated with trains – it carries passengers according to certain rules, which are either exploited (where are they all going?) or emphatically enforced (a ticket collector immediately appears, and Alice immediately finds herself excluded as an illegal passenger, an object of curiosity and contempt – the 'social evaluation' here comes in the form of a painful everyday experience). The contradictory results of my analysis are the following: in the case of the train in *Through the Looking-Glass*, there is *inscription* of certain *social evaluations* produced by the extralinguistic; but this inscription is not 'natural' (as in the case when Johnson's image schemata are involved), but arbitrary. I must refine my model.

The trouble with the 'reflection' theory of inscription, even in its refined Bakhtinian form of 'refraction', is that it conforms to the logic of representation. The process of refraction produces an image of the light source, even if it is a 'deformed' one compared to simple reflection. To put it briefly, the logic of representation involves at least three aspects (a) a separation, a break, between the representing and the represented elements (the image and the object, the sign and its referent, the MP and her constituents); (b) a replacement of the represented by the representing element (the sign's main function is to represent the referent in its absence; the constituents are not admitted to the parliament building, except on limited occasions; the image may persist when the object is no longer there; presentation is not representation); (c) a hierarchy between the representing and the represented elements – there is an ordering of representation. We must have first the object and then the image, otherwise this is no representation but hallucination; this relation of chronological sequence tends to become a metaphorical relation of consequence, in the causal or in the moral sense ('this is of no consequence'). Various philosophies will establish this hierarchy in various ways, but the common point is the ordering. In our case the reflection theory of inscription entails that (a) the text that bears the inscription is separated, and qualitatively different, from the inscribed reality; (b) it represents the inscribed reality in its absence (the text is a monument to a vanished conjuncture); and (c) there is ordering in the process: the text is always secondary to the extralinguistic from which it borrows the raw material for inscription.

The metaphor for this ordering, if we follow the philosophy of Gilles Deleuze, is the tree,[49] which seems to play the same role as one of Johnson's schemata. To this, Deleuze opposes another schema, the rhizome: not an ordered hierarchy but an anarchic arrangement of unpredictable branchings out. This, in turn, is the schema that corresponds to another logic, the logic not of representation, but of arrangement (*agencement*), what he calls the 'logic of the AND'. This logic turns the logic of representation upon its head: it works not through separation but through contiguity (the scandalous contiguity of heterogeneous elements or fields); not through replacement but through coexistence (the various elements are co-present, so that no one element is abstracted from the rest to represent them); not through hierarchy but through conjunction. The result of course is heterogeneous, even as separation ensures that representation is homogeneous – images with images, objects with objects. This, it seems to me, provides a better account of the train in *Through the Looking-Glass*, which is obviously not a symbol, but an arbitrary arrangement, whereby a segment of the social, the train, is forcibly plugged, like a square peg into a round hole, into a fairy tale, which is already a strange object, as it is combined (through sheer conjunction – the logic of the 'AND') with a chess game. In this, *Through the Looking-Glass* is a perfect illustration of what Lyotard calls the *différend*.[50] Incompatible 'regimens of phrase' are made to coexist – the result is a rather strange object, a new genre of discourse, nonsense.

To go back to Figure 4.2, the relationship between the line (here nonsense as a genre) and the anchoring points (the social) appears in a new light. The advantage of the figure is that it shows the contiguity between line and anchoring point (there is no separation). The disadvantage is that it separates the singularity (the individual text) from the line (the discourses), thus confessing that it is still in part a product of the logic of representation. There would be no sense, of course, in offering here an improved version of the figure, as this would not make a break with representation. The only way is to go beyond it and attempt to describe a heterogeneous arrangement of literary text, social discourses and ideological apparatuses, or institutions. This is what I am trying to capture under the name 'the institution of nonsense'. And my thesis here is that nonsense texts are an integral part of a complex Victorian arrangement, or social apparatus, which we will call 'the School' for short – an arrangement of spaces (the buildings and grounds), bodies (the scholars and the teachers), books (the textbooks), discourses (at the school and about the school) and texts (*Tom Brown's Schooldays*, but also *Alice's Adventures in Wonderland*, as well as innumerable 'primers'). Because nonsense texts are contiguous with, coexisting with and conjunct to all those elements, they somehow 'contain' them.

The first form of this co-presence is the importance of the school as theme and discourse in nonsense texts, or rather (the language of re-presentation, of meta-phor from one field to another is difficult to avoid – the rejection of metaphor is one of Deleuze and Guattari's firmest tenets)[51] the pervasiveness of the nonsense-cum-school rhizome. A series of hints will convince us that in Victorian Britain the school is steeped in nonsense, and nonsense inscribes the school within its text.

I have already had occasion to comment on Alice's only solecism: 'Curiouser and curiouser.' But the context is the locus for a dialogue with the narrator, who comments on this in an aside:

> 'Curiouser and curiouser!' cried Alice (she was so much surprised, that for the moment she quite forgot how to speak good English). 'Now I'm opening out like the largest telescope that ever was! Good-bye, feet!' (for when she looked down at her feet, they seemed to be almost out of sight, they were getting so far off).[52]

This is an interventionist narrator, bent on fulfilling Genette's communicational function for narrators, that is to address the reader in his own voice, in order to comment on the action and guide the interpretation – this is the obvious role of the second parenthesis. But something more is happening in his first intervention: beyond the interpellation of the reader, or rather through it, another addressee is convoked: Alice, the quality of whose language is severely judged. This is the interpellation *cum* exclusion of pedagogic dialogue: the addressee stands up, which makes her stand out, to hear the sentence passed on her performance. The jocularity of the intervention is characteristic of the fake chumminess of pedagogic address. The narrator of nonsense tales makes the pedagogic nature of all narrative relationships explicit. The school is always somehow present in the text, explicitly so in nonsense.

I have insisted on the patchwork aspect of the nonsense pastiche. This is a characteristic the texts share with numerous textbooks, the contents of which are often, as the Victorians used to say, 'elegant extracts'. As instruments of vulgarisation, textbooks naturally draw on all sorts of texts and discourses. In Victorian textbooks, the result was often absurd, an absurdity which nonsense barely exaggerates. Victorian young ladies, the non-fictional Alices, were sometimes made to absorb meaningless extracts and lists: Latin declensions, lists of important dates and capital cities – the whole thing was as absurd to the Victorian child as Lear's nonsensical geography appears to us. The classical education of Tom Tulliver and the effect it had on his mind are excellent examples of this. This is how, in 1825, the *Westminster Review*, from a progressive Benthamite point of view, describes the education given in grammar schools: the scholars are busy eight hours a day,

> in attempting, not to read and understand the matter of a classical author, to know the history, the poetry, the philosophy, the policy, the manners and the opinions of Greece and Rome, but the grammar, the syntax, the parsing, the quantities and the accents; not in learning to write and speak the language, but in getting by rote a few scraps of poetry, to be again forgotten, and in fabricating nonsense, or sense verses, it is indifferent which.[53]

No doubt there is an aspect of political caricature in the quotation. But apart from the fact that the word 'nonsense' has been uttered, which implies that the school is one of the places where nonsense is produced, the text identifies the insistence on grammar and parsing as the main shortcomings of this type of education – and also the source for the nonsense produced: the verses are nonsensical because they are written with a view to grammatical correctness and metrical regularity, not as means of expressing feelings and ideas.

There is in fact a strong link between parsing as the core of old-fashioned education in Victorian Britain, and nonsense as a literary genre. I have shown that nonsense was preoccupied with the rules of language. Nonsense is a metalinguistic genre because it has the same goals (but not the same methods) as school education: to teach children the rules of language (this is why the purity of language is so important, both in the narrator's aside in *Alice's Adventures in Wonderland* and in Carroll's practice), and more generally the rules of conduct. In the terms of Roger Caillois,[54] nonsense appears to give in to *paidia*, the rule-free playing of the unruly child, in order to promote *ludus*, the rule-governed playing that acclimatises the child to the rules of adult society through imitation and constraints. It is easy to understand why metaphor is unacceptable in those circumstances – for the same reason that it constitutes a problem to objectivist accounts of truth and meaning: it ultimately defies computation, it always breaks the rules set up to police it.

As a result, nonsense and the school interpenetrate. There is rich nonsense in school life. This is how Winston Churchill describes his first lesson at Harrow in 1888: he was asked to learn by rote the declension of *mensa*, a table. Being of an inquisitive mind, he asked for an explanation of the vocative case:

'What does O table mean?'
'Mensa, O table, is the vocative case,' he replied.
'But why O table?' I persisted in genuine curiosity.
'O table – you would use that in addressing a table, in invoking a table.' And then seeing he was not carrying me with him, 'You would use it in speaking to a table.'
'But I never do,' I blurted out in honest amazement.
'If you are impertinent, you will be punished . . . was his conclusive rejoinder.[55]

We need not have absolute confidence in the reminiscences of an adult who has become a model of respectability (and who has

216

perhaps read *Alice's Adventures in Wonderland*), and who sees himself as a naughty but intelligent child, genuinely amazed at the stupidity of a narrow pedant. Yet the scene, the words uttered and the tone of the exchange are familiar – this is he world of the Alice books, the world of nonsense. We understand where the conjunction of nonsense and the child occurs – in the child's prolonged experience of being submitted to the school's curriculum and mores. The pedagogue behaves like the Mouse in Chapter 3 of *Alice's Adventures in Wonderland*, when he is interrupted by the Duck, or like the Queen of Hearts, whenever anything that displeases her occurs. There are more ways than one of saying 'Off with his head!' There are even closer links between Alice and young Winston – the absurdity of the vocative (which is the emblem of both the fundamental absurdity of rules of grammar – when their abstractness is compared with the actual use of living language – and of their necessity – if you wish to learn Latin you have to know what the vocative case is) seems to be a common point. This is how Alice, in Chapter 2, addresses the Mouse:

> 'O Mouse, do you know the way out of this pool?' . . . (Alice thought this must be the right way of speaking to a mouse: she had never done such a thing before, but she remembered having seen, in her brother's Latin Grammar, 'A mouse – of a mouse – to a mouse – a mouse – O mouse!'[56]

We know who Alice is – she is Winston's younger sister. And the role of nonsense is to provide a context for the impossible utterances that the language of the school daily forces us to utter, thus at the same time justifying their existence (I must learn the vocative for 'a table', because in a nonsense text I may read about a table being addressed in this fashion, as indeed a live wall is addressed by Pyramus and Thisbe in *A Midsummer Night's Dream*) and denouncing their absurdity (the situation is nonsensical, i.e. both impossible and yet, in the world of fiction, real).

So it is not difficult to show that, if there is nonsense in schools, the reverse is also true. There are schoolboys in nonsense, like Tweedledum and Tweedledee, and school subjects are mentioned, like Laughing and Grief, Mystery and Seography. The puns are a good image not so much of the refraction of school in nonsense, as of the portmanteau creations that the conjunction of two heterogeneous fields produces – impossible objects created by rhizomatic branchings out, even as the Mock Turtle is an

217

impossible creature, created by the linguistic rhizome of the remainder.

Nonsense, therefore, is part of a rhizome, that is of what Deleuze and Guattari call an 'arrangement of utterance' – the School, for short. It involves the co-presence of elements belonging to incompatible realms of being. In the feudal arrangement of utterance, according to them, various elements are conjoined: the knight, his horse, weaponry and armour, but also the epic narratives of chivalric deeds, perhaps even the courtly love poems of the troubadours, and the feudal relation of production, involving processes of territorialisation and de-territorialisation. In the School *qua* arrangement of utterance, Lewis Carroll's and Edward Lear's poems are in direct contiguity with (they are 'plugged into') a number of institutions, individuals, buildings and discourses. The School in Victorian Britain is a complex arrangement of institutions, the result of a compromise between (a) the state, whose responsibilities in the field of education have begun to increase; (b) the various churches, who compete between themselves, with the help of the state (but also, to a certain extent, against its intervention) for the traditional right to educate the masses; and (c) the lay reformers, the founders of modern educational institutions, often Utilitarians and Benthamites, who criticise the inadequacy of the system, which fails to prepare the students for the tasks the economy demands. The School is also a historically recent arrangement (an Althusserian might say: this is the conjuncture of the constitution of the School into the dominant Ideological State Apparatus): Victorian Britain is the period of the capture of an increasing proportion of the male population by the educational institutions, the time of the cementing of the alliance between the upper and the middle classes through the individual opportunities for social mobility offered by education – even if the global function of the system is still the streamlining of children into distinct social strata.

The position of nonsense in this conjuncture savours of paradox, on three counts: its exponents are at best marginal members of the institution, at worst totally cut off from it; its privileged readers are not part of the masses of children captured by the institution – Victorian little girls do not usually go to school, at least not if they belong to the middle classes: Alice has her own governess; and the pedagogic positions that can be derived from nonsense texts can hardly be said to reflect mainstream Victorian educational practices. But this (self-)exclusion of nonsense from the School is a form of participation in the arrangement. An arrangement of utterances thrives on the heterogeneity of its component parts; it requires co-presence, not coherence. In our case, this incoherence provides nonsense with a point of view on the educational institutions which makes it the embodiment of their transversion – the locus for the educational dialectics of subversion and support.

Exclusion first. Lewis Carroll, at first sight, is a caricatural product of the most authorised institutions of the Victorian School: he went to Rugby and Oxford, where he remained all his life as a don. But presence does not necessarily mean integration. Carroll hated Rugby, and although he was very attached to Oxford and the life of leisure it allowed its dons to enjoy, he never took much part in the educational aspect of this life (at the time, there was no absolute necessity for him to do so). He was so inefficient as a teacher (his shyness and stammer hardly helped) that his rare ventures into the field of education ended in boredom or disaster. Besides, Oxford at the time could not claim to be at the forefront of educational progress. As a member of an over-reformed academia, I have always relished the answer given in 1850 by the university to some government reform committee: the university was reformed two hundred years ago by Archbishop Laud, and, human nature not having changed since, there is no need of further change. Carroll's position is thus doubly marginal: an old-fashioned member of an archaic institution. As for Lear, he hardly went to school at all, and had to earn his living as a draughtsman early – he had no connections whatever with the School.

The same applies to the children whom nonsense addresses. Either they are too young (Lear's first limericks were read aloud in the nursery at Knowsley, the Earl of Derby's seat) or they belong to the wrong sex – the School in Victorian times developed by capturing boys, not girls. So there is no lack of 'social evaluation' implicit in Carroll's famous quip; 'I like children, except boys.' Nonsense addresses those children whom the School still excludes. As such, one could argue that it complements the usual institutions by providing material for home schooling – after all, that is what nursery rhymes and cautionary tales are meant to do. There is an element of truth in this, although the situation is made more complex by the third factor mentioned earlier: the pedagogic position that can be derived from the text.

One can derive a pedagogic position from nonsense texts. And it is pleasantly anti-Victorian. *Alice's Adventures in Wonderland*, even if it quotes and parodies textbooks, for instance the boring history book which the Mouse quotes in Chapter 3: 'and even Stigand, the patriotic archbishop of Canterbury, found it advisable —', is emphatically *not* a textbook. It is everything that a Victorian textbook is not, and everything that it should be, if it took any account of the personality and educational needs of its prospective readers. (This is where Lewis Carroll again has extraordinary intuitions: he was a failure with students and pupils, but he instinctively knew what little girls wanted – he was attentive to their desires probably because he was attentive to his own.) Nonsense, thus, stands Victorian textbooks on their heads.

But the pedagogy of nonsense does not stop at this subversion and inversion. It also engages in conversion and transversion. Conversion, because in a playful manner it passes on essential educational material – a belief in the necessity of rules: rules of grammar, of linguistic behaviour, of politeness and manners. Irony and inversion turn out to be the best pedagogic devices, the only way to capture the audience in the psychological, as opposed to the physical, sense of the term. There is also transversion, because nonsense introduces an element of seduction and desire (Carroll belongs to the tradition of amorous Victorian curates – Kilvert, who tramped four miles for the pleasure of kissing a little girl on the cheek, is another instance),[57] or rather it accepts and makes almost explicit this element, which is present in any 'agogic' relationship (this is the common point between pedagogues and demagogues). The consequence is that far from being a marginal branch of the rhizome, a patch on the carefully woven cloth of the School, nonsense is an integral, nay a crucial, part of the arrangement. It is the point where the various incompatible branches converge, the point of crisis – nonsense both upholds and ruins the values of Victorian education, it both mimics and mocks the educational institutions, it both captures and frees the children still excluded by the system, it echoes, stages and intervenes upon the contradictions of language as both object and vehicle of Victorian pedagogy. Nonsense it is that turns an incipient ideological school apparatus into a rhizome.

We can account for this in Bakhtinian terms by talking of the *exotopy* of nonsense. The concept names the dialectics of inclusion and exclusion that hold between the subject and the world, including the world of other subjects. As an 'I', I hold a privileged position in so far as the lived world (*my* lived world) is constructed around me – I am in a relation of exotopy in so far as I am *out* of the world (at a distance from it) and yet *in* the world, which constitutes my horizon (I am at the centre). This dialectic is essential, Bakhtin notes, to the genre of autobiography – this is my life, and yet I must be outside it, at a distance from it, in order to narrate it as a story. The contradictory position of exotopy, he adds, has one considerable advantage – it gives the subject a *surplus of vision*. It is also beneficial in that it enables the subject to construct a world of values around her, to establish the boundaries of her world, of the possible and of the acceptable. Exotopy is the position from which a *Lebenswelt* is possible. But there is a negative form of exotopy – it can also be the point from which the *Lebenswelt* is subverted, from which the values are ruined, the boundaries dissolved. This occurs in comic genres, and the form it takes is madness or senselessness. For exotopy not only founds values, it also guarantees the unity of a *style* and the coherence of *meaning*. The negative exotopy of senselessness subverts all this.

Nonsense is both positive and negative exotopy. As negative exotopy, it subverts values, meaning and style (pastiche is the contrary of style) – it even threatens to subvert grammar. But as positive exotopy, it reconstructs and reasserts the values it has appeared to subvert, so that there is a style of nonsense (a nonsense text is eminently recognisable), and some meaning, in the guise of 'social evaluations', re-emerges out of an appearance of incoherence and chaos.

The contradiction between positive and negative exotopy has an embodiment which is easily perceived by the reader, in the contradiction between the archaism, the nostalgia of nonsense, and its modernity, its power of intuition and anticipation. There is a strong flavour of archaism to nonsense texts – they all look back to a lovely July afternoon, to an Oxford still immune from the nastier consequences of modernity, to the golden age of childhood, before the unwelcome change of puberty set in. At the same time – this has been the main contention of this book – they look forward, even if unconsciously, to a more advanced state of knowledge and understanding, in matters linguistic for instance, and the result of this is that they are in tune with the modernity of today's reader – they have not aged as most Victorian texts have. The exotopy of nonsense subverts Victorian values in that it mocks their sentimental, or self-righteous, seriousness (and it is a sad fact that, nowadays, any of Dickens's villains is more acceptable to the reader than that preposterous bore, little Dorrit – we prefer to read about Mrs Jellyby, because she is ridiculous, than about the saintly death of Jo the roadsweeper, because we can no longer bear the pathos). And yet it also preserves what is essential in them, in the form of rules of language and social behaviour – we still recognise our modern preoccupations in the dialogic struggles in *Alice's Adventures in Wonderland*. This is the content of what I have repeatedly called the transversion of nonsense.

CONCLUSION

If we try to account for nonsense by using the terms of Lyotard's *Le Différend*, we shall find that the position of nonsense is again one of contradictory exotopy. On the one hand, nonsense is close to a 'regimen of phrase' (as appears in the exclamation, 'Don't talk nonsense!'). There are nonsensical, as there are assertive and interrogative, phrases. Or rather nonsense is a meta-regimen, an operation that takes any phrase of any regimen and renders it incoherent – a translation machine which disrupts any linguistic organisation, and turns coherence into incoherence, sense into non-sense. At the same time, and this has been the subject of this chapter, this regimen of phrases has crystallised into a 'discursive genre', a set of phrases with its internal laws and characteristics. This discursive genre is part of the arrangement of utterance which I have called the School – it has deep-seated links with a historical conjuncture. And it constitutes a narrative, perhaps even a 'grand narrative' in the sense of Lyotard – the genre is also a myth. It will come as no surprise to the reader if I say that the content of the myth is the figure of the child (nonsense as a genre is a modern version of the great Romantic myth of the child). The modernity of the nonsensical version of the myth lies in the fact that it concentrates not on the child's soul (its intimations of immortality) but on the child's language. The essential childishness of the child, as nonsense pictures it, lies in the fact that she is a language-learner: the important thing for Alice is not that she goes through the looking-glass, but that she undergoes the mirror stage, and lives up to all the linguistic consequences of this.

CONCLUSION

READING PHILOSOPHICALLY

It is never too late to justify one's title. The justification I have to offer for linking the name of a literary genre, nonsense, to the word 'philosophy' is that I have attempted a philosophical reading of literary texts in a double, reversible movement. First I have, in traditional fashion, used philosophical concepts and theories in order to cast light upon the workings of nonsense texts. In this context, the literary texts run the risk of being mere pretexts, opportunities for an essentially exploitative relationship. I am not the first in the field, and the exploitation is sometimes subtle.[1] But there is provocation – nonsense texts, as we have seen, exert strong fascination on philosophers, so that there is a second, inverse, movement in my reading. I have also attempted to use Victorian literary texts to read philosophical texts, sometimes much later texts, so that the interpretation of philosophical texts in and through nonsense is given anachronistically, in advance – an interpretation of yet unwritten texts. I have, in short, attempted a reading of, by and with the texts of Victorian nonsense.

This, it seems to me, enables us to account for two striking characteristics of nonsense texts: their modernity, and the quality of their intuitions. There is indeed an achronic quality in nonsense texts which accounts for their effortless survival in a drastically altered literary and ideological conjuncture. As is well known, Victorian texts can no longer be read ahistorically, without an effort towards sympathy for their ethical and ideological background assumptions. Even the best of Victorian novels need, on the part of the reader, some adaptation to the Victorian frame of mind – witness the treatment of the Jews in George Eliot's *Daniel Deronda* (I deliberately choose a novel where the treatment of

Jewish culture is sympathetic: it is even more manifest that such treatment is based on a vision of Jewishness which we no longer entirely share). If we take as another example an almost extinct novel, Charlotte Yonge's *The Heir of Redclyffe*, the reason for this distancing becomes obvious. The plot revolves around an engagement, not condoned by the young couple's parents, and not immediately made public, which is the direct cause of tragedy and ruin. We no longer believe in the possibility of such causal chains, because our ethical and literary values have changed. The surprising thing, in this context, is that nonsense, that arch-Victorian genre, is hardly affected by the changes, that it easily bursts out of the Victorian frame of mind and seems directly to address ours. There are, after all, advantages to lack of seriousness – the playful reversal of values in temporary topsy-turvydom is the harbinger of a more serious devaluation or transvaluation. The retrospective diachrony of nostalgia, in which many nonsense texts indulge (Carroll's golden July afternoon in a dream-like Oxford; Lear's regression to childhood) has at least this advantage that, by distancing itself from contemporary values, it is not threatened when these vanish or are deeply altered – distance from values, whatever they are, there still is because there always was.

The diachrony of nonsense works both ways: it looks back in nostalgia, but it also looks forward in anticipation. Most of this book has been devoted to what is, to my mind, the most striking feature of Victorian nonsense – the quality of its intuitions, this mixture of diachrony (the genre reflects, refracts and arranges the elements of a historical conjuncture) and anachrony: it anticipates, and it criticises in advance, the developments of philosophy and linguistics. We now fully understand why Artaud could accuse Lewis Carroll of having plagiarised him in advance.

The phrase 'reading philosophically'[2] seeks to capture this dual, and reversible, mode of reading: a philosophical reading which is also a way of reading philosophy. With the usual hubris of conclusions – at the moment when the writer labours under the illusion that he has provided not only an account of his topic, but also a more general method – I shall offer a last illustration of this type of reading by revisiting *The Hunting of the Snark*.

THE HUNTING OF THE SNARK REVISITED

The interpretation of Carroll's mock-epic so far proposed, *en passant*, in this book, hesitates between two critical moods. On the one hand, *The Hunting of the Snark* can be given a material, or semantic, interpretation, in terms of existential angst, the Romantic quest for the void, etc. It is all too easy, for instance, to note that the comic tone of the poem verges on the sublime to such an extent that the dividing line becomes indistinct. Here is the Baker, in the last fit:

> Erect and sublime, for one moment of time.
> In the next, that wild figure they saw
> (As if stung by a spasm) plunge into a chasm,
> While they waited and listened in awe.[3]

The suspicion soon occurs, of course, that this is the exaggeration of caricature (a few stanzas before the 'unnamed hero' has been hailed as 'Thingumbob'); yet the gloom and general heaviness of the atmosphere tend to smother the mirth, and seem to justify Elizabeth Sewell's exclusion of such texts from nonsense.[4] On the other hand, however, the poem can be given a formal, or linguistic, interpretation, concentrating on the reflexivity and distance of parody – this is a mock-epic, a *Reader's Digest* version of an epic, the composition of which obeys a mirror-image law of inversion. It is difficult to take this as anything but a formal literary game, an early example of the use of metafictional devices. The problem is not to adopt one interpretation at the expense of the other, but to account for their simultaneous occurrence. The semantic reading is too serious, but cannot be dismissed altogether. The formal reading is evident, but too technical – it threatens to render the text illegible because lifeless. In order not to reconcile the two interpretations but to show their underlying unity as interpretations of the same text, we must embark on a detour through philosophy – this is where the 'reading philosophically' method shows the tip of its ears.

In his 'Essay on the introduction of the concept of negative quantity into philosophy',[5] a pre-critical work, Kant explores not logical negation or contradiction, but what he calls 'real' opposition, where quantity is 'negated' by being opposed to its inverse, a negative quantity. The formula for this is '$a - a = 0$'. In scholastic terms, he seeks to distinguish between two types of 'nothing', the absolute nothing of logical contradiction, *nihil negativum*, and the relative, or positive nothing of opposition, *nihil privativum* (we may recall that in the *Critique of Pure Reason*, at the very end of the analytic of principles, there is a brief account of the concept 'nothing', through a fourfold distinction between two entities, *ens rationis* and *ens imaginarium*, and the two forms of 'nothing' just mentioned). Kant further analyses the *nihil privativum* in terms of the distinction between privation (one could almost risk 'deprivation' – a positive structure, where two opposed quantities cancel each other: the ' – a' in the 'a – a = 0' formula fits this form of negation) and lack (the sign for which might be simply the zero sign in the preceding formula, as it denotes mere absence, a passively negative state of affairs). Thus, if pleasure is a positive quantity, displeasure is its privative opposite; also a quantity, albeit negative. Whereas indifference is simply lack-of-pleasure-and-displeasure. The formula thus becomes, once its variables have been replaced by their values: 'pleasure – displeasure = indifference'.

Two other examples, which Kant uses in his essay, will be of interest to us: death is not lack but privation, a negative quantity, the active opposite of birth rather than mere absence. And, in the same vein, abstraction is described as negative attention: it is not mere lack of attention, or absent-mindedness (which is indeed what the word means in English in its psychological acceptation: an abstracted look), but an active destruction of certain representations in order that what is left should be clearer and more striking – thus one abstracts the concept, or the ontological metaphor, from the indistinct mass of phenomena. I shall use Kant's distinction in two ways, according to my method: I shall show that it provides a unified reading of *The Hunting of the Snark*, taken as an illustration of the privation v. lack opposition; and I shall show that the text, in turn, 'reads' the conceptual distinction by introducing a third term, difference, into the dichotomy.

Indeed, rather than a quest for the void, *The Hunting of the Snark* can be taken as a journey through negation, which makes it an emblem of the negative prefix that defines the genre. I shall limit myself to a few hints. Privation in the Kantian sense, as negative quantity, is personified in the poem in the character of the Boojum, who is part of the series of Bs (the crew, we may recall, have been chosen not on account of their skills and experience, but because their names begin with B), but it is also what will annul the series, if the crew meet a Snark which happens to be a Boojum. If 'B' is read as 'be', the chain of beings that the crew forms is bound to meet with non-being, its corresponding negative quantity, by which it will be cancelled in mutual disappearance. This is what happens in the last stanza of the poem, when the Baker meets a Boojum and 'softly and suddenly vanished away':

> They hunted till darkness came on, but they found
> Not a button, or feather, or mark,
> By which they could tell that they stood on the ground
> Where the Baker had met with the Snark.[6]

'Baker − Boojum = Vanishing'. The question, however, remains of the Baker's predestination. His fate is announced as early as the end of the second fit, when he faints away at the mention of a Boojum: he it is of all the crew who is doomed to meet with his negative quantity. My interpretation of this election is that the Baker illustrates the other aspect of the dichotomy, lack. All the other members of the crew have some solid claim to existence − first of all, a name, or rather the name of a profession, which is the ostensible reason for their inclusion. Thus,

> The crew was complete: it included a Boots −
> A maker of Bonnets and Hoods −
> A Barrister, brought to arrange their disputes −
> And a Broker, to value their goods.[7]

In this mock-ideal community, based on a division of labour worthy of Fourier (there is even a Beaver, whose function it is to make lace in the bow), the Baker is the odd man out. He is not introduced by name ('There was one who was famed for the number of things / He forgot when he entered the ship'),[8] and indeed he cannot be, as he has 'wholly forgotten' it. He comes as a Baker, but he can only bake Bridecake, for which no materials are to be had, so that he is useless. His moral character might save him, as 'his courage is perfect! And that, after all, / Is the thing that one needs with a Snark'),[9] except that, as we have seen, he faints in terror at the mere mention of his enemy's name. The most important aspect, however, is his lack of a name:

> He would answer to 'Hi!' or to any loud cry,
> Such as 'Fry me!' or 'Fritter my wig!'
> To 'What-you-may-call-um!' or 'What-was-his- name!'
> But especially 'Thing-um-a-jig!'[10]

This is not the active nothing of privation (the Baker is not subject to Adamic deprivation, since all names fit him), but the inert nothing of lack. It is not even a case of forgetting as inverse memory — the Baker's name has not been repressed into the unconscious by some infantile trauma, it has just been passively forgotten, like the forty-two boxes, 'all carefully packed, / With his name painted clearly on each'[11] which were left behind on the beach, because he never mentioned their existence to anyone.

The second hint I wish to offer is provided by the map that the Bellman uses to reach the Snark (Figure C1). It is a singular object.[12]

On the face of it, this map is as fine an illustration of negation *qua* lack as I can hope to find. And such appears to be the opinion of the crew:

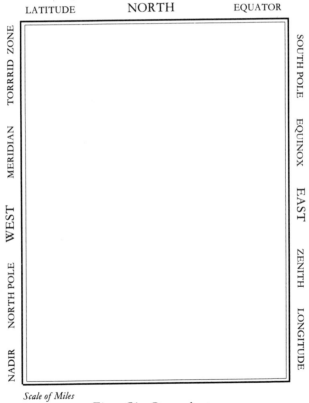

Figure C1   Ocean-chart

'What's the good of Mercator's North Poles and Equators,
Tropics, Zones, and Meridian Lines?'
So the Bellman would cry: and the crew would reply,
'They are merely conventional signs!

'Other maps are such shapes, with their islands and capes!
But we've got our brave Captain to thank'
(So the crew would protest) 'that he's bought us the best –
A perfect and absolute blank!'[13]

If lack means absence, this blank is the very emblem of it. Yet
positivity soon creeps back. It does so on the map itself, or rather
just outside it, in the (somewhat reorganised) geographical terms
that give the map its structure and meaning, and we may note that
the North is on top, in its usual place, so that the Bellman's map is
an example not so much of absence as of abstraction, that negative
form of attention, even as the medieval *Mappa Mundi* kept in
Hereford Cathedral reorganises the world so that it fits into a
circle, with the East on top, in which T is inscribed (the vertical
shaft of the T is the Mediterranean, the right horizontal branch the
Nile). The welcome consequence (or cause) of such reorganisation
of the haphazard phenomena of geography is that Jerusalem is seen
to be at the very centre of the world (Figure C2).
The result of this restructuring is that lack as absence is being
semiotised into a positive form of privation, as happens with the
modern successors of Carroll's map, two monochrome engravings

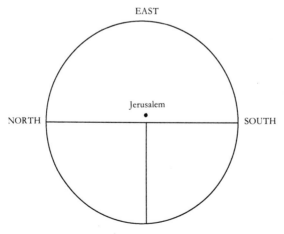

Figure C2   Medieval *Mappa Mundi*

229

by T. Atkinson and M. Baldwin, both entirely blank, and respectively entitled: 'Map to not indicate: Canada, James Bay . . . Straits of Florida' and 'Map of a 36 square mile surface of the Pacific Ocean west of Ohahu'. Not to mention, of course, Malevitch's *White Square on a White Background*, which Carroll's map anticipates. There is a linguistic analogue of this in the various blanks that punctuate the text: the characters do not always finish their sentences, because they faint, vanish, are interrupted, or do not bother to go on till the end. A good instance of this is provided by the Bellman:

> For England expects – I forbear to proceed:
> 'Tis a maxim tremendous, but trite'[14]

The joke (whether intended by Carroll or not) is that, out of the famous saying, the Bellman keeps only those words, 'England expects', which were never uttered by Nelson (who wanted to say: 'Nelson confides that every man will do his duty'), but were substituted for ease of transmission in flag language. The important word, however, has been uttered: the blank maps, like the linguistic blanks are *semiotic* blanks; they introduce neither privation nor lack, but difference, a positive form of opposition. This is where, in turn, *The Hunting of the Snark* reads Kant, and beyond him.

At first sight, my reading of *The Hunting of the Snark*, inspired and informed by philosophical concepts, has given me an interpretation of the poem. The Snark, therefore, has received a meaning (which was sadly lacking): he may be seen as an emblem of non-sense, embodying negation both as privation (Snark − Boojum = 0) and lack (its 'five unmistakable marks' are so incoherent that they delineate nothing, sheer absence). Nonsense as a genre always hesitates between these two forms of negation. But such a global interpretation of the poem is open to doubt, and the first to doubt it was Lewis Carroll himself, as he viewed all global interpretations of his text ironically:

> As to the meaning of the *Snark*? I'm very much afraid I didn't mean anything but nonsense! Still, you know, words mean more than we mean to express when we use them: so a whole book ought to mean a great deal more than the writer meant. So, whatever good meanings are in the book, I'm very glad

to accept as the meaning of the book. The best I've seen is by a lady (she published it in a letter to a newspaper) – that the whole book is an allegory of the search after happiness. I think this fits beautifully in many ways – particularly about the bathing machines.[15]

I find myself in the embarrassing company of the lady who read allegories into the text and wrote to newspapers about it. But the quotation from Carroll's letter, where a more modern theory of the meaning–saying relationship is proposed than the one contained in the famous proverb, 'Take care of the sense and the sounds will take care of themselves', offers a way out of my quandary. Indeed, it welcomes a proliferation of interpretations, emblematised in the poem in the proliferation of dreamed or imaginary Snarks, which compensates for the absence of the real Snark. The way out is not, of course, the idea that, in the field of interpretation, anything goes. It is rather the awareness, which the proliferation of meaning triggers, that it is a fundamental characteristic of language that utterances are independent of meanings, thus allowing meaning to proliferate. Language distinguishes and separates (the formula for this form of 'negation' is 'a $\neq$ b' – the Snark is *not* a Boojum), but the separation is not merely introduced in the two parallel chains, between words and between referents, but also in the correspondence, or lack of it, between the two chains – between each word and its referent(s). The Snark is not only *not* a Boojum – it is also definitely *not* an object in the external world, not even an object in the world of ideas, a concept (its five distinguishing marks are incoherent) – it is the kind of nothing *qua* free-floating difference that language allows. This is the only allegorical reading the poem may accept – a meta-allegory, the allegory of the linguistic sign as free-floating difference, as the *case vide*, the empty square that is nothing in itself but, in classic structuralist fashion, gives the whole structure its meaning (even as the absent Snark, in spite or because of its absence, structures the text of the poem – the beast is not there, but the occurrences of the word multiply). The fundamental characteristic of language that is disclosed in *The Hunting of the Snark* is that language has the capacity to turn 'real' negation (*nihil privativum*) into semiotic negation, or difference. If I were to adopt the language of Lyotard's *Discours, figure*,[16] I might say that in *The Hunting of the Snark* we are made to witness the process whereby the figural turns into the semiotic. Carroll's keen awareness of the workings of the language takes him beyond

Kant's theory of negation, and amounts to an intuitive grasp of a philosophical problematic that clearly emerged almost a century after his death.

NOTES

INTRODUCTION: READING NONSENSE READING

1 C. Lévi-Strauss, 'La structure des mythes', in *Anthropologie structurale 1*, (Paris: Plon, 1958), pp. 227–56; J.P. Vernant and P. Vidal-Naquet, *Mythe et tragédie en Grèce ancienne* (Paris: Maspero, 1972).
2 J.J. Lecercle, *Philosophy through the Looking-Glass* (London: Hutchinson, 1985), pp. 74–9.
3 M. Pierssens, *La Tour de babil* (Paris: Minuit, 1976).
4 P. Bourdieu, *Ce que parler veut dire* (Paris: Fayard, 1982).
5 H. Bloom, *A Map of Misreading* (New York: Oxford University Press, 1975).
6 E. Hobsbawm and T. Ranger (eds) *The Invention of Tradition* (Cambridge: Cambridge University Press, 1983).
7 J.P. Brisset, *La Grammaire logique* (Paris: Tchou, 1970); L. Wolfson, *Le Schizo et les langues* (Paris: Gallimard, 1970).
8 Lecercle, op. cit., ch. 1.
9 J. Derrida, *Glas* (Paris: Galilée, 1974).
10 M. Gardner (ed.) *The Annotated Alice* (Harmondsworth: Penguin, 1965); this edition will be used throughout the book.
11 A. Ettelson, *Through the Looking-Glass Decoded* (New York: Philosophical Library, 1966), p. 21.
12 ibid., p. 12.
13 ibid., p. 24.
14 ibid., p. 19.
15 D. Davidson, 'What metaphors mean', in *Inquiries into Truth and Interpretation* (Oxford: Oxford University Press, 1984).
16 J.F. Lyotard, *Le Différend* (Paris: Minuit, 1983).
17 M. Thevoz (ed.) *Ecrits bruts* (Paris: Presses Universitaires de France, 1979); *Le Langage de la rupture* (Paris: Presses Universitaires de France, 1978).
18 L. Wolfson, *Ma Mère, musicienne, est morte . . .* (Paris: Navarin, 1984).
19 H. Steele, *Lord Hamlet's Castle* (London: André Deutsch, 1987).
20 W. Abish, *Alphabetical Africa* (New York: New Directions, 1974).

21 G. Hartman and S. Budick (eds) *Midrash and Literature* (New Haven: Yale University Press, 1986).

22 Pierre Ménard is the fictional critic in Borges's story, who, as the acme of critical practice, rewrote a chapter of *Don Quixote* word for word, thus producing an entirely different text from Cervantes's.

23 J.F. Lyotard, *Instructions païennes* (Paris: Galilée, 1977).

24 *Annotated Alice*, p. 271.

25 ibid., p. 270.

26 For instance S. Marret, 'Lewis Carroll, la logique à l'œuvre' (University of Paris III, 1990).

27 G. Deleuze, *Logique du sens* (Paris: Minuit, 1969).

28 G. Deleuze and F. Guattari, *Kafka* (Paris: Minuit, 1975).

29 W. Benjamin, 'The task of the translator', in *Illuminations* (New York: Harcourt, Brace, 1955).

30 ibid., p. 75.

31 ibid., pp. 78–9.

32 *Annotated Alice*, p. 191.

33 ibid., p. 126.

34 Adapted from E. Souriau, 'Sur l'esthétique des mots et des langages forgés', *Revue d'Esthétique* 18(1) (Paris, 1965): 19–48.

35 *Annotated Alice*, p. 197.

36 L. Sterne, *Tristram Shandy*, Book V, ch. 43.

37 *Annotated Alice*, p. 190.

38 V. Propp, *Morphology of the Folktale* (Austin, Tex.:University of Texas Press, 1968).

39 L. Carroll, *The Works of Lewis Carroll* (London: Hamlyn, 1965), p. 1106.

40 See R. Barthes, *La Chambre claire* (Paris: Seuil, 1980).

41 M. Heidegger, *An Introduction to Metaphysics* (Newhaven: Yale University Press, 1959), p. 151, quoted in A. Benjamin, *Translation and the Nature of Philosophy* (London: Routledge, 1989), p. 19.

42 *Alice*, dir. J. Svankmajer, Czechoslovakia, 1988.

1 THE LINGUISTICS OF NONSENSE

1 C. Wells (ed.) *A Nonsense Anthology* (New York: Charles Scribner's Sons, 1902), p. 23 (repr. New York: Dover, 1958).

2 M. Peake, *A Book of Nonsense* (London: Peter Owen, 1972), p. 29.

3 H.W. Fowler and F.G. Fowler, *The King's English*, 2nd edn (Oxford: Clarendon Press, 1924), pp. 4–7.

4 Wells, op. cit., p. 158.

5 E. Souriau, 'Sur l'esthétique des mots et des langages forgés', *Revue d'Esthétique* 18, (1) (1965): 19–48.

6 I. Fonagy, *La Vive voix* (Paris: Payot, 1983).

7 ibid., p. 81 ff.

8 E. Lear, *The Complete Nonsense of Edward Lear*, ed. H. Jackson, (London: Faber & Faber, 1947), p. 237.

9 For a detailed analysis of this letter see J.J. Lecercle, *The Violence of Language* (London: Routledge, 1991), Introduction.

10 M. Gardner (ed.) *The Annotated Alice* (Harmondsworth: Penguin, 1965), p. 60.
11 A.C. Gimson, *An Introduction to the Pronunciation of English* (London: Edward Arnold, 1962), p. 239.
12 Souriau, op. cit., pp. 44–5.
13 Wells, op. cit., p. 26.
14 E. Lear, *Letters*, ed. V. Noakes, (Oxford: Oxford University Press, 1988), p. 195.
15 *Annotated Alice*, p. 90.
16 ibid., p. 28.
17 Wells, op. cit., p. 10.
18 ibid., pp. 10–11.
19 ibid., p. 14.
20 H. Haughton (ed.) *The Chatto Book of Nonsense Poetry* (London: Chatto & Windus, 1988), pp. 139–40.
21 K. Amis, *Ending Up* (Harmondsworth: Penguin, 1987), pp. 152, 178.
22 Lear, *Complete Nonsense*, p. 243.
23 J. Milner, 'De quoi rient les locuteurs?', *Change*, 29 (Paris, 1976).
24 See Lecercle, op. cit., Ch. 2.
25 Lear, *Complete Nonsense*, p. 255.
26 Anon., in Wells, op. cit., p. 36.
27 Oliver Herford, ibid.
28 G. Lakoff and M. Johnson, *Metaphors We Live By* (Chicago: University of Chicago Press, 1980), Ch. 6.
29 *Annotated Alice*, p. 271.
30 A. Grésillon, *La Règle et le monstre: le mot valise* (Tübingen: Niemeyer, 1984), pp. 189–92.
31 *Annotated Alice*, p. 272.
32 ibid., p. 195.
33 ibid., p. 194.
34 ibid., p. 171.
35 ibid., p. 191.
36 L. Carroll, *The Works of Lewis Carroll* (London: Paul Hamlyn, 1965), p. 734.
37 S. Freud, *Jokes and their Relation to the Unconscious*, trans. J. Strachey (London: Routledge & Kegan Paul), 1960.
38 J.C. Milner, *L'Amour de la langue* (Paris: Seuil, 1978), ch. 7; English trans. A. Banfield, *For the Love of Language: Language, Discourse, Society* (London: Macmillan, 1989).
39 J.M. Cohen (ed.) *The Penguin Book of Comic and Curious Verse* (Harmondsworth: Penguin, 1952), p. 221.
40 Wells, op. cit., p. 41.
41 E. Sewell, *The Field of Nonsense* (London: Chatto & Windus, 1952), ch. 4.
42 I call Brissetising, as a tribute to the French logophiliac, J.P. Brisset, the illegal re-analysis of a sequence which has already been analysed into its proper constituents; and I call Wolfsonising, as a tribute to the American schizophrenic, Louis Wolfson, the synthesis of linguistic elements which should not be combined. On this, see Lecercle, op. cit., chs. 1 and 2.
43 See Lecercle, op. cit.
44 S. Leclaire, *Psychanalyser* (Paris: Seuil, 1968).

45 M. Heidegger, *What is Called Thinking?*, trans. D. Wieck and J.G. Gray (New York: Harper & Row, 1968), part II, ch. 7.
46 *Annotated Alice*, p. 47.
47 Lecercle, op. cit., ch. 1.
48 *Annotated Alice*, p. 35.
49 J. Angus, *Hand-Book of the English Tongue* (London: Religious Tract Society, 1870), p. 190.
50 *The Works of Lewis Carroll*, p. 537.
51 See D. Wood, *Philosophy at the Limit* (London: Unwin Hyman, 1990), ch. 2.
52 *Annotated Alice*, p. 122.
53 ibid., p. 67.
54 Lear, *Complete Nonsense*, p. 93.
55 Grésillon, op. cit., p. 45.
56 Wells, op. cit., p. 24.
57 J. Haslam, *Illustrations of Madness* (London: Routledge, 1988).
58 P. Grice, *Essays in the Ways of Words* (Cambridge, Mass.: Harvard University Press, 1989), Ch. 2.
59 J. Searle, *Expression and Meaning* (Cambridge: Cambridge University Press, 1979).
60 Lear, *Complete Nonsense*, p. 93.
61 *Annotated Alice*, p. 268.
62 ibid., p. 158.
63 Wells, op. cit., p. 149.
64 ibid. p. xxxi.
65 *Annotated Alice*, p. 129.
66 Sewell, op. cit.

2 THE PRAGMATICS OF NONSENSE

1 B. Della Casa, *Galateo*, trans. R.S. Pine-Coffin (Harmondsworth: Penguin, 1958), p. 59.
2 ibid., p. 98.
3 L. Carroll, *The Annotated Alice*, ed. M. Gardner (Harmondsworth: Penguin, 1965), p. 96.
4 E. Lear, *The Complete Nonsense of Edward Lear*, ed. Holbrook Jackson (London: Faber & Faber, 1947), p. 199.
5 F. Recanati, 'La pensée d'Austin et son originalité', in P. Amselek (ed.) *Théorie des actes de langage, éthique et droit* (Paris: Presses Universitaires de France, 1986), pp. 19–36.
6 R. Girard, *La Violence et le sacré* (Paris: Grasset, 1972).
7 *Annotated Alice*, p. 25.
8 ibid., p. 233.
9 P. Grice, *Essays in the Ways of Words* (Cambridge, Mass.: Harvard University Press, 1989), part I.
10 J. Habermas, *Communication and the Evolution of Society* (London: Heinemann, 1979), and *Reason and the Rationalisation of Society* (London: Heinemann, 1984).

11 G. Lakoff and M. Johnson, *Metaphors We Live By* (Chicago: University of Chicago Press, 1980).
12 B. Latour and S. Woolgar, *Laboratory Life. The Construction of Scientific Facts* (London: Sage, 1979), and B. Latour, *Science in Action* (Cambridge, Mass.: Harvard University Press, 1987).
13 P. Hamilton, *The West Pier* (Harmondsworth: Penguin, 1986, first published 1951), p. 14.
14 D. Lewis, *Convention* (Oxford: Blackwell, 1969).
15 Hamilton, op. cit., p. 15.
16 *Annotated Alice*, pp. 87–8.
17 D. Sperber and D. Wilson, *Relevance* (Oxford: Blackwell, 1986), p. 160.
18 *Annotated Alice*, pp. 238–40.
19 ibid., p. 89.
20 G. Bateson, 'Towards a theory of schizophrenia', in *Steps to an Ecology of Mind* (London: Paladin, 1973).
21 *Annotated Alice*, p. 161.
22 A.J. Ayer, *Language, Truth and Logic* (Harmondsworth: Penguin, 1971, first published 1936), 153.
23 R.A. Duff, *Intention, Agency and Criminal Responsibility* (Oxford: Blackwell, 1990), pp. 60–80.
24 O. Leith and F. Myerson, *The Power of Address: Explorations in Rhetoric* (London: Routledge, 1989).
25 *Annotated Alice*, p. 147.
26 ibid., pp. 155–8.
27 S. Kripke, *Naming and Necessity* (Cambridge, Mass.: Harvard University Press, 1980).
28 *Annotated Alice*, pp. 156–7.
29 ibid., pp. 158–61.
30 See J. Searle, *Intentionality* (Cambridge: Cambridge University Press, 1983).
31 H. Lee, *To Kill a Mocking-Bird* (London: Heinemann, 1960), p. 3.
32 See J. Derrida, 'Signature événement contexte', in *Marges* (Paris: Minuit, 1972).
33 D. Davidson, 'What metaphors mean', in *Inquiries into Truth and Interpretation* (Oxford: Clarendon Press, 1984), pp. 245–64.
34 G.P. Baker and P.M.S. Hacker, *Language, Sense and Nonsense* (Oxford: Blackwell, 1984), p. 224.
35 T.B. Macaulay, *Critical and Historical Essays* (London: Dent, Everyman's Library, 1907), pp. 325–6.
36 H. Bloom, *The Anxiety of Influence* (New York: Oxford University Press, 1973); *A Map of Misprision* (New York: Oxford University Press, 1975).
37 G.N. Leech, *Principles of Pragmatics* (London: Longman, 1983).
38 ibid., p. 64.
39 ibid.
40 L. Carroll, *Lewis Carroll's Symbolic Logic*, ed. W.W. Bartley (Hassocks: Harvester, 1977), p. 51.
41 Leech, op. cit., pp. 81–2.
42 ibid., p. 83.
43 ibid.
44 Adapted from Leech, p. 132.

45 *Annotated Alice*, p. 81.
46 ibid., p. 72.
47 ibid., p. 68.
48 Lakoff and Johnson, op. cit., pp. 132–3.
49 *Annotated Alice*, p. 212.
50 R.L. Green (ed.) *A Century of Humorous Verse* (London: Dent, Everyman's Library, 1959), p. 270.
51 *Annotated Alice*, p. 280.
52 ibid., p. 267.
53 ibid., pp. 94–5.
54 ibid., p. 101.
55 ibid., p. 276.
56 ibid., p. 201.
57 ibid., p. 255.
58 ibid., p. 203.
59 ibid., p. 83.
60 ibid., p. 103.
61 ibid., pp. 286–7.
62 D. Rackin, 'Alice's journey to the end of the night', *PMLA*, October 1966: 313–26.
63 *Annotated Alice*, p. 287.
64 Lear, op. cit., p. 163.
65 ibid., p. 170.
66 ibid., p. 207.
67 ibid., p. 203.
68 M. Heidegger, *Being and Time*, trans. J. Macquarrie and E. Robinson (Oxford: Blackwell, 1962), p. 164.
69 ibid., p. 166–7.
70 Lear, op. cit., pp. 50, 41, 36.
71 ibid., p. 39.
72 Heidegger, op. cit., p. 213.
73 V. Woolf, 'Kew Gardens', in *A Haunted House* (Harmondsworth: Penguin, 1973, first published 1944), p. 38.
74 Heidegger, op. cit., p. 208.
75 Lear, op. cit., p. 57.
76 J.R. Kincaid, 'Alice's invasion of Wonderland', *PMLA*, January 1973: 92–9.
77 J. Rawls, *A Theory of Justice* (Oxford: Oxford University Press, 1972).
78 *Annotated Alice*, p. 164.

3 NONSENSE AND THE PHILOSOPHY OF LANGUAGE

1 L. Carroll, *The Annotated Alice*, ed. M. Gardner (Harmondsworth: Penguin, 1965), pp. 281–2.
2 J.N. Findlay, *Meinong's Theory of Objects and Values* (Oxford: Clarendon Press, 1963).
3 E.M. Anscombe, *Intention* (Oxford: Blackwell, 1958), p. 58.
4 ibid., p. 84.

5 ibid.
6 *Annotated Alice*, p. 72.
7 ibid., p. 67.
8 ibid., p. 95.
9 ibid.
10 ibid.
11 ibid.
12 ibid., p. 84.
13 ibid., pp. 120–1.
14 J. Searle, 'Reiterating the differences: a reply to Derrida', *Glyph* 2 (1977); J. Derrida, 'Signature événement contexte', in *Marges* (Paris: Minuit, 1972). *Limited Inc* (Evanston, Ill.: Northwestern University Press, 1988).
15 J. Searle, *Speech Acts* (Cambridge: Cambridge University Press, 1969), Ch. 1, section 5.
16 J. Searle, *Intentionality* (Cambridge: Cambridge University Press, 1983).
17 D. Davidson, *Inquiries into Truth and Interpretation* (Oxford: Clarendon Press, 1984), p. 98.
18 J. Searle, *Expression and Meaning* (Cambridge: Cambridge University Press, 1979), Ch. 2.
19 ibid.
20 Derrida, op. cit.; see also G. Bennington and J. Derrida, *Jacques Derrida* (Paris: Seuil, 1991).
21 Derrida, op. cit., p. 389.
22 J.L. Borges, 'Pierre Menard, author of the Quixote', in *Ficciones* (New York: New Directions, 1964).
23 D. Davidson, 'What metaphors mean', in Davidson, op. cit.
24 Derrida, op. cit., p. 375.
25 J.F. Lyotard, *Instructions païennes* (Paris: Galilée, 1977), pp. 64–5.
26 Shakespeare's 'will' sonnets are nos. 135 and 136.
27 J.J. Lecercle, *Philosophy Through the Looking-Glass* (London: Hutchinson, 1985); *The Violence of Language* (London: Routledge, 1991).
28 *Annotated Alice*, p. 261.
29 ibid., pp. 27–8.
30 ibid., p. 261.
31 S. Kripke, *Naming and Necessity* (Cambridge, Mass.: Harvard University Press, 1980).
32 *Annotated Alice*, pp. 263–9.
33 P. Veyne, *Comment on écrit l'histoire* (Paris: Seuil, 1971).
34 E.C. Bentley, *The Complete Clerihews* (Oxford: Oxford University Press, 1981), p. 30.
35 J. Keats, *The Complete Poems* (Harmondsworth: Penguin, 1973), p. 345.
36 *Annotated Alice*, p. 276.
37 ibid., p. 262.
38 ibid., p. 266.
39 G.A. Cohen, *Karl Marx's Theory of History: A Defence* (Oxford: Clarendon Press, 1978), pp. 13–15.
40 *Annotated Alice*, p. 276.
41 P. Watzlawick (ed.) *The Invented Reality* (New York: Norton, 1984); see also J. Grenier on Nietzsche's ontology ('being is being interpreted'), in

Le Problème de la vérité dans la philosophie de Nietzsche (Paris: Seuil, 1966), pp. 323–4.

42 *Annotated Alice*, pp. 262–3.

43 D. Bolinger, *Forms of English* (Cambridge, Mass.: Harvard University Press, 1965).

44 I. Fonagy, *La Vive voix* (Paris: Payot, 1983).

45 *Annotated Alice*, p. 265.

46 R. Caillois, *Les Jeux et les hommes* (Paris: Gallimard, 1958).

47 H. Bergson, *Le Rire* (Paris: Presses Universitaires de France, 1940), p. 29.

48 *Annotated Alice*, p. 265.

49 ibid., p. 266.

50 See J. Bouscaren, J. Chuquet and L. Danon-Boileau, *Introduction to a Linguistic Grammar of English* (Paris: Ophrys, 1992), pp. 111–12.

51 *Annotated Alice*, pp. 266–7.

52 ibid., pp. 268–70.

53 See B. Pautrat, *Versions du soleil: figures et système de Nietzsche* (Paris: Seuil, 1971).

54 Quoted in *Annotated Alice*, p. 268. The quotation originally comes from *Symbolic Logic*.

55 J.J. Goux, *Les Monnayeurs du langage* (Paris: Galilée, 1984).

56 *Annotated Alice*, p. 273.

57 ibid., p. 275.

58 ibid., p. 276.

59 ibid., pp. 226–7.

60 ibid., p. 134.

61 N. Goodman, 'The end of the museum?', in *Of Mind and Other Matters* (Cambridge, Mass.: Harvard University Press, 1984).

62 Carroll, *Annotated Alice*, p. 114.

4 THE POLYPHONY OF NONSENSE

1 G. Lakoff and M. Johnson, *Metaphors We Live By* (Chicago: University of Chicago Press, 1980), ch. 6.

2 ibid., Ch. 1.

3 A. Kojève, *Introduction à la lecture de Hegel* (Paris: Gallimard, 1947).

4 J.J. Lecercle, *The Violence of Language* (London: Routledge, 1991), ch. 5.

5 See Holquist, *Dialogism* (London: Routledge, 1990), p. 109.

6 M. Bakhtin, 'Discourse in the novel', in *The Dialogic Imagination: Four Essays by M. Bakhtin*, ed. M. Holquist (Austin: University of Texas Press, 1981).

7 See M. Bakhtin, *Speech Genres and Other Essays*, ed. C. Emerson and M. Holquist (Austin: University of Texas Press, 1986).

8 L. Carroll, 'Theme with variations', in *The Works of Lewis Carroll* (London: Paul Hamlyn, 1965), pp. 802–3.

9 R. Barthes, *S/Z* (Paris: Seuil, 1970), ch. 21, p. 51.

10 L. Carroll, *The Annotated Alice*, ed. M. Gardner (Harmondsworth: Penguin, 1965), pp. 307–13.

11 Quoted in W. Wordsworth, *The Poems*, vol. I (Harmondsworth: Penguin, 1977), p. 986.

12 ibid., pp. 554–5.
13 M. Bakhtin, 'Speech genres', in *Speech Genres*.
14 M. Bakhtin, 'Remarques sur l'épistémologie des sciences humaines', in *Esthétique de la création verbale* (Paris: Gallimard, 1984), p. 386.
15 M. Bakhtin, 'Les Carnets 1970–71', ibid., p. 366.
16 J. Addison, R. Steele *et al., The Spectator*, vol. I (London: Dent, Everyman's Library), 1907, p. 166.
17 M. Bakhtin, *Speech Genres*.
18 I. and P. Opie, *The Lore and Language of Schoolchildren* (London: Paladin, 1977).
19 I. and P. Opie (eds) *The Oxford Dictionary of Nursery Rhymes* (Oxford: Clarendon Press, 1951).
20 Opie and Opie, *Lore and Language*, p. 25.
21 C. Dickens, *Little Dorrit* (London, 1857), ch. 23.
22 ibid.
23 R.L. Green (ed.) *A Century of Humorous Verse, 1850–1950* (London: Dent, Everyman's Library), 1959, p. 18.
24 H. Bloom, *The Anxiety of Influence* (New York: Oxford University Press, 1972).
25 M. Bakhtin, 'The problem of speech genres', in *Speech Genres*.
26 E. Sewell, *The Field of Nonsense* (London: Chatto & Windus, 1952).
27 L. Carroll, *The Annotated Snark*, ed. M. Gardner (Harmondsworth: Penguin, 1967), p. 66.
28 J.J. Lecercle, 'Le Nonsense: genre, histoire, mythe', dissertation, University of Paris VII, 1981, pp. 377–82.
29 See the chapter on *The Hunting of the Snark* in R.M. Adams, *Nil: Episodes in the Literary Conquest of Void during the Nineteenth Century* (Oxford: Oxford University Press, 1966).
30 M. Bakhtin, *Problems of Dostoevsky's Poetics* (Minneapolis: University of Minneapolis Press, 1984; first published 1929, revised and enlarged edn 1963).
31 Quoted in H. Aarsleff, *The Study of Language in England, 1780–1860* (Princeton: Princeton University Press, 1967), p. 233.
32 R.C. Trench, *On the Study of Words*, 9th edn (London, 1859), p. 210.
33 M. Müller, *Lectures on the Science of Language* (London, 1864), p. 525.
34 ibid., pp. 346–7.
35 R.C. Trench, *On the Study of Words*, p. 110.
36 P. Alexander, 'Logic and the humour of Lewis Carroll', *Proceedings of the Leeds Philosophical and Literary Society* 7(1) (1944–7): 551–6.
37 See S. Marret, 'Lewis Carroll: la logique à l'oeuvre', dissertation, University of Paris III, 1990.
38 C. Darwin, *The Voyage of the 'Beagle'* (London: Dent, Everyman's Library), 1966, p. 158.
39 ibid., p. 268.
40 H. Reichert, *Lewis Carroll, Studien zum literarischen Unsinn* (Munich, 1970).
41 Foucault, *Madness and Civilization: A History of Insanity in the Age of Reason* (New York: Random House, 1965).
42 E. Sitwell, *English Eccentrics* (Harmondsworth: Penguin, 1971).
43 ibid., pp. 49–50.
44 *Perceval's Narrative*, ed. G. Bateson (New York: William Morrow, 1974).

45 Lecercle, 'Le Nonsense', ch. 8.
46 M. Johnson, *The Body in the Mind* (Chicago: University of Chicago Press, 1987), ch. 2.
47 V.N. Vološinov (M. Bakhtin), 'Discourse in life and discourse in poetry', in *Bakhtin School Papers*, Russian Poetics in Translation, vol. 10, ed. A. Shukman (Oxford, RPT Publications, 1983), p. 19.
48 *Annotated Alice*, p. 172.
49 G. Deleuze and C. Parnet, *Dialogues* (Paris: Flammarion, 1977), p. 33.
50 J.F. Lyotard, *Le Différend* (Paris: Minuit, 1983); English trans. G. van den Abbeele (Manchester: Manchester University Press, 1988).
51 For instance G. Deleuze and F. Guattari, *Kafka* (Paris: Minuit, 1975), pp. 39–40.
52 *Annotated Alice*, p. 35.
53 B. Simon, *The Two Nations and the Educational Structure, 1780–1870* (London: Lawrence & Wishart, 1974), p. 100.
54 R. Caillois, *Les Jeux et les hommes* (Paris: Gallimard, 1958), p. 75 ff.
55 Quoted in J. Gathorne-Hardy, *The Public School Phenomenon 597–1977* (Harmondsworth: Penguin, 1979), p. 155.
56 *Annotated Alice*, p. 41.
57 F. Kilvert, *Kilvert's Diary*, ed. W. Plomer (London: Jonathan Cape, 1964), p. 35.

CONCLUSION

1 See, for instance, A. MacKay, 'Mr Donnellan and Humpty Dumpty on referring', *Philosophical Review* 77 (1968): 197–202, and K. Donnellan, 'Putting Humpty Dumpty together again', *Philosophical Review* 77 (1968): 203–15.
2 The phrase is coined in imitation of the title of an introductory textbook in philosophy, F. Vivian, *Thinking Philosophically* (London: Chatto & Windus, 1965).
3 L. Carroll, *The Annotated Snark*, ed. M. Gardner (Harmondsworth: Penguin, 1962), p. 94.
4 E. Sewell, *The Field of Nonsense* (London: Chatto & Windus, 1952).
5 I. Kant, *Versuch den Begriff der Negativen Grössen in die Weltweisheit einzuführen* (Königsberg: Kauter, 1763).
6 *Annotated Snark*, p. 96.
7 ibid., p. 47.
8 ibid., p. 48.
9 ibid., p. 51.
10 ibid., p. 50.
11 ibid., p. 48.
12 ibid., p. 56.
13 ibid., pp. 55–6.
14 ibid., p. 70.
15 Quoted ibid., p. 22.
16 J.F. Lyotard, *Discours, figure* (Paris: Klincksieck, 1978).

INDEX